SILVERFARE
BRITAIN'S

C000154466

DA47.9.I7

BRITAIN'S INFORMAL EMPIRE
IN THE MIDDLE EAST

BRITAIN'S INFORMAL EMPIRE IN THE MIDDLE EAST
A Case Study of Iraq, 1929–1941

DANIEL SILVERFARB

Foreword by Majid Khadduri

New York · Oxford
OXFORD UNIVERSITY PRESS
1986

Oxford University Press

Oxford   New York   Toronto
Delhi   Bombay   Calcutta   Madras   Karachi
Petaling Jaya   Singapore   Hong Kong   Tokyo
Nairobi   Dar es Salaam   Cape Town
Melbourne   Auckland

and associated companies in
Beirut   Berlin   Ibadan   Nicosia

Copyright © 1986 by Oxford University Press, Inc.

Published by Oxford University Press, Inc.,
200 Madison Avenue, New York, New York 10016

Oxford is a registered trademark of Oxford University Press

All rights reserved. No part of this publication may be reproduced, stored in a retrieval
system, or transmitted, in any form or by any means, electronic, mechanical,
photocopying, recording, or otherwise, without the prior permission of
Oxford University Press

Library of Congress Cataloging-in-Publication Data

Silverfarb, Daniel, 1943–
Britain's informal empire in the Middle East.

Bibliography: p.
Includes index.
1. Great Britain—Foreign relations—Iraq.
2. Iraq—Foreign relations—Great Britain.
3. Iraq—History—Hashemite Kingdom, 1921–1958.
4. Great Britain—Foreign relations—1910–1936.
5. Great Britain—Foreign relations—1936–1945.
I. Title.
DA47.9.I72S55   1986   327.410867   85-25830
ISBN 0-19-503997-1

Printing (last digit):   9 8 7 6 5 4 3 2 1

Printed in the United States of America
on acid-free paper

Foreword

This book is a case study of Iraq's role in Britain's imperial history. After its occupation of Iraq during the First World War, Britain began to find that that country was not only important as a defense outpost but also vital for other purposes. These purposes were the product of the new conditions created by the First World War which prompted policy makers to design a new form of control that would link the country with the larger British imperial superstructure. Perhaps a little background about Iraq under British control and the new conditions that emerged after the First World War may be useful to explain the form of that unique relationship between Iraq and Britain.

Before Iraq was occupied during the First World War, Great Britain had already been the predominating power in the neighboring Gulf area. Earlier Britain had extended its control to East Africa and southern Arabia when Napoleon descended upon Egypt in 1798 and threatened to cut British overseas routes to India. Iraq—then geopolitically marked on the map as the three *vilayets* (provinces) of Mosul, Baghdad, and Basra—had been under Ottoman domination since the sixteenth century and Britain seems to have been quite satisfied with Ottoman control as a barrier against rival powers. Nor were British commerical interests, though gradually expanding, in need of protection, since the Ottoman administration was on the whole well disposed toward British traders.

But the balance of power began to change early in the nineteenth century when the Ottoman Porte appeared too weak (often referred to as the Sick Man) and rival powers—first Russia and then Germany—began to encroach on his dominions and exert an increasing influence in the internal affairs of his country, which were looked upon as detrimental to British interests and prestige in the eastern Mediterranean and the Indian Ocean. So concerned was Britain about the Russian threat during the Crimean War (1854–56) that she went to war with Russia to save the Ottoman Porte from collapse. She also opposed Russia when its forces again attacked Ottoman territory in 1877.

The danger, however, did not come only from Russia. After the fall of Bismarck from power, Germany became involved in full competition with Britain in colonial ventures and Kaiser William II began to cultivate the friendship of the Ottoman sultan. Not only did the sultan grant commercial and other economic concessions to German firms, but he also allowed them to construct a railroad across the hinterland from Istanbul to Baghdad—known in European diplomacy as the Berlin-Baghdad Railway—with an extension to Basra. Considering this a threat to its position in the Gulf and the Indian Ocean, Britain strongly opposed the whole project. In time of hostilities, it argued, Germany could use Basra as a base for submarine activities in the Indian Ocean against British shipping. Had the First World War not broken out in 1914 and given Britain the opportunity first to occupy Basra in 1914 and Baghdad and Mosul in 1917 and 1918, it was simply a matter of time before Britain would have extended its control over the head of the Gulf—Basra and possibly beyond—to ensure the security of its imperial communications.

The British occupation of the three Ottoman provinces, which were united and officially called Iraq after the First World War, raised the whole question whether Britain should withdraw from the country since the German threat had disappeared. The question was debated in London after a revolt suddenly erupted in Iraq (1920), demanding the withdrawal of British military forces. After a review of the situation at a conference held in Cairo (1921), the British cabinet decided that the new conditions created in the region after the war—the threat of the Bolshevik Revolution to the Gulf and India, the possible occupation of the Mosul province by the new nationalist regime in Turkey, and the prospect of oil potential in Iraq—necessitated the establishment of a national regime in Iraq to replace the military administration and reduce British expenditure, although some argued in favor of complete withdrawal while others urged administering the country as part of the Indian Empire. As a compromise, an Arab government headed by Faysal, son of the sharif of Mecca (ally of

Britain in the war), was established in 1921, designed to satisfy Arab national aspirations and allow indirect British control to protect vital imperial interests. Moreover, this arrangement fulfilled British obligations toward the League of Nations whose covenant provided that countries (in the words of the covenant) "not yet able to stand by themselves" should be entrusted to a mandatory to provide administrative assistance "until such time as they are able to stand alone" (article 22).

Britain thus found ample justification to perpetuate its control over Iraq but not without qualifications. The new national regime, often referred to as the "Arab façade," promised ultimate independence, as the country was deemed not yet ready for full independence. Independence, however, under nationalist pressures, was finally achieved and the mandate came to an end in 1932. Moreover, Britain entered into treaty arrangements with Iraq (1930) which regulated the new relationship between the two countries. By virtue of this arrangement Britain recognized Iraq's independence and retained full control over two airbases as well as the use of all means of communication during war. As a *quid pro quo,* Britain promised to assist Iraq in case of foreign attack. This kind of rapport between Britain and her former ward is rightly described by Dr. Silverfarb as a form of an "informal empire," since Iraq had not been fully freed from foreign control. For when Iraq tried to make an independent judgment on foreign policy in 1941, pressure was brought to bear culminating in a thirty-day war that forced Iraq to meet British imperial requirements. Even when the treaty of 1930 came to an end in 1954, Iraq was prevailed upon to enter into a new agreement (1955) pledging joint cooperation with Britain on the occasion of signing a regional security pact with Turkey and Iran called the Baghdad Pact. Both the special agreement with Britain and the Baghdad Pact were repudiated by an angry public when it rose in revolt against the monarchy in 1958. The monarchy was swept away because it was created by Britain in 1921 to protect British imperial interests. But the emotional outburst subsided after the fall of the monarchy, as the country under a new regime committed to development and social reforms sought to achieve national aspirations.

The material used in the present study is drawn primarily from British official documents that have been made recently available to the public as well as from works by scholars and writers on subjects relating to British imperial policy. Dr. Silverfarb, however, has not used these sources uncritically, since he has verified his material with works by Iraqi leaders and writers who provided us with their version of the events and developments in the country that have bearing on British imperial policy. The product of his research may be taken as a balanced assessment of both British imperial interests and legitimate Iraqi national aspirations. He has also provided the reader with an interpretation of the movements and events which shaped the "informal empire" that may be taken to sum up Britain's imperial experience in Iraq. Nor did he shrink from giving his own personal views on some of the important issues that arose between Britain and Iraq. In all these endeavors, Dr. Silverfarb did his utmost to maintain a high level of objectivity and impartiality.

Majid Khadduri

Preface

This work is an account of Anglo-Iraqi relations from Britain's decision in 1929 to grant Iraq independence until the conclusion of hostilities between the two countries in 1941. In particular, it shows how Britain tried to maintain its political influence, economic ascendancy, and strategic position in Iraq after independence. It is thus a study in the possibilities and limitations of the method of indirect rule. It is also a description of an important episode in the fairly rapid disintegration of the dominant position that at great cost Britain established in the Middle East during the First World War. Finally, it is the story of how a recently independent Arab nation struggled to free itself from the lingering grip of a major European power.

This book is based mainly on unpublished British documents located at the Public Record Office in London. The volumes on Iraq in the foreign office 371 series were the most valuable, although for the period before Iraqi independence in 1932 the files in the colonial office 730 series were important. I also used cabinet, air ministry, war office, and Baghdad embassy papers. For matters relating to Kuwait, India office and Kuwait political agency documents located at the India Office Library and Records in London were useful. For the Iraqi side of the story, I found published works by Majid Khadduri, Taha al-Hashimi, Mahmud al-Durra, Eliezer Beeri, Khaldun Husry, Ayad al-Qazzaz, Hanna Batatu, and Mohammad Tarbush very helpful.

All quotations from documents at the Public Record Office appear by permission of the Controller of Her Majesty's Stationery Office.

The map entitled Syria and Iraq Mid 1941 was drawn specifically for this book and is based on a map in I. S. O. Playfair, *The Mediterranean and Middle East*, Vol. II (London, 1956). It is printed with the permission of the Controller of Her Majesty's Stationery Office.

For the sketch map of Kuwait I am indebted to Pat Kattenhorn of the India Office Library and Records.

I am grateful to Nur el-Deen Masalha for assisting me with Arabic translations.

I would like to take this opportunity to thank Dr. John B. Kelly, who first stimulated my interest in Middle Eastern history and who in numerous ways has assisted me ever since; and Professor Robert Koehl, my former adviser at the University of Wisconsin who has never ceased to be of great help to me. For reading all or part of my manuscript and offering useful suggestions, I would also like to thank Dr. James Piscatori of Australia National University, Dr. Joseph Kostiner of Tel Aviv University, Professor Eric Davis of Rutgers University, Dr. Peter Wetzler, Leonard Wetzler, Michael Van Vleck, Aviel Roshwald, Nur el-Deen Masalha, and Jeffrey Gunning. Needless to say, any errors or shortcomings in this work are solely my own responsibility.

Finally, I would like to express my deepest gratitude to my parents for their generous support and constant encouragement over a period of many years.

Madison, Wisconsin   D.S.
September 1985

Contents

BRITAIN'S INFORMAL EMPIRE
IN THE MIDDLE EAST

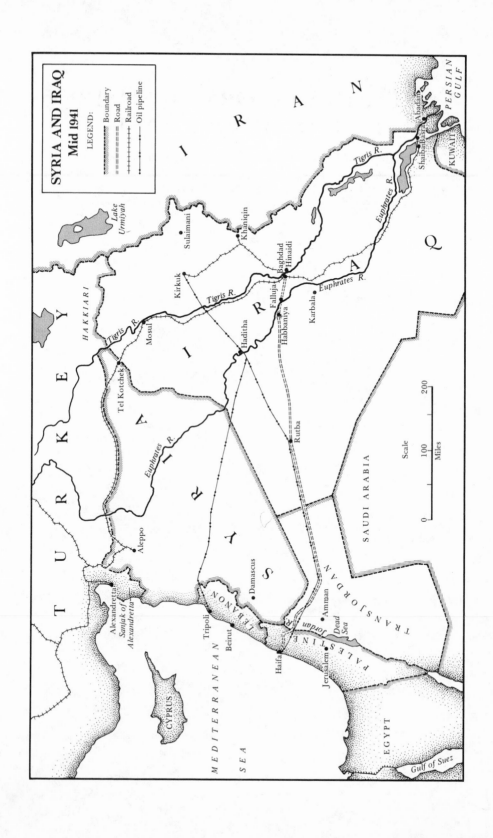

SYRIA AND IRAQ
Mid 1941

LEGEND:
Boundary
Road
Railroad
Oil pipeline

IRAN

PERSIAN
GULF

Lake
Urmiyah

Sulaimani

Khaniqin

Tigris R.

Euphrates R.

Abadan

Shaiba
Basra

KUWAIT

Kirkuk

Tigris R.

Baghdad
Himaidi

Q

HAKKIARI

Tigris R.

Mosul

Falluja
Habbaniya

Euphrates R.

Karbala

Haditha

Tel Kotchek

I

Euphrates R.

Rutba

SAUDI ARABIA

R

Scale

100   200

Miles

Aleppo

0

Alexandretta
Sanjak of
Alexandretta

Tripoli

Beirut

Damascus

S

Amman

TRANSJORDAN

LEBANON

Jordan R.

Dead
Sea

Haifa

PALESTINE

Jerusalem

MEDITERRANEAN

SEA

CYPRUS

EGYPT

Gulf of Suez

TURKEY

CHAPTER 1

Introduction

During the First World War, after prolonged and costly fighting, Britain expelled the Ottoman empire from Iraq. By the end of the conflict all vestiges of Ottoman authority had been eliminated, and British and Indian troops were in occupation of the entire country.[1] Now the British government had to decide what to do with Iraq.

For various reasons, Britain did not simply withdraw from Iraq. To begin with, it viewed the country as a vital link in a chain of airfields that would eventually connect Egypt with India and extend onwards to Australia. Already in 1921 British aircraft were flying regularly from Egypt to Iraq with intermediary landings for refuelling in Palestine and Transjordan. By facilitating trade, travel, and mail deliveries, British leaders believed that the air route would help tie the widely separated parts of their empire together. They also believed that the air route had considerable military potential because in an emergency it would enable Britain rapidly to reinforce its garrisons in Egypt, Palestine, Transjordan, Iraq, Aden, the Sudan, or India with planes normally stationed in other locations.[2]

Aside from the need to develop and safeguard the air route, after the First World War the British government remained in Iraq because it wanted to have military forces near the large British owned oilfields in southwestern Iran and the important oil refinery at Abadan. During the war this oil had greatly facilitated Britain's military operations, and British leaders believed that in a future conflict it might again become important. Even in peacetime, in the early 1920s it supplied more than half of the admiralty's total requirements. However, British leaders feared

3

that if they withdrew from Iraq Russia would increase its influence in Iran and eventually threaten these oilfields.[3]

In addition to the oil in Iran, the British government strongly suspected that there were large quantities of commercially exploitable oil in northern Iraq. Although the existence of this oil was not finally proved until 1927, after the First World War the British government was determined to remain in Iraq in order to keep this oil-bearing region within a British sphere of influence.[4]

Britain stayed in Iraq also because it wanted to keep other major powers away from the Persian Gulf. For over 100 years it had viewed those waters as a vital outpost on the western approaches to India and had prevented any European nation from establishing a naval base there. During the First World War it had moved into Iraq in part because it feared that Germany, with the assistance of Turkey, would establish a submarine base at Basra and thereby jeopardize British shipping in the Persian Gulf and the Indian Ocean. Now, after the war, the British government was concerned that if it withdrew from Iraq Turkey would resume control over the country and, with Russian assistance, again threaten Britain's position in the Persian Gulf.[5]

For Britain a resumption of Turkish control over Iraq would have the additional disadvantage of inflicting great damage on British prestige throughout the east since it would now appear that Britain and not Turkey had lost the war. Because they controlled large territories in Africa and Asia with a relatively small number of their own troops, British leaders were very sensitive to the question of prestige.[6]

After the First World War the British government feared the rise of a large bloc of anti-British states in the Muslim world extending from Egypt and Turkey in the west to Iran and Afghanistan in the east. It was especially concerned that anti-British agitation in these states would jeopardize its hold on the allegiance of the Muslim community in India. By retaining control of Iraq British leaders believed that they could drive a wedge down the center of the bloc of Muslim states and thereby gravely weaken it.[7]

Finally, the British government stayed in Iraq because it wanted to obtain some long-term benefit for the great military effort it had made to conquer the country.[8] During the First World War nearly 900,000 British and Indian troops had fought in Iraq. Almost 100,000 of these men had become casualties, and the fighting on this front had cost the British treasury £200,000,000.[9] Now that the war was over it would be difficult for the British government to justify these sacrifices if it simply abandoned Iraq.

Once the British government resolved to stay in Iraq it had to decide upon the method or manner of its rule. For various reasons in 1920 it chose a form of indirect rule through an Arab government rather than direct rule through British officials. To begin with, in 1915, in an effort to foment an Arab uprising against the Ottoman empire, it had promised the Sharif Husayn of the Hijaz that it would support the independence of most of the Arab inhabited districts of the Ottoman empire. True, Sir Henry McMahon, the British high commissioner in Egypt who conducted the negotiations with Husayn, qualified this commitment in several respects. For example, he stipulated that the Baghdad and Basra areas in Iraq would remain under fairly close British supervision, and he said that his pledge to support Arab independence would only apply to the extent that Britain could act without detriment to the interests of France.[10] But, in spite of these reservations, after the war McMahon's promise to Husayn made it difficult for the British government to treat Iraq as a *tabula rasa* upon which it could without inhibition or restraint construct an absolutist type of administration.

In another effort to secure Arab cooperation with the British war effort, in March 1917, when British troops occupied the city of Baghdad, Lieutenant-General F. S. Maude, the British commander, acting under instructions from the foreign office, issued a proclamation stating that the British had come as liberators not conquerors and that Britain would not impose alien institutions upon Iraq. Maude then invited the inhabitants "through your Nobles and Elders and Representatives, to participate in the management of your civil affairs in collaboration with the Political Representatives of Great Britain who accompany the British Army so that you may unite with your kinsmen in the North, East, South and West in realizing the aspirations of your race."[11] Like McMahon's pledge to Husayn, Maude's proclamation to the people of Baghdad was vaguely formulated and open to various interpretations. Nonetheless, like McMahon's pledge, it was sufficiently specific to make it difficult for Britain to impose a form of direct rule upon Iraq after the war without a breach of faith.

In a public proclamation of British war aims, in January 1918 Prime Minister David Lloyd George stated that the various Arab inhabited districts of the Ottoman empire "are in our judgement

entitled to a recognition of their separate national conditions."
Lloyd George intended his speech as a reply to the Bolshevik
campaign for a peace without annexations. He also wanted to
frustrate France's imperial ambitions in the Middle East.[12] Regardless of the motivation, Lloyd George's speech, although am-
biguous, certainly appeared to preclude the imposition upon Iraq
of an undisguised form of British rule.

So did the publication, a few days later, of United States President Woodrow Wilson's fourteen-point peace platform. Point
twelve pertained to Iraq and stated that "nationalities which are
now under Turkish rule should be assured an undoubted security of life and an absolutely unmolested opportunity of autonomous development." Although the fourteen points were a purely
American document, in November 1918 the British government
endorsed them in order to avoid a breach with the United States
and to encourage Germany to agree to an armistice.[13]

In November 1918 Britain, together with France, issued a declaration stating that the policy of the two countries in Iraq and
Syria was to facilitate "the establishment of national Governments and Administrations drawing their authority from the initiative and free choice of the indigenous populations." British
leaders hoped that this declaration, coming on the eve of the Paris
peace conference, would appeal to President Wilson because of
his well-known anti-imperialist sentiments. They also hoped that
the declaration would allay Arab suspicions of the Sykes-Picot
agreement of 1916 which divided the Arab lands of the Ottoman
empire into British and French spheres of influence.[14] In any
event, the Anglo-French declaration, like McMahon's pledge,
Maude's proclamation, Lloyd George's speech, and Wilson's
fourteen points, did much to foreclose the possibility of the establishment of direct British rule in Iraq.

Under the terms of the treaty of Versailles of June 1919 the
British government became a party to the covenant of the League
of Nations. Article 22 of the covenant laid down that certain
communities which formerly belonged to the Ottoman empire
(Iraq was obviously intended to be one of them although it was
not specifically mentioned) "have reached a stage of development where their existence as independent nations can be pro-
visionally recognised subject to the rendering of administrative
advice and assistance by a Mandatory until such time as they are
able to stand alone." In April 1920, at the San Remo conference
of the principal allied powers, the British government accepted

the mandate for Iraq under the terms of article 22.[15] As a result of this acceptance of the mandate, accompanied as it was by the recognition of Iraq as a quasi-independent state and by the assumption of an obligation to prepare the country for self-rule, it would have been difficult for the British government to justify the imposition of a purely or even predominantly British administration upon Iraq.

In the immediate postwar period British leaders were confronted with strong internal pressure for reduced military expenditures and increased outlays on social welfare. Much of the public pressure for reduced military expenditures centered around Iraq, which in the summer of 1919 was costing the British treasury about £2,700,000 per month.[16] By 1920 British leaders were convinced that only by creating under strict British supervision an Arab government in Baghdad, complete with its own army and police force with which to maintain internal order, could they withdraw most of their troops from Iraq, thereby saving a great deal of money, and still safeguard essential British interests.[17]

At the beginning of July 1920, while Iraq was still under direct British rule, there was a serious anti-British uprising. The rebellion was incited by nationalists in Baghdad who were angered by Britain's refusal to grant independence in seeming contradiction to its various pledges. They were especially eager for independence because they hungered for the highly remunerative government jobs that were occupied by British officials. These nationalists were aided by the Arab government in Syria which contained numerous Iraqis who wanted to return to Iraq to take power. The uprising was also promoted by Shiite religious leaders in the holy cities of Karbala and Najaf in southern Iraq who disliked living under Christian rule and viewed the expulsion of the Turks as an opportunity to increase their authority in the country. The most numerous participants in the rebellion were Shiite tribesmen along the Euphrates River in southern Iraq who were influenced by their religious leaders and by the propaganda from Syria; angered by the regularity and efficiency of British tax collections and by the British-imposed obligation to labor on constructing river banks and other public works; opposed to certain tribal leaders who, supported by Britain, had become tyrannical and oppressive; encouraged by recent troop withdrawals that seemed to indicate British weakness; and inspired by tribal victories in the early stages of the rising.[18]

At the outset of the rebellion there were 60,200 British and

Indian troops in Iraq. To reinforce this garrison, which initially was hard pressed, in the next few months Britain sent about 40,000 additional British and Indian troops to Iraq.[19] By the beginning of 1921 this force crushed the revolt, but only after serious fighting that left 426 British and Indian troops dead (plus the great majority of the 451 troops reported missing) and 1,228 wounded.[20]

The uprising was not a factor in Britain's decision to create an Arab government in Iraq. This decision was announced in Baghdad on 20 June 1920, just before the outbreak of the rebellion, with the date of implementation scheduled for the autumn of that year. Nonetheless, the uprising had an important impact because throughout the 1920s fear of a renewed outbreak of rebellion was a factor in Britain's decision to move Iraq rapidly toward independence.[21]

In November 1920, two years after the end of the war, Britain created a provisional Arab government in Iraq and thereby brought to an end the period of direct British rule. Under the terms of this new arrangement there was a council of state whose members headed the various government departments. The members of the council, all of whom were Iraqi, were appointed by and served under the leadership of Abd al-Rahman al-Gaylani, an elderly and highly respected dignitary known as the Naqib of Baghdad. However, each member of the council was closely supervised by a British adviser, and the entire government was under the ultimate control of the British high commissioner in Iraq, Sir Percy Cox. Indicating the extent of Cox's authority, it was he who suggested to the Naqib the names of most of the members of the council, and he had the right to veto any of the council's decisions.[22]

In January 1921, soon after the formation of the provisional government, British leaders invited Faysal ibn Husayn to assume the kingship of a more permanent regime in Iraq. Faysal was the son of King Husayn of the Hijaz to whom, in exchange for his participation in the fighting against the Ottoman empire, in 1915 Britain had made some rather vague pledges regarding Arab independence. By making Faysal king of Iraq British leaders thought that they could to a considerable extent fulfill their pledges to Husayn while simultaneously rewarding both father and son for having loyally served the allied cause during the war. They chose Faysal for the kingship also because, aside from being appropriately anti-Turkish, he could command the allegiance of the several hundred former Ottoman army officers from Iraq whom Britain hoped would form the nucleus of an Iraqi army that would defend British interests in the region. In addition, no Iraqi candidate for the throne had widespread support and approbation while Faysal, although not an Iraqi, had some prestige and status in the country because of his father's position as guardian of the holy places of Islam, because of his commanding role in the Arab revolt against the Ottoman empire, and because of his leadership after the war of the independent Arab government in Syria. For Britain Faysal was an obvious choice too because in July 1920 France had evicted him from Syria and thus he was now available to assume new responsibilities.[23]

With full British support, in August 1921 Faysal became king of Iraq. The British government now wanted to conclude a treaty with Faysal, not to replace the mandate which it valued highly because it gave Britain the juridical right to remain in Iraq, but rather to define and regulate the unequal relationship between the two countries. Initially, Iraqi leaders refused to conclude a treaty with Britain unless it would replace the mandate and guarantee their complete independence. Ultimately, however, they yielded because Britain had superior force and, by arresting some of the leading opponents of the treaty, demonstrated a willingness to use it if necessary.[24] As a result, in October 1922 a treaty, which was generally written to British specifications and scheduled to last for twenty years unless Iraq was admitted to the League of Nations before the expiration of that period, was concluded between the two countries. According to the terms of the treaty, the Iraqi king promised to be guided by British advice in all important matters affecting Britain's international and financial interests.[25] In a subsidiary document known as the military agreement which was signed in 1924, Britain also acquired the right to station its military forces in Iraq, raise and command a local military force in Iraq, use Iraqi roads, railways, rivers, and ports to move British troops across Iraq, inspect the Iraqi army at will, control the movements of the Iraqi army, control any joint Anglo-Iraqi military force which was placed in the field, and compel the king of Iraq to declare martial law and entrust its administration to a British officer.[26] In another subsidiary document signed at the same time as the military agreement, Iraq was obligated upon British request to employ, at its own expense and at a high rate of pay, a British official in a large number of important government positions.[27]

In this manner Britain retained a substantial amount of control over Iraq even after the end of direct British rule in 1920. This control enabled Britain to fulfill its duties and obligations to the League of Nations under the terms of the mandate, withdraw most of its military forces from Iraq while still ensuring the safety of the remaining garrison, and generally protect its strategic interests in the Middle East. However, Iraqi leaders accepted such great restrictions on their freedom only under compulsion. Predictably, they constantly struggled to remove these restrictions. Thus during the 1920s Britain's control over Iraq was less secure than appeared at first glance because Iraqi governments, complete with their own army, police force, and administrative machine, did not willingly accept it. In addition, British control rested on a weak military foundation because, mainly for reasons of economy, during the course of the 1920s Britain withdrew all of its ground troops from Iraq.[28] As a result, by 1929 Britain's position in Iraq had become so insecure that British leaders hastily agreed to terminate the mandate and grant full independence, long before they were legally obligated to do so and without first insisting upon adequate safeguards for important British interests in the region, in large measure because they feared incurring the displeasure or, more frightening, the active opposition of the Iraqi government.

CHAPTER 2

The End of the Mandate

In September 1929 Britain informed the Iraqi government, without qualification or proviso, that it would support Iraq's candidature for admission to the League of Nations in 1932.[1] Because admission to the League necessarily meant the end of the British mandate (in fact, in the opinion of the British government it was the only way in which the mandate could be legally terminated)[2] and the grant of full independence to Iraq, this promise was of considerable importance.

In some respects the British pledge was surprising. True, as a result of domestic political pressure to withdraw from Iraq, in April 1923 the British government had agreed to a protocol that reduced the twenty-year duration of the treaty of 1922 to a period of four years.[3] However, in July 1925 the commission of the League of Nations which examined the question of the disputed frontier between Turkey and Iraq decided that the *vilayet* (province) of Mosul should pass to Iraq only on the condition that the British mandate continued for the next twenty-five years in order to allow sufficient time for the Iraqi state to consolidate and develop. Acting on the commission's recommendation, in December 1925 the council of the League of Nations resolved that the award of Mosul to Iraq would not become definitive until Britain had concluded a new treaty with Iraq that would ensure that the mandate remained in effect for the next twenty-five years unless Iraq were admitted to the League before the expiration of this period. Iraqi leaders were amenable to the council's decision because they desperately wanted to keep the *vilayet* of Mosul, which was widely believed to contain large quantities of oil, and because they thought that they could induce Britain to recommend Iraq for membership in the League long before the expiration of the twenty-five year time period. The British government was amenable to the council's decision because it wanted to keep the oil-bearing region of Mosul within a British sphere of influence. Consequently, in January 1926 Britain and Iraq duly concluded a new treaty that extended the treaty of 1922 in accordance with the council's decision.[4] Thus Britain's promise in 1929 to recommend the termination of the mandate and the admission of Iraq to the League, coming less than four years after it had accepted the council's decision awarding Mosul to Iraq on the implied condition of a lengthy continuation of the mandate, might be seen, at least by some, to smack of sharp practice. For the foreign office this possibility was indeed a matter of some concern.[5]

At first sight, Britain's promise to recommend Iraq for admission to the League of Nations was striking also because by 1929 the entire cost of the mandate to the British treasury was less than £500,000 per year.[6] Even this relatively low figure probably overstated the mandate's true cost because quite likely the British economy benefited from some export orders it would not otherwise have received.[7] In exchange for this modest sum, the British government maintained three modern, fully equipped airbases in Iraq.[8] These bases enabled Britain in an emergency to move military aircraft rapidly between Egypt and India, to protect the valuable oilfields in both Iraq and Iran, and generally to safeguard vital British interests in the Persian Gulf. Thus for little financial cost the British government gained important strategic advantages, but all of these advantages would be lost if an independent Iraq refused to allow a continued British military presence.

And this option was open to Iraq because Britain's promise to recommend Iraq for admission to the League of Nations was unqualified. It did not include any reservation that would ensure the future protection of vital British interests in the region—for example, the right to retain airbases in Iraq or the right to move troops across Iraq. True, the message to the Iraqi government which contained the promise also stated that it would be necessary to conclude a new treaty before 1932 in order to regulate Anglo-Iraqi relations after independence. However, the promise to recommend Iraq for admission to the League was not conditional upon the conclusion of this treaty. Thus in 1930, during the lengthy and difficult negotiations for the new treaty, Britain was unable to bring pressure to bear upon Iraq for concessions by threatening to retain the mandate if a satisfactory agreement were not concluded. In this manner the British government abandoned an important bargaining card, the consequences of which were significant for the ultimate shape of the Anglo-Iraqi treaty of 1930.

Nor was it clear that most Iraqis wanted the mandate to end at this time. In September 1929 Iraq was calm and peaceful, and no British ground troops were required to hold the country. True, King Faysal and the relatively small group of urban Sunni Arab politicians and military leaders who constituted the bulk of the ruling class in Iraq wanted Britain to withdraw so that they could assume complete control over the country. So too did their sizable block of followers among the Sunni Arab population (in all about 20 percent of Iraq's total population of around 3,000,000)[9] and especially that highly politically conscious portion of it such as teachers, students, lawyers, and civil servants who lived primarily in the major cities like Baghdad and Mosul. The *Watani* (National) party, which was led by the distinguished Shiite politician Jafar Abu al-Timman and which drew most of its support from Shiite handicraft workers and petty tradesmen in urban areas, also wanted an immediate end to the mandate.[10]

However, in the late 1920s probably most of the Shiite community, which dwelled mainly in the southern part of the country and comprised slightly more than half of the total population,[11] was not eager for Britain to leave Iraq. At first glance this attitude was surprising because Shiites had been in the forefront of the anti-British rebellion of 1920. Certainly this attitude was not because the Shiites had become genuinely pro-British in sentiment or outlook, or because they wanted to maintain an enduring administrative or constitutional link with Britain, or because they were undesirous of ultimately achieving independence for Iraq. Rather it was because they now viewed the mandatory as a possible check on the power and avariciousness of the Sunni elite who dominated the government and the army.[12] Illustrating the extent of this domination and the resultant sense of grievance among the Shiites, during the period from 1921 to 1932 no Shiite was appointed to the office of prime minister and only 17.7 percent of the other ministerial positions went to Shiites.[13] To perpetuate itself in office the small Sunni ruling class manipulated parliamentary elections: for example, in the elections of 1928 Shiites won only twenty-six out of a total of eighty-eight seats in the chamber of deputies.[14] The situation was similar in the provinces: in 1921 all five of Iraq's *mutasarrifs* (governors of *liwas* or provinces) were Sunni, and eight of the country's *qaimmaqams* (the chief executive officer of a *qadha* or district) were Sunni while only one was Shiite;[15] and in 1933 thirteen *mutasarrifs* were Sunni while only one was Shiite, and forty-three *qaimmaqams* were Sunni while only four were Shiite.[16]

Aside from anger at being deprived of political power, in the late 1920s most Shiites were opposed to the government's attempt to introduce conscription which, they suspected, would involve mainly Shiite conscripts serving under mainly Sunni officers. The fact that British opposition was the primary reason why the Iraqi government had failed to introduce conscription was not lost on the Shiite community.[17] Nor were the Shiites mistaken in their belief that Sunnis controlled the army. Indicating the extent of this control, in a sample of sixty-one army officers who were serving in 1936, one authority could discover only one Shiite.[18] According to another account, in 1946 out of eighty staff officers serving in the army only three were Shiites.[19]

In addition to these considerations, certain Shiite tribal leaders had benefited greatly from Britain's policy of promoting their authority in the countryside. Britain initiated this policy during the First World War as an inexpensive means of collecting tax revenue, protecting the army's line of communications, and denying supplies to the enemy. It worked reasonably well, and Britain continued it after the war in order to ensure, with minimal British effort, peace and order in the rural regions of the country. The policy involved giving arms, money, land, and tax remissions to certain shaykhs whom the British administration designated as tribal leaders. It also involved promoting the judicial authority of these shaykhs by means of the tribal criminal and civil disputes regulation. This measure, which the British promulgated in 1916, gave tribal leaders the power to settle conflicts and disputes among the inhabitants of their areas. Iraqi governments opposed this regulation because it excluded from their judicial authority large sections of the rural part of the country, but on several occasions during the 1920s the British high commissioner prevented them from abrogating it. He also prevented them from taking other fiscal and administrative measures to curb the wealth and power of these tribal leaders.[20] Thus for these tribal leaders, who had gained so much from Britain's presence in Iraq, the prospect of British withdrawal, which might possibly be followed by the loss of their land, privileges, and power, was particularly alarming.

Many Kurds, too, were dismayed and worried by the prospect of British withdrawal. Kurds, who constituted nearly 20 percent of the total population,[21] were congregated in the northern part of Iraq. They spoke a language quite distinct from Arabic, and had many customs and traditions of their own. In July 1925 the commission of the League of Nations which recommended that the Mosul *vilayet* should pass to Iraq stated that "Regard must be paid to the desires expressed by the Kurds that officials of Kurdish race should be appointed for the administration of their country, the dispensation of justice, and teaching in the schools, and that Kurdish should be the official language of all these services."[22] In December 1925 the council of the League of Nations, which adopted the commission's report, insisted that the British government inform the council of "the administrative measures which will be taken with a view to securing for the Kurdish populations mentioned in the report of the Commission of Inquiry the guarantees regarding local administration recommended by the Commission in its final conclusions."[23] Thus Britain was obligated to ensure that the terms of the League of Nations award in regard to the Kurdish districts of Iraq were fulfilled. However, the Iraqi government did not want to see any form of local autonomy or administration in Kurdistan which, it feared, would limit its authority and possibly undermine national unity. It suspected that British efforts to ensure special treatment for the Kurds were part of a plot to weaken or even dismember the country. Consequently, in the middle and late 1920s it refused to implement the terms of the League of Nations award. In light of this background it is understandable that the British government's announcement in September 1929 that it would recommend Iraq for admission to the League of Nations in 1932 caused serious concern in Kurdistan. At this time most Kurds favored separation from Iraq and some form of independence under the protection of Britain or the League of Nations. Alternatively, they preferred a continuation of the mandate which represented their best hope for the creation of the special regime in Kurdistan that the League of Nations had stipulated and which the Iraqi government had promised but failed to implement. In any event, from Kurdistan there was little pressure on Britain to end its supervisory role in Iraq.[24]

The non-Muslim communities, consisting primarily of Jews, various Christian denominations, and Yazidis, comprised in all nearly 7 percent of the total population of Iraq.[25] Generally these groups were well disposed toward Britain and did not want the mandate to end. The Jews, for example, a community of about 100,000 who resided mainly in Baghdad and were heavily involved in trading activities, had especially good relations with the British.[26] So did the Assyrian Christians, a group of about 30,000 in the northern part of Iraq. Many Assyrians had served in the levies, a British military force quite distinct from the Iraqi army, and feared that after independence this service would mark them for retribution. Indeed, the Assyrians were so fearful of living in an independent Iraqi state that in 1931 they petitioned the League of Nations, without success, to find a home for them under the rule of a European Christian power.[27]

Why then did the British government issue the promise to Iraq of September 1929? To begin with, the decision should be seen in the context of a general modification of imperial policy which resulted in large measure from the terrible physical and moral debilitation Britain suffered during the First World War. This great loss came at a time when nationalist movements in several countries under British control, for example, Ireland, Egypt, and India, as well as Iraq, were rapidly gaining in strength. As a result of this conjunction of events, after the First World War British leaders concluded that only by granting increasing amounts of self-rule to the indigenous peoples of their empire could they retain the essential parts of their imperial position in the world.[28]

For Britain the human and economic cost of the war was very high. 745,000 British soldiers were killed (about 9 percent of all of the men in the United Kingdom aged 20 to 45) and 1,700,000 were wounded. Part of Britain's overseas wealth had to be liquidated in order to pay for the war. Other British assets in central Europe and Russia were seized by hostile powers. Because British industry was obligated to concentrate almost entirely on war production, and because there was a shortage of shipping, many foreign markets were lost to American and Japanese competitors, or to locally made products, and were not recovered after the conflict.[29] Illustrating the extent of this loss of markets, between 1913 and 1923 the export of British cotton piece goods to India declined by 53 percent.[30] During the same period, and allowing for the change in the value of the pound, the total value of British exports to South America fell by over one-third.[31] And between the periods 1911–13 and 1931–38 Britain's share of the world export trade in manufactured goods declined from 27.5 percent to 18.5 percent.[32]

During the war tax revenues had only covered 36 percent of

expenditures, and the remaining money had been borrowed. Consequently, after the war British governments reduced military outlays in order to meet interest payments on the national debt. Indicating the magnitude of this financial obligation, by the late 1920s 40 percent of the government's spending was devoted to meeting interest payments on the national debt compared with only 12 percent in 1913.[33]

After the war British governments also reduced military expenditures in order to meet popular pressure for increased outlays on domestic needs such as housing, education, pensions, and unemployment compensation.[34] Thus while social service payments in financial year 1913–14 were £41,500,000, in 1921–22 they rose to £234,000,000 and in 1933–34 totaled £272,500,000.[35] By comparison, expenditure on the army and navy combined in 1932 was only £86,000,000, which was the same amount that was spent immediately before the First World War even though costs had risen greatly during the interval and total government spending had increased more than fourfold.[36] Clearly illustrating the government's changing sense of priorities, on the eve of the First World War the armed forces received 43 percent of the total government budget, while by 1932 this figure was reduced to 12 percent.[37]

Combined with the reduction of economic strength and military power, in the 1920s the belief in the moral righteousness of the imperial mission, which before the war had permeated British society and was an essential ingredient for the maintenance of the empire, was sapped by the widespread propagation of liberal ideals like democratic government and self-determination of nations for which the war had ostensibly been fought. Imperialism not only conflicted with these liberal ideals but also, in the minds of many, had been a major cause of the war. As a result, in Britain in the 1920s it became a much maligned doctrine that no longer commanded broad support.[38] Indicating the disrepute into which imperialism fell, during the 1920s most of the British press advocated completely abandoning or at least strictly curtailing British responsibilities and commitments in Iraq.[39] In 1927, during a period of Conservative government in Britain, one minister actually recommended prompt withdrawal from Iraq largely because he thought it would be electorally popular.[40]

Thus in the 1920s the British government, weakened economically and militarily, and with reduced public support for imperial ventures, had to confront strengthened nationalist movements in various parts of the empire. In this difficult situation, in order to retain the essence of its imperial position—which in India consisted of control of the Indian army but which elsewhere often consisted primarily of military bases at strategic locations—Britain granted increasing amounts of self-rule to India, Ireland, Egypt, Transjordan, and, as we have observed in the previous chapter, Iraq. Perhaps this attempt to accommodate local nationalists by withdrawing from some imperial responsibilities was slightly hastened by the advent to power of a Labour government in June 1929, but it had begun much earlier and had commanded widespread support in all three major political parties.[41]

Thus Britain's promise of September 1929 was part of a wider policy of retreat from an absolutist form of empire toward a more liberal or informal type of empire. But it was also consonant with previous policy in Iraq itself. Since Britain had established an Arab government in Baghdad in 1920 it had tried to prepare the country for self-rule. Arguably, such a policy was incumbent because article 22 of the covenant of the League of Nations, the legal basis for Britain's position in Iraq, did not give Britain sovereignty or the right permanently to remain in control of Iraq under some other guise such as a protectorate. On the contrary, although the time period was not stipulated precisely, article 22 clearly envisaged the establishment of an independent state in Iraq as soon as that country was able to stand alone without the advice and assistance of the mandatory.[42]

Aside from this consideration, in July 1927 the British government had promised King Faysal that it would recommend Iraq for admission to the League of Nations in 1932 "If all goes well in the interval and the present rate of progress is maintained."[43] The following December, in a formal treaty with Iraq, the British government again pledged to recommend Iraq for admission to the League of Nations in 1932 "Provided the present rate of progress in Iraq is maintained and all goes well in the interval."[44] The officials at the colonial office in London, who supervised Britain's relations with Iraq, believed that this qualification referred only to the possibility of widespread internal disorder or serious interruption of constitutional government. Since neither event had occurred, in September 1929 they felt obligated to implement the government's promise. They did not believe that the government could renege on its promise simply because, for example, Iraqi leaders refused to agree to allow Britain to retain airbases in Iraq after independence. To do so, they feared, would invite, and not without justification, accusations of bad faith.[45]

The British government's decision to terminate the mandate was also influenced by the unsound legal position of its military forces in Iraq. This position was sanctioned and regulated by the Anglo-Iraqi military agreement of 1924.[46] However, the agreement expired in December 1928, and the Iraqi government refused to conclude a new agreement except in exchange for the elimination of all British control over the Iraqi army plus the right to determine the nature and size of the British garrison in Iraq.[47] The British government would not accept these conditions because it believed that they were incompatible with Britain's obligations to the League of Nations, and because it feared that they would endanger the remaining British forces in Iraq.[48] As a result of this impasse, the British government in 1929 no longer had any treaty sanction for the presence of its military forces in Iraq or for the legal privileges and immunities they enjoyed. Nor did it have any treaty sanction for its recruitment of Iraqi subjects into a British imperial military force stationed in Iraq known as the levies, or for its previously held right in time of emergency to compel the king of Iraq to proclaim martial law and entrust its administration to a British officer.[49] Of course, the British government could and did maintain that it needed military forces in Iraq in order to implement its obligations to the League of Nations, and that consequently it regarded the existing military agreement as remaining in force after the date of expiration.[50] But the Iraqi government did not accept this proposition, and British leaders feared that this unsettled and disputatious situation would lead to continual friction to the detriment of important imperial interests in the Middle East.[51] British officials were unhappy with this situation too because they did not believe they had a strong legal case for insisting that the military agreement of 1924 remain operative after the date of expiration.[52] By agreeing to recommend Iraq for membership in the League of Nations they hoped to create a favorable atmosphere for the negotiation of a new treaty that would give firm legal sanction to the continued stationing of British military forces in Iraq.[53]

British leaders also agreed to recommend Iraq for membership in the League of Nations because they were concerned that continuation of the mandate would eventually lead to internal unrest and upheaval, possibly fomented by the Iraqi government itself. In the late 1920s Sir Henry Dobbs, the British high commissioner in Iraq, and his successor, Sir Gilbert Clayton, frequently made this point.[54] These warnings affected British leaders, who were haunted by fear of a repetition of the violent insurrection against British rule in Iraq in 1920.[55] Ultimately, 102,000 British and Indian troops had been required to suppress the rising.[56] But by 1929 the British government had withdrawn all British and Indian ground troops from Iraq. Aside from military aircraft and one and a half armored car companies manned by Royal Air Force personnel, the British authorities in Iraq had at their disposal only 2,000 locally recruited levies.[57] True, they also had a considerable degree of control over the 9,000 man Iraqi army. For example, there were thirty-six British officers in key positions,[58] and the Iraqi government could not move any unit without British permission.[59] However, the great majority of its officers were Iraqi, and British leaders doubted whether they could count on this force in a crisis, especially if the Iraqi government itself instigated the disturbances.[60]

Of course, in an emergency Britain could reinforce its garrison in Iraq with Indian troops. But by the late 1920s the British government could no longer send Indian troops abroad without encountering strong opposition and protests from political leaders in India who did not believe that their people should bear the military and financial burden of defending British imperial interests in the Middle East and elsewhere.[61] Indicating the depth of feeling on this subject in India, in 1921 the legislative assembly of India passed a resolution defining the role of the Indian army as "the defence of India against external aggression and the maintenance of internal peace and tranquillity." For any other purpose, the resolution stated, the obligations resting on India were to be optional and self-imposed as they were in the case of the self-governing British dominions.[62] In 1929 the practical repercussions of this sentiment could be observed by the fact that, excluding the adjacent territory of Burma, there were only two Indian army battalions stationed abroad (one in Hong Kong and one in Malaya) assisting Britain in maintaining control of its far-flung empire.[63] In 1929 the practical repercussions of this sentiment could be observed also when, in response to a request from the war office in London, the chief of the general staff of the Indian army refused to promise to provide Indian troops to defend the valuable British controlled oilfields in southwestern Iran or the largely British controlled oilfields in northern Iraq, even in the event of a Russian attack on those countries.[64]

Nor could Britain easily send troops to Iraq from its garrison in Egypt because in August 1929 serious riots broke out in Palestine as a result of a dispute between Jews and Arabs at the western wall in Jerusalem. To restore order the British government sent three battalions and an armored car squadron from Egypt to Palestine.[65] But this move meant that there were now few British troops in Egypt available for dispatch to Iraq.

And for Britain in August and September 1929 the security situation in Iraq was especially worrying because there was much sympathy for the Arab protesters in Palestine.[66] Indeed, on 30 August nationalist politicians in Baghdad organized a large anti-Zionist and anti-British demonstration.[67] Compounding the problem, the Iraqi government led by Tawfiq al-Suwaydi had just resigned and no leading political figure would attempt to form a government in the absence of a clear statement from Britain regarding Iraqi independence. If internal upheaval broke out in the midst of this indeterminate and volatile political situation, British leaders feared that they might have to reintroduce considerable numbers of British troops and administrative personnel and resume direct control over the country. But Britain had abandoned direct rule in 1920 in favor of indirect rule through an Arab government. Aside from considerations of financial cost and overextension of limited military resources, reintroduction of direct control would involve a serious admission of failure. All the more reason then, in the minds of British leaders, to conciliate nationalist aspirations by promising to recommend Iraq for admission to the League of Nations.[68]

But the British government's decision of September 1929 to accommodate nationalist opinion in Iraq was not only prompted by a desire to avoid internal unrest and upheaval. British officials also believed that by terminating the mandate at a relatively early date they would earn the goodwill and gratitude of most of Iraq's governing class and thereby, in the long run, maintain Britain's political influence and strategic position in Iraq more assuredly and effectively, and with less strain and inconvenience, than by clinging to a supervisory role in the country's affairs.[69]

Although the British government relinquished the mandate in 1932, long before it was legally obligated to do so, in the 1930s and early 1940s many Iraqi leaders viewed Britain with resentment and anger. Much of the explanation for this paradox lies in the Anglo-Iraqi treaty of alliance of 1930, which was designed to regulate the relationship between the two countries for a twenty-five year period after Iraq became independent.[70] The most important provisions of the treaty are discussed in detail in the following chapters and need concern us here only briefly. Suffice it to say that this agreement allowed the British government to maintain two airbases in Iraq and to move its military forces across Iraqi territory. It also obligated Iraq to purchase virtually all of its military equipment in Britain, employ at its own expense the services of a British military mission, send its officers exclusively to British military academies, and use British subjects whenever it needed foreign experts. The British government insisted upon including these provisions in the treaty because it wanted to retain its strategic position and political influence in Iraq after independence. The Iraqi government accepted these restrictions on its sovereignty because it believed that it needed a treaty of alliance with Britain in order to be certain of gaining admission to the League of Nations and thereby ending the mandate. Thus while Iraq became an independent state in 1932, it was still involuntarily bound to Britain in a subordinate relationship. As time passed Iraqi leaders increasingly found this relationship humiliating. In various ways they struggled to liberate themselves from it. Ultimately, in 1941 an Iraqi attempt to restrict Britain's privileges in Iraq led to military conflict between the two countries and thereby exposed the limitations of Britain's policy of indirect rule.

CHAPTER 3

The British Airbases

The most difficult matter that arose during the negotiations for the treaty of June 1930 which gave Iraq independence was the question of the British airbases. By the beginning of 1930 the British government had withdrawn all British and Indian ground troops from Iraq but it still maintained five squadrons of military aircraft. These planes were stationed at three widely separated airbases: Mosul, Hinaidi (five miles from Baghdad), and Shaiba (ten miles from Basra), plus a seaplane anchorage at Basra. While not opposing the termination of the mandate, the air ministry was determined to retain these bases, or at least as many of them as possible, after independence.[1]

Because of the relatively short range and unreliable nature of aircraft at this time, the air ministry believed that these bases were an essential link in the British military and civil air route to India. Indeed, the air ministry argued that the abandonment of the bases and the consequent rupture of the Iraqi link in the air route would be as grave a setback for Britain as the closure of the Suez Canal. For the air ministry this route was particularly important because in an emergency it planned quickly to reinforce the British garrisons in Aden, the Sudan, Egypt, Palestine, Transjordan, Iraq, or India with warplanes from the other countries. The air ministry realized, of course, that technological developments would eventually lead to more reliable longer ranged aircraft and thereby reduce the need for intermediary landing grounds such as those in Iraq. Nonetheless, it believed that for the forseeable future it would still require several airbases between Cairo and Karachi because the army cooperation type of aircraft, which was especially useful for military operations in the Middle East and India,

was likely to remain short ranged. Nor was the air ministry willing to rely on Iraqi controlled airbases for refuelling purposes
because, aside from the need to be absolutely certain about its
fuel supplies, it needed to stockpile large quantities of spare parts,
tools, and munitions, and to maintain sophisticated meteorolog-
ical and communication facilities. The air ministry also needed to
have sufficient numbers of highly trained British personnel constantly available to perform essential maintenance and repair work
on the aircraft. In 1930, after years of laborious effort and great
expense, all the stockpiles, facilities, and personnel existed at the
British airbases in Iraq, and the air ministry was strongly opposed to abandoning them.[2]

In addition to these imperial considerations, the air ministry
argued that the bases were necessary to enable the British government to fulfill its obligations under the mandate, and later
under the treaty of 1930, to defend Iraq against aggression. In
the opinion of the air ministry it was important for the British
government to honor this commitment not only for moral reasons and because of Iraq's strategic location on the air route to
India but also because of the rich oilfields in northern Iraq in
which British interests were heavily represented. During the 1920s
Iraq had been menaced by both Turkey and by Ibn Saud's kingdom of Najd-Hijaz; and the air ministry feared that, if the Royal
Air Force withdrew, these countries, plus Iran and possibly even
Russia, would again threaten Iraq. Conversely, the air ministry
maintained that the continued presence of the R.A.F. in Iraq
would be a formidable deterrent against aggression.[3]

The air ministry also believed that the continued presence of
the R.A.F. in Iraq after independence would discourage dissident groups in Iraqi society like the Kurds or the Shiite tribes
from brigandage or revolt. In 1930 Iraq had no air force, and
the air ministry was convinced that the Iraqi army alone, which
then stood at about 9,000 men, would be incapable of preventing
serious outbreaks of disorder. Although the British government
had no intention of remaining legally responsible for internal security after independence, the air ministry maintained that in the
event of internal upheaval Britain would still have to intervene
in order to restore domestic tranquillity because British lives and
property would be endangered and the British line of communications across Iraq would be jeopardized. In the event of such
upheaval, the air ministry argued that the British government
would have to intervene also because otherwise neighboring states,

taking advantage of Iraq's debilitated condition, would move into the country. Thus the air ministry wanted to retain the British airbases because it believed that their very existence would help to preserve internal order and thereby obviate the need for British military intervention in the domestic affairs of Iraq. If, however, the R.A.F.'s deterrent value were insufficient and internal disorder still ensued, the air ministry thought that the bases would enable the British government to intervene quickly and efficaciously.[4]

Aside from these purely Iraqi considerations, the air ministry wanted to keep the bases because of their proximity to the large British owned oilfields in southwestern Iran and the valuable oil refinery at Abadan. In the event of a Russian attack on Iran the air ministry believed that the British government could use the bases to help defend these installations. The air ministry also thought that the withdrawal of the R.A.F. from Iraq would remove a powerful deterrent to Russian aggression against Iran.[5]

The air ministry further believed that the British airbases in Iraq inhibited Iran and Ibn Saud's kingdom of Najd-Hijaz from menacing British interests in the Persian Gulf. The air ministry was alarmed about this possibility because Iran had a territorial claim to the entirety of the British protected shaykhdom of Bahrain, and Ibn Saud had territorial claims to portions of the British protected shaykhdoms of Qatar and Abu Dhabi.[6]

The Iraqi government did not want the British airbases to remain after independence. It believed that their continued presence on Iraqi territory would be derogatory to national sovereignty and tantamount to an indefinite prolongation of the British military occupation. If the bases stayed, Iraqi officials thought that Britain would inevitably interfere in the domestic affairs and the administration of the country. The Iraqi government, which in 1930 was led by genuinely pro-British figures like King Faysal, Prime Minister Nuri al-Said, and Defence Minister Jafar al-Askari, also feared that the bases would be a running sore that would damage Anglo-Iraqi relations for as long as they remained. In addition, the Iraqi government was concerned that France would cite the continued presence of British airbases in Iraq as a precedent and an excuse to keep its ground troops in Syria indefinitely, thereby preventing Syria from attaining true independence and also preventing Iraq and Syria from uniting.

Nor did Iraqi leaders think that the bases were necessary to protect Iraq from attack. On the contrary, they maintained that the Anglo-Iraqi military alliance by itself would probably be sufficient to deter aggression. Aside from the moral value of the alliance, they argued that fear of the British fleet in the Mediterranean would deter Turkish aggression. If an attack still occurred, they said that Britain could rapidly fly warplanes to Iraq from neighboring countries. As far as internal security was concerned, Iraqi leaders did not believe that they would need British assistance, especially since they planned to develop their own air force as rapidly as possible. Indeed, in 1930 there were already ten Iraqi pilots and twenty-one mechanics under instruction in Britain and at the British airbase at Hinaidi. As a possible alternative to the continued presence of the British airbases in Iraq, in April 1930 the Iraqi government proposed that Britain transfer the bases to Transjordan and Kuwait. From these locations it thought that Britain could still maintain the integrity of the air route to India. As compensation for the removal of the bases, the Iraqi government offered to allow Britain to fly over Iraqi territory and to use Iraqi airfields for refuelling purposes at any time.[7]

Influenced by the views of the air ministry, the British government insisted on keeping some form of military presence in Iraq. At this stage Iraqi leaders were concerned that without an agreement on the airbases Britain might create an excuse to retain the mandate and thereby deprive Iraq of independence.[8] There was also the nagging fear that without a treaty of alliance with Britain the League of Nations would conclude that Iraq was incapable of standing alone and deny Britain's request to relinquish the mandate.[9] After all, in 1925 the council of the League had said that the mandate should probably continue for the next twenty-five years. For these reasons, in late April 1930 the Iraqi government offered to allow Britain to keep the airbase at Shaiba and the seaplane anchorage at Basra if Britain agreed to withdraw from Mosul and Hinaidi.[10] The Iraqi government was especially anxious to secure Britain's withdrawal from Hinaidi because it found the presence of British forces so close to the capital particularly offensive.[11]

The air ministry, however, did not want to leave Mosul and Hinaidi. It maintained that it would cost Britain at least £1,000,000 to expand the facilities at Shaiba sufficiently to accommodate all the British aircraft in Iraq. The air ministry also pointed out that from Shaiba the British government would be unable to protect the oilfields in northern Iraq or the envisaged oil pipeline to the Mediterranean.[12] The air ministry believed that the British base at Mosul was especially useful for deterring a Turkish attack and, in the event of need, would be an excellent location for resisting such an attack. In addition, the air ministry argued that Mosul was valuable because it enabled British pilots to become intimately familiar with the terrain in northern Iraq over which they would have to fight in the event of war with Turkey. The air ministry wanted to retain Mosul too because it was the most pleasant station in the country during the hot summer months and for this reason was quite popular with the crews.[13]

However, Mosul was off the British air route to India and thus from the imperial perspective less important than Hinaidi. For the air ministry Hinaidi was more important than Mosul too because it was a much larger base with more accommodation for aircraft and personnel and more elaborate repair and maintenance facilities. Indeed, the air ministry had spent £600,000 developing Hinaidi since it took over the base from the army in 1922, and the war office had spent considerable money before that date. For the air ministry Hinaidi had the further advantage of being linked by both railway and river transportation to Basra, Iraq's only port. Mosul, on the other hand, was isolated in northern Iraq, about 600 miles from the Persian Gulf. The air ministry also wanted to retain Hinaidi because its location near Baghdad enabled the British air officer commanding readily to stay in touch with the British high commissioner and the Iraqi government. From this contact the air ministry believed that the air officer commanding gained valuable intelligence information about conditions in the country which allowed him to anticipate possible sources of disturbance. In addition, the air ministry maintained that Hinaidi's location in the center of Iraq just outside the capital provided an excellent deterrent to internal disorder and, if necessary, a perfect position from which to launch swift and decisive intervention against lawless elements. If the R.A.F. vacated Hinaidi the air ministry feared that internal disorder would ensue which would rapidly lead to external aggression and the necessity for British intervention under the terms of the proposed treaty of alliance. In view of these considerations, in late April 1930 the air ministry said that it would withdraw from Mosul provided it could retain the base at Hinaidi.[14]

With the withdrawal from Mosul generally agreed, by the end of April 1930 the question of the British airbase at Hinaidi was the major issue preventing the successful conclusion of the treaty negotiations. In contrast to the air ministry, the colonial office, which was the department responsible for supervising Britain's relations with Iraq, was willing to accept the Iraqi offer to vacate Hinaidi in exchange for retaining Shaiba. The colonial office believed that under this arrangement the British government could still maintain the air route to India by flying directly from a landing ground at Rutba in the desert in western Iraq to Shaiba. Unlike the air ministry, the colonial office thought that after independence the Iraqi government would be able to keep a reasonable degree of order in the country even without the presence of a British airbase at Hinaidi. The colonial office also argued that if the British government retained Hinaidi it would remain morally responsible for maintaining internal security in Iraq without either the legal sanction or the adequate means for discharging that responsibility. In addition, the colonial office noted that in practical terms it would be difficult and possibly even dangerous for Britain to stay at Hinaidi in the face of opposition by the Iraqi government. Because the Iraqi army would no longer have any British officers, the colonial office feared that after independence it would be an unreliable force that might one day threaten the remaining British garrison in Iraq. However, in the opinion of the colonial office this risk would be considerably reduced if all of the British forces in Iraq were congregated at Shaiba because the area was virtually under the guns of British warships in the Shatt al-Arab, and because in an emergency the British government could easily reinforce or withdraw the garrison by sea. The colonial office also emphasized that Shaiba would be more secure than Hinaidi because the Basra area was probably the most pro-British region in the country.[15]

Perhaps most important, however, the colonial office was willing to withdraw from Hinaidi because it feared that otherwise the negotiations with Iraq would break down. In the opinion of the colonial office, this result would be very undesirable because Iraq might then gain independence without a treaty of alliance with Britain. After all, in September 1929 the British government had promised to recommend Iraq for membership in the League of Nations in 1932 without making this promise conditional upon the prior negotiation of a treaty of alliance. In this situation, with Iraq independent but not tied to Britain in a treaty of alliance, if Britain but not Iraq were engaged in war, the British government would be unable to keep military forces at Shaiba or anywhere else in Iraq, or to move troops across Iraqi territory, without contravening generally accepted principles of international law governing the behavior of neutral powers in wartime. The colonial office also pointed out that without a treaty of alliance Iraq would be able freely to grant military bases or spheres of influence to other countries in an area of great strategic importance to Britain. In addition, the colonial office believed that even without an alliance the British government would probably have to defend Iraq against aggression because of its own important commercial and strategic interests in the area; consequently an alliance was desirable to act as a deterrent to aggression. Finally, the colonial office argued that without a treaty of alliance the League of Nations might conclude that Iraq was incapable of standing alone and therefore refuse the British government's request to terminate the mandate. In this case the colonial office feared that there would be outbreaks of disorder throughout Iraq that Britain would be able to suppress only with considerable effort and at great expense.[16]

In late April 1930, and again several times the following month, Sir Francis Humphrys, the British high commissioner who conducted the treaty negotiations in Baghdad with the Iraqi government, suggested a compromise solution. Like the air ministry, he believed that it was necessary for Britain to retain an airbase in central Iraq because otherwise internal disorder would soon spread and the entire fabric of administration would rapidly deteriorate. However, Humphrys sympathized with the Iraqi government's opposition to a British base so close to Baghdad. He also thought that a British military presence so near the capital would be a continual source of acrimony between the two countries and would probably increase rather than decrease the chances of internal unrest. In the event of internal unrest, Humphrys feared that Hinaidi would be difficult to defend precisely because it was located so close to Baghdad, the likely source of the disturbances. In addition, he pointed out that Hinaidi was situated below the flood level of the Tigris River, and that its artificial bank might be breached in time of trouble. He also argued that one of Hinaidi's main advantages—the fact that in an emergency it was accessible from Basra and the sea via the Tigris—would soon cease to exist as increasing quantities of water from the river were diverted to agriculture. In view of these considerations, Humphrys recommended that the British government should build a new airbase in central Iraq near Lake Habbaniya about fifty miles west of Baghdad.[17]

Initially, the air ministry resisted the high commissioner's proposal because it would mean abandoning the well-developed and, from the air ministry's perspective, ideally situated base at Hinaidi. Moreover, the air ministry believed that at Habbaniya the Royal Air Force would be too far from Baghdad to be conveniently able to maintain regular and close communication with the British embassy and the Iraqi government, and would therefore be deprived of valuable sources of intelligence information about events in the country. The air ministry also said that removed from the immediate vicinity of Baghdad the R.A.F. would be a less effective deterrent to internal disorder. In the event of such disorder, the air ministry feared that at Habbaniya the R.A.F. would be too far from Baghdad to be able to intervene rapidly and effectively before the turmoil achieved serious dimensions that threatened important British commercial or strategic interests in Iraq and possibly led to external aggression. In addition, the air ministry maintained that it would cost the British government nearly £2,000,000 to construct a proper airbase at Habbaniya, that the Habbaniya area was subject to flooding and had poor communications with Basra, and that British airmen in that isolated location would lack the amenities and diversions previously found at Baghdad.[18]

However, in mid-May 1930 the air ministry reluctantly accepted the possibility of moving to Habbaniya.[19] Probably the air ministry was influenced by a report by the air officer commanding in Iraq, Sir Robert Brooke-Popham, which claimed that the new location was really quite desirable. In particular, Brooke-Popham maintained that Habbaniya would be more secure than Hinaidi in case of internal disorder, that it was nearer the projected oil pipeline, that there was a good site on high ground for construction, that the area would soon be connected to Baghdad by rail, that the region was non-malarial, and that there were readily available shooting, fishing, boating, and bathing facilities superior to those existing near Hinaidi.[20]

In early June 1930 the Iraqi government also accepted the high commissioner's compromise proposal, probably because it was relieved to get the British air force out of Hinaidi and because only through a treaty of alliance with Britain could it be certain of gaining independence.[21] Accordingly, the Anglo-Iraqi treaty of 30 June 1930 stated that the British government had to withdraw all of its forces from Mosul and Hinaidi within five years of the treaty's entry into force, which was scheduled to occur when Iraq was admitted into the League of Nations. However, the treaty allowed Britain to maintain its airbase at Shaiba and its seaplane anchorage at Basra, and to construct a new airbase west of the Euphrates presumably in the region of Lake Habbaniya.

In accordance with the terms of the treaty, in 1936 and 1937 the British government duly withdrew all of its military forces from Mosul and Hinaidi and relocated them at the newly constructed base at Habbaniya.[22] Four years later, in May 1941, the Iraqi army besieged Habbaniya. The British forces withstood the assault in part because Habbaniya's isolated location increased Iraqi supply problems while giving British commanders considerable warning of the impending danger. Moreover, Habbaniya's position in western Iraq made it relatively easy for the British government to reinforce the garrison by road from Palestine.[23] It is unlikely that the garrison would have fared so well if it had still been located at Hinaidi. Thus, ironically, for the air ministry, which long opposed the withdrawal from Hinaidi, the move to Habbaniya was really very fortunate. Equally ironically, for the militantly anti-British government that came to power in Iraq in 1941, Britain's withdrawal from Hinaidi proved to be quite disastrous.

In 1929–30 the British government could have retained the mandate for Iraq. The League of Nations would not have objected, and there would have been considerable support for the policy within Iraq. It was this policy of retaining the mandate which in the 1920s and 1930s Britain followed in Palestine and France followed in Syria. Possibly this course of action would have continued to safeguard the air route to India, protect the oilfields in Iraq and Iran, and generally secure British strategic interests in the region.

Alternatively, the British government could have relinquished the mandate, withdrawn all British military forces from Iraq, and relied on the strength of Iraqi nationalism to keep foreign military bases and political influence out of the country. It was this policy of complete military withdrawal which after the early 1920s Britain followed in Turkey and Iran. Perhaps this course of action would have won the goodwill of most influential Iraqis and laid the groundwork for an enduring friendship between the two countries on the basis of complete equality.

But rather than either of these two options the British government chose a middle path: it relinquished the mandate and withdrew its ground troops but retained airbases in Iraq. This course of action neither properly safeguarded British strategic interests in the area nor gained the goodwill of most of those who by the

early 1940s dominated Iraq. The latter generally, and especially
the military leaders, viewed the British airbases as an infringe-
ment on Iraqi sovereignty and a possible source of intervention
in Iraqi internal affairs. To them the bases were a constant af-
front and a continual reminder of Iraq's subservient status vis-à-
vis Britain.[24] Nor did the bases properly safeguard British strategic interests because they were inadequately protected by only
a small force of native levies.[25] Thus the bases were secure only
as long as the Iraqi government was friendly to Britain and insecure as soon as that government became unfriendly. Indeed,
for the anti-British government that came to power in 1941 the
very weakness and vulnerability of the bases—a condition originally intended by Britain to appease Iraqi sensibilities—was an
irresistible temptation to attack in the hope of finally eliminating
the long resented British military presence. Thus in 1941 the un-
wisdom of Britain's decision in 1929–30 to relinquish the mandate while only retaining minimally guarded airbases became
painfully apparent. At this time, at a particularly awkward moment in the middle of a world war against a powerful enemy, the
British government had to divert precious resources from other
hard-pressed fronts in order to launch a major military operation to protect the base at Habbaniya which was originally intended by itself to protect British interests in the region.

CHAPTER 4

The Assyrian Minority

On the eve of the First World War about 40,000 Nestorian Christians lived in a mountainous district of the Ottoman empire northeast of Mosul known as Hakkiari. The Nestorians were frequently referred to as Assyrians because they claimed descent from the ancient Assyrians who had ruled a powerful state in Mesopotamia until it was destroyed in 606 B.C. The Assyrians were primarily an agricultural and pastoral people. They spoke Syriac which was derived from Aramaic, the language of Christ. They were officially recognized by the Ottoman government as a millet or religious community, which meant that they enjoyed a certain degree of autonomy. The Assyrians were led by a patriarch, known as the Mar Shimun, who was not only the ecclesiastical head but also the paramount chief of the community. The patriarchate was hereditary in the same family, although it did not descend from father to son because the patriarch was forbidden to marry.[1]

After the outbreak of the First World War in 1914 the Russian government, seeking to weaken the Ottoman empire, encouraged the Assyrians to revolt. To assist the revolt the Russians promised arms and other help. Enticed by these promises, emboldened by Russia's success in the fighting against the Ottoman empire and in particular by Russia's reoccupation of that section of northwestern Iran near Hakkiari, angered by the recent murder of numerous Assyrians by neighboring Kurdish tribes, and perhaps alarmed by reports of widespread killings of Armenian Christians in eastern Anatolia, in May 1915 the Assyrians rose against the Turks. But due to the exigencies of war the Russians were unable to provide assistance, and soon the Assyrian homeland was surrounded by Ottoman troops and Kurdish irregulars.

With considerable skill the entire Assyrian community maneuvered its way through Turkish lines and, after a lengthy and difficult march, in October 1915 reached the comparative safety of the Russian position west of Lake Urmiyah in northwestern Iran. There the Russians rearmed the Assyrians, organized them into three infantry battalions under the command of Russian officers, and on several occasions during the next two years sent them into combat against the Turks.[2] Thus after the war the Assyrians could fairly claim not only that they had unequivocally committed themselves to the allies by rebelling against the Ottoman empire but that they had served as a regular military force in the front line against the central powers. As we shall soon observe, they believed that this service obligated Britain, the leading allied power in the Middle East, to pay due regard to their interests or, at the least, to grant them physical protection.

Soon misfortune again befell the Assyrians. As a result of revolutionary upheavals in Russia, in late 1917 the Russian front in northwestern Iran collapsed, and the Assyrians were left alone at Urmiyah to defend themselves as best they could. In the spring and summer of 1918 they were attacked by the Turks. At first the Assyrian troops held their own in the fighting but eventually they were defeated. To avoid annihilation, the entire Assyrian community from Hakkiari, together with a considerable number of Armenian refugees and several thousand Assyrians who had long resided at Urmiyah, fled south in a desperate effort to make contact with the British forces then operating in Iran. This march was far more tragic than the earlier escape from Hakkiari. There was a greater shortage of food and water, and the retreating columns were frequently attacked by Turks, Kurds, and Iranians. Of the roughly 70,000 who began the march more than 20,000 perished on the way. Finally, after a terrible journey of nearly 300 miles, in August 1918 the remainder reached the British base at Hamadan in western Iran between Kermanshah and Tehran.[3]

But the British military authorities at Hamadan were unable to provide for all of these destitute people. Consequently, in August and September 1918 they moved the bulk of the refugees over 200 miles west to Iraq where they were lodged in a large camp at Baquba, about thirty miles northeast of Baghdad. However, the British retained the able-bodied Assyrian men at Hamadan and used them to create four infantry battalions under the command of British officers. Thus once again the Assyrians formed a regular military force in the service of the allied powers. But before the Assyrians could be employed in combat, in October 1918 hostilities ceased. These Assyrian troops were then demobilized and soon followed the rest of the community to the refugee camp at Baquba.[4]

After the war most of the Assyrians who had long resided at Urmiyah gradually returned to their former homes in Iran. The Assyrians from Hakkiari wanted to return to their former homes also, although preferably under some form of British protection. However, the Hakkiari area was north of the provisional frontier between Turkey and Iraq. Because the Assyrians were Christians, former rebels, and closely linked with Britain, the Turks did not want them in the country. In 1924 the Turks actually expelled a group of Assyrians who had recently returned to Hakkiari to settle. In 1925, when a commission of the League of Nations was adjudicating the Turko-Iraqi border, the British government argued that the Hakkiari district should be included in Iraq so that the Assyrians could return to the area, settle as a homogenous community, and still remain under British protection. But the League commissioners drew the frontier south of the Hakkiari district because they did not believe that Turkey should lose territory simply because with little provocation some of its subjects, in alliance with an enemy power, had rebelled in 1915. As a result of this decision, the Assyrians had to remain in Iraq.[5]

With British encouragement and financial assistance, and with the cooperation of the Iraqi government, during the 1920s most of the Assyrians settled on land in northern Iraq. However, because there was not a sufficiently large block of uninhabited land available, the Assyrians were unable to settle together as a group in a single area. For the Assyrians this dispersal was distressing because for reasons of security they thought it necessary to live together. Thus from their perspective the settlement program was not successful, and they retained a strong sense of grievance.[6]

During the 1920s the Assyrians generally did not try to assimilate into Iraqi society. Most of them did not learn Arabic. Frequently, they adopted a condescending attitude toward the Arabs. Usually they regarded themselves as refugees only temporarily residing in Iraq, and clung to the belief that eventually they would be able to return to their former homes in Hakkiari.[7]

For economic reasons, and because they closely identified with the British, during the 1920s many Assyrians joined the levies. The levies were a British controlled and primarily British officered military force that Britain recruited in Iraq to supplement and then replace British and Indian troops. The force was entirely separate from the primarily Arab officered Iraqi army and in no way under the control of the Iraqi government. From 1921 Britain hired mainly Assyrians for the levies because Arabs were needed to serve in the Iraqi army, and because the Assyrians were fine soldiers and politically reliable. Indeed, in 1919 Assyrians whom Britain had hastily pressed into service distinguished themselves in combat during a Kurdish revolt in the Amadia district in northern Iraq. Again in 1920 Assyrians performed a valuable military service for Britain during the widespread rebellion against British rule in Iraq. By the late 1920s there were about 2,000 levies, nearly all of whom were Assyrians.[8]

Because of their service with the levies and their tendency generally to identify themselves with the British and to adopt a contemptuous attitude toward Arabs, the Iraqi government viewed the Assyrians with dislike and mistrust. In 1924 Iraqi animosity and concern increased when two companies of Assyrian soldiers from the levies, after some provocation from the local inhabitants, ran amok in the town of Kirkuk and killed fifty people. The Iraqi government was especially worried about the Assyrians because they had long had a reputation for military prowess, and because Britain allowed each veteran of the levies to retain his rifle and 200 rounds of ammunition after leaving the service. In particular, the Iraqi government feared that one day the Assyrians would attempt by force to establish, possibly with British assistance, an autonomous region for themselves in northern Iraq. Iraqi leaders strongly opposed the creation of such a region because they believed it would upset the unity of the country and possibly create a precedent for other dissident groups in Iraq such as the Kurds or the Shiites.[9]

Thus Britain's decision to employ the Assyrians as levies had fateful consequences. It increased the Assyrians' separation from the rest of Iraqi society by encouraging their feelings of superiority while simultaneously making them objects of suspicion and hostility. Although in the 1920s Britain's decision to recruit Assyrians was militarily sound and financially inexpensive, it entailed the assumption of a moral obligation to protect this community which in the 1930s Britain was unable or unwilling to fulfill.

In the Anglo-Iraqi treaty of 1930, which was designed to regulate the relationship between the two countries after Iraq be-

came independent in 1932, the British government did not press
for the inclusion of safeguards for the Assyrians or any of the
other minority communities. It did not believe that provisions to
this effect were appropriate in an agreement between two sov-
ereign states because they would imply a continuing British right
to intervene in the internal affairs of Iraq. If such safeguards were
necessary, the British government thought that it was the responsibility of the League of Nations to insist upon them while
considering the question of the termination of the mandate and
the admission of Iraq into the League. Such a procedure would
not be unusual since on several occasions in the past the League
had required applicants for membership in the organization to
give pledges regarding the good treatment of minorities. Beyond
such pledges British officials did not feel that other measures, such
as the grant of local autonomy or the appointment of a League
of Nations commissioner to reside in northern Iraq, were necessary to protect the Assyrians. In their opinion the Iraqi government was basically tolerant and would not oppress the minority
communities. British officials also believed that in the long run
the best safeguard for the Assyrians was rapid assimilation into
Iraqi society. In their view, any measures, however well-
intentioned, that impeded this process by encouraging the Assyrians to maintain their separate identity would be harmful because they would lead the Iraqi government to regard the
Assyrians as tools of a British scheme designed to limit Iraq's independence.[10]

In 1931 the council of the League of Nations instructed the
permanent mandates commission to consider the question of the
termination of the British mandate in Iraq. Some members of the
commission were concerned about the future security of the minority communities and expressed the opinion that guarantees
such as those given in the past by some European nations upon
entry into the League would not afford adequate protection in
this case. However, in June 1931 Sir Francis Humphrys, the British
high commissioner in Iraq, assured the commission that the minorities were not in danger and, in a remark the British government later found extremely embarrassing, said that "Should Iraq
prove herself unworthy of the confidence which had been placed
in her, the moral responsibility must rest with His Majesty's Government." The commission was much influenced by Humphry's
testimony. Indeed, in its report of November 1931 it stated that
"Had it not been for this declaration, the Commission would, for

its part, have been unable to contemplate the termination of a regime which appeared some years ago to be necessary in the interest of all sections of the population." Concluding its report, the commission recommended that Iraq should be admitted to the League but only after it had presented a declaration guaranteeing protection and good treatment for the minority communities. The council of the League accepted the commission's recommendation, and in May 1932 the Iraqi government presented the required declaration. The following October the British mandate was formally terminated and Iraq was admitted to the League of Nations.[11]

The British government's unequivocal promise of September 1929 to recommend Iraq for membership in the League of Nations, coupled with the complete absence of minority guarantees in the Anglo-Iraqi treaty of June 1930, alarmed the Assyrians in Iraq. Many of them feared repression or even a massacre. Nearly all felt abandoned and betrayed.[12] They maintained that they had served Britain loyally both during the war and afterwards, and in the process had considerably worsened their relationship with the Muslim population of Iraq. But now, in return, Britain was planning to leave them entirely at the mercy of an Arab government in Baghdad which, they believed, hated them. The Assyrians also pointed out that in July 1925 the commission of the League of Nations which adjudicated the disputed frontier between Turkey and Iraq had said that they should be given a meaningful degree of local autonomy, and that a representative of the League should be appointed to reside in northern Iraq to ensure that this condition was fulfilled. Moreover, in December 1925 the council of the League had instructed Britain to act in accordance with the commission's recommendation. But the Iraqi government had not given the Assyrians autonomy, Britain had not insisted upon it, and a representative of the League had never been appointed.[13] In exoneration, the British government argued that local autonomy was impossible because the unavailability of a sufficiently large tract of uninhabited land had made it necessary to settle the Assyrians in small groups over a wide area in northern Iraq.[14] Still the Assyrians were aggrieved and, more important, frightened.

In 1931 and 1932 the Assyrians petitioned the League of Nations for redress. They asked for control of an autonomous region in the area north of Mosul because they believed that only under this condition could they live safely in Iraq after the termination of the British mandate.[15] But the League refused because it believed that the scheme would imperil the unity of the Iraqi state, because it calculated that the Assyrians would only constitute a minority of the population of the proposed autonomous region, and because it did not think that an autonomous region was necessary for the Assyrians' security.[16] As an alternative, the Assyrians asked the League to find a home for them under the control of a European Christian power. But no other country wanted to pay the financial and social cost of transporting and then settling a poor alien community, especially in the middle of a world depression.[17]

After legal methods had proved inefficacious, the Assyrians tried to force the issue. At the beginning of June 1932, a few months before Iraq was scheduled to become independent, the 1,500 Assyrians who were now serving in the levies collectively announced that since the British government had not safeguarded the interests of the Assyrian people they would terminate their engagements on 1 July. Assyrian leaders said that the resignations would be withdrawn only if the Assyrian community were given an autonomous enclave or homeland in northern Iraq. If their demand were rejected, Assyrian leaders hinted that they would concentrate all of their people in the Amadia district north of Mosul and establish by force an Assyrian kingdom.[18]

The British government opposed the Assyrians' demand because it believe that the entire community could not be grouped together in a single area in northern Iraq without displacing a large number of Kurds who were already settled there. It also believed that the creation of an autonomous region would impede the absorption of the Assyrians into Iraqi society and thereby not serve their long-term interest.[19] In addition, the British government considered the Assyrians' demand impractical because it knew Iraqi leaders would never accept a scheme that threatened national unity.[20]

Although they opposed the creation of an Assyrian enclave in northern Iraq, British officials feared that unless they prevented the abrupt disbandment of the levies the Iraqi government would blame Britain for conniving in and possibly even instigating the Assyrian plan.[21] Consequently, on 22 June 1932 the British government began to move a British infantry battalion in Egypt by air to Iraq. The British authorities in Iraq intended to use the troops, together with air force personnel already in Iraq, to prevent the Assyrian soldiers serving in the levies from disbanding collectively and joining the concentration in the north. However, the British government's show of force induced Assyrian leaders to abandon their plan, and at the end of June the great majority of the levies withdrew their resignations and agreed to remain in the service.[22]

Nonetheless, the incident worried Iraqi leaders. They viewed it as a serious threat to the unity and integrity of the country. They also feared that other racial or religious groups like the Kurds or the Shiites might imitate the Assyrians and attempt by force to achieve autonomy. Probably some of them believed that the British government would use the Assyrian agitation to retain a foothold in northern Iraq or even to delay Iraqi independence altogether. Thus the levy mutiny increased Iraqi leaders' apprehension and dislike of the Assyrians. To some extent it helps explain their behavior during the tragic events of the following summer.[23]

In May 1933, after Iraq had become independent, Hikmat Sulayman, the minister of the interior, invited the Mar Shimun to Baghdad in an effort to arrange a settlement of outstanding differences. Hikmat Sulayman offered to recognize the Mar Shimun as spiritual leader of the Assyrian community with a regular financial subsidy from the Iraqi government. But he adamantly refused to grant the Mar Shimun any temporal power because he feared that this would subvert the government's authority and create an undesirable precedent for other racial and religious groups in Iraq. Because the Mar Shimun insisted upon receiving a rather vaguely formulated degree of temporal power, and because he would not cooperate in the Iraqi government's efforts to complete the settlement of Assyrians on scattered pieces of land in northern Iraq, the talks soon collapsed. In late June the Mar Shimun wanted to return to his home in Mosul. However, without charge or accusation Hikmat Sulayman ordered him to remain in Baghdad because he feared that the government's prestige would suffer if the Mar Shimun departed after an ostentatious display of defiance. Thus the negotiations exacerbated the tension and increased the ill will between the Iraqi government and the Assyrians. The Mar Shimun's insistence upon temporal authority and his refusal to cooperate in the government's land settlement program reinforced the conviction of Iraqi leaders that they could not deal amicably with him or the Assyrian community he represented. Similarly, the unlawful detention of the Mar Shimun vindicated the belief of many Assyrians that they could

not live safely in Iraq and increased their determination to find
another home for themselves.[24]

In July 1933 a small party of Assyrians under the leadership
of Yacu, an associate of the Mar Shimun and a former officer in
the levies, crossed the Iraqi border into Syria. Yacu asked the
French authorities to allow the entire Assyrian community to enter Syria on the grounds that it was impossible for them to remain in Iraq any longer. Yacu based his belief not only on the
detention of the Mar Shimun but also on a profound apprehension, which was probably justified, that the Iraqi army intended
to disarm all of the Assyrians in Iraq. Without waiting for a reply
to his query, Yacu informed the Assyrians in Iraq that the French
were prepared to receive them and to provide suitable land for
settlement. Following Yacu's advice, nearly 800 armed Assyrian
men crossed into Syria. Apparently they wanted to inspect the
land before bringing over their women and children and belong-
ings. But the French decided not to allow them to remain, and
in early August a sizable group of the Assyrians recrossed the
frontier into Iraq in order to return to their villages. However,
by this time the Iraqi government had become concerned about
the movement through the countryside of large numbers of armed
Assyrians. Consequently, it sent troops to the border with orders
to allow the Assyrians to re-enter Iraq only if they surrendered
their arms. In this tense situation, with communication between
the two groups difficult and with so much distrust and animosity
on both sides, it is hardly surprising that on 4 August serious
fighting broke out. As both parties accused the other, it is impossible to determine which side fired the first shot. In any event,
the Iraqi army suffered over seventy casualties and the Assyrians
about forty. All fighting stopped the following morning as most
of the Assyrians fled back into Syria.[25]

Iraqi leaders were now thoroughly alarmed. They believed that
the government was confronted with a full-scale revolt of well-
armed Assyrians, possibly abetted for nefarious purposes by
France and Britain. They greatly overestimated the number of
Assyrians who had fought in the battle at the frontier, as well as
the number—actually about 200—who had not retreated into Syria
after the fighting and were now trying to reach their villages in
Iraq. They were concerned that Assyrians who had not participated in Yacu's adventure, including those in the levies, might
now join his forces and fight against the government. They were
also worried that rebellious Kurds in the Barzan area in north-

eastern Iraq and disaffected Shiite tribes along the Euphrates would capitalize on any Assyrian success by repudiating the government's authority.[26]

In addition to sincerely felt apprehension about the Assyrian menace, many Iraqis hankered for revenge because they believed that the army had been treacherously attacked and because some Iraqi troops had been found burnt and mutilated, or so the army alleged. The desire to hit the Assyrians hard was increased by inflammatory newspapers that unhesitatingly printed grossly exaggerated or entirely unfounded accounts of Assyrian atrocities. It was increased too by the fact that the Assyrians were Christians of alien origin who were closely linked to Britain by ties of friendship and service. Possibly the desire to retaliate against the Assyrians was also fanned by Iraqi ministers in an effort to unite all Iraqi Muslims, including the many Kurds and Shiites who were not yet reconciled to rule by a government composed primarily of a small group of Sunni Arabs, in a common struggle against a single Christian enemy.[27]

It is uncertain whether the Iraqi government encouraged the military forces, Kurdish villagers, and Arab tribesmen to initiate a pogrom against the Assyrians, but this is what happened.[28] During the next few days the army summarily executed every Assyrian survivor of the battle whom it managed to capture. Troops also killed any other male Assyrian whom they encountered. The army's most awful deed was at the village of Simmel on 11 August when it massacred 315 Assyrians who had just surrendered their rifles on the promise of protection. In all, the army killed about 550 Assyrians in a period of little over a week, and neighboring Kurds about fifty more. The great majority of the victims had not participated in the exodus to Syria or in any other activity against the government. Aside from the massacre, sixty-four Assyrian villages were looted by Kurds or Arab tribesmen, generally with no interference or restraint from the army or police. In all, the Assyrians lost at least £50,000 worth of property. Afterwards the Iraqi government did not hold an inquiry into these events, nor did it punish any of the participants. Indeed, Bakr Sidqi, the Iraqi military commander in the north, who almost certainly deserves much of the responsibility for the massacres, was feted and promoted by the Iraqi government.[29]

In August 1933 there was a widespread feeling in Iraq that Britain would intervene with armed force in order to protect the Assyrians. For fifteen years the Assyrians had been close friends and devoted servants of the British, and it was difficult for most

Iraqis to believe that Britain would abandon them now when they were under such terrible pressure. Indeed, many Iraqis thought that Britain was already aiding the Assyrians by dropping food and ammunition to them from R.A.F. planes based in Iraq. Some even feared that Britain was preparing to use the disturbances as an excuse to regain control of the country.[30]

But the British government did not intervene with armed force in the civil strife in Iraq. In part, British restraint was due to fear that intervention would lead to further atrocities against the Assyrians and possibly other Christians also. More important, however, British officials believed that their strategic interests in the Middle East generally, and particularly the security of their airbases in Iraq, would be best served by continuing to adhere to their longstanding policy of supporting the central government in Baghdad. Although they laid much of the blame for the original disturbance on the Iraqi government for detaining the Mar Shimun and attempting to disarm the Assyrians returning from Syria, they had no intention of jeopardizing their relations with this government by rushing to the assistance of a small beleaguered minority group which obstinately refused to integrate itself into Iraqi society. The fact that the Assyrians were the object of so much obloquy in large measure because of their long years of loyal service to Britain in the levies was not sufficient even to induce the British government publicaly to condemn Iraq, still less to motivate it to send a military expedition to that country.[31]

Rather than intervene with armed force on the side of the Assyrians, on 7 August, three days after the fighting began, Air Vice-Marshal C. S. Burnett, the British air officer commanding in Iraq, responded to an Iraqi request for assistance by providing 100 bombs for use in military operations against the Assyrians.[32] Burnett felt obligated to give the bombs because article 5 of the annexure of the Anglo-Iraqi treaty of 1930 stated that "His Britannic Majesty undertakes to grant whenever they may be required by His Majesty the King of Iraq all possible facilities in the following matters . . . [including] The provision of arms, ammunition, equipment, ships and aeroplanes of the latest available pattern for the forces of His Majesty the King of Iraq." Foreign office officials in London were not pleased with the haste with which Burnett fulfilled the Iraqi request. They would have preferred to temporize until the situation was calmer, for example, by claiming that the bombs could not be spared at the moment or that they would have to be sent by ship from Britain.[33] But they recognized, as did Prime Minister Ramsay MacDonald who was consulted, that eventually the British government would have to provide the bombs because article 5 of the annexure of the treaty did not contain any qualification that would enable Britain conveniently to evade its commitment, and because they feared that if they did not adhere to this provision of the treaty then Iraq would retaliate by not fulfilling certain of its responsibilities.[34] Thus, ironically, the British government was obligated militarily to assist the Iraqi army, which was permeated with anti-British sentiment, in its efforts brutally to crush the most pro-British group of people in Iraq. Such was the unhappy consequence of Britain's policy of employing large numbers of Assyrians in the levies for many years and then terminating the mandate without first evacuating them from Iraq.[35]

It is doubtful whether the British government won much goodwill or gratitude in Iraq from its refusal to assist the Assyrians. More likely it earned contempt for its inability or unwillingness to support its friends in their time of need. In any event, during this period there was a great surge of anti-British feeling in Iraq. The British government was widely accused of creating the entire problem by bringing the Assyrians to Iraq, employing them as soldiers, giving them rifles and ammunition, encouraging their pretensions to superiority, and generally using them as a tool to preserve British influence in the country. Thus the defeat of the Assyrians was viewed with satisfaction by many Iraqis as a defeat for Britain and a step on the road toward the elimination of the entire remaining British presence in Iraq.[36]

After August 1933 the British government believed that as long as the Assyrians remained in Iraq there would be a strong possibility of further outbreaks of violence against them. In such an event, British leaders were concerned that they might feel morally obligated to intervene in Iraq in order to prevent additional and perhaps even greater massacres. If the disturbances spread, they feared that they might have to intervene also in order to protect the very vulnerable British airbases in Iraq and the Iraq Petroleum Company's extremely valuable installations and pipeline to the Mediterranean. British leaders dreaded the prospect of intervention because it would be financially expensive, tie up a large number of troops, and do terrible damage to Anglo-Iraqi relations. Consequently, in order to obviate the need for intervention they tried to remove all of the Assyrians from Iraq and settle them elsewhere.[37]

But finding a new home for the Assyrians was difficult. Although they numbered only about 28,000, all of the self-governing British dominions refused to accept them. In part this rejection was due to economic problems brought on by the world depression, but probably it was attributable more to the fact that the Assyrians were Asiatics.[38] The government of India would not admit the Assyrians because it believed that India was already overpopulated, and because it feared widespread internal opposition on the grounds that without benefit to itself India was being forced to bear the entire burden of solving an exclusively British problem.[39] For various reasons, such as intemperate climate, existing large-scale unemployment, shortage of vacant land suitable for agriculture which was not already reserved for British settlers, and objection to adding another group to societies already torn by racial strife, the colonial office said that it could not accommodate the Assyrians in any British colony.[40]

Non-British countries did not want the Assyrians either. There was a widespread view that the British government was morally obligated to provide a home for these people because its decision to employ the Assyrians in the levies was largely responsible for making them so unpopular in Iraq, and because its decision to relinquish the mandate at the earliest possible opportunity led to the current problem. It was also widely believed that Britain must have space for the Assyrians somewhere within the confines of its vast empire.[41]

At this point the British government could have settled the Assyrians in various urban areas within the United Kingdom itself. Although traditionally the Assyrians had been an agricultural and pastoral people, in recent years many of them had settled in Mosul and Baghdad where they were employed as artisans. Others worked on the railways or for the Iraq Petroleum Company. Still others served in the levies. In all, about half of the male Assyrian population in 1933 no longer had any direct connection with the land.[42] Thus there was no obvious reason why over time this relatively small group of people, many of whom had already abandoned agricultural and pastoral labor, could not have been successfully integrated and absorbed into several large British cities. And even if some of the Assyrians had had difficulty adjusting to a different way of life in an alien culture, at least they would have been physically safe and the British government would have fulfilled its moral obligation toward them. However, in all of the voluminous correspondence on this question in the 1930s there is not the slightest indication that any of the British officials concerned, including ministers, ever considered this option.

Since the troubles of August 1933 France had sheltered in Syria some 550 Assyrians who had participated in the original battle with the Iraqi army at the frontier. In exchange for the payment of £10,000 from the Iraqi government, in the summer of 1934 France accepted 1,500 women and children who were dependents of these men. In exchange for the payment of a further £60,000 from Iraq, an equal sum from Britain, and a lesser amount from the League of Nations, during the next two years France admitted additional batches of Assyrians totalling 8,500 people by the end of 1936. The French authorities settled the entire group on the Khabur River in northeastern Syria, about forty miles from the Iraqi border. To assist their establishment in the area, French officials provided material to build houses and irrigation machinery to cultivate the land. The French also distributed some rifles to enable the Assyrians to defend themselves against marauding bedouin.[43] While it was generous of France to accept people who were not wanted in Iraq or elsewhere, the government's motives were probably not entirely altruistic since it could now cite the need to protect the Assyrians as a reason to prolong French rule in Syria.

Aside from the group that went to Syria, the Assyrians remained in Iraq. By the end of 1937 the British government abandoned hope of placing the Assyrians elsewhere and decided that their best chance for a secure future would be to settle down as loyal Iraqi citizens.[44] But Britain's policy of continuing to employ Assyrians in the levies after independence in 1932 made it difficult for the community to be accepted in Iraq.[45] In May 1941, during the hostilities between Britain and Iraq, the Assyrians in the levies performed notably in the defense of the British airbase at Habbaniya against the Iraqi army.[46] As a result, the British government again became concerned about the future safety of the Assyrians and once more investigated the possibility of removing them from Iraq. But, as in the prewar period, nothing resulted from these efforts because no foreign country, British dominion, or British colony wanted them.[47] Consequently, the Assyrians stayed in Iraq where, fortunately, there were no further outbreaks of violence against them. Gradually, the Assyrians integrated themselves into Iraqi society and ceased to be regarded as an instrument of foreign domination. This process was facilitated by the disbandment of the levies in 1955.[48]

CHAPTER 5

The Levies

Beginning in 1915 during the First World War the British government recruited a special military force in Iraq under British officers known as the levies. By the end of the war in 1918 this force numbered about 5,500 men. Initially, the levies were mainly Arabs. However, starting in 1921 Britain recruited primarily Assyrians in order to give employment to these people, most of whom were refugees from Hakkiari, and because the Assyrians had long had a reputation for combativeness. The British also preferred Assyrians because, as a small Christian minority recently arrived in Iraq with its own language and customs, the Assyrians felt alienated from the predominantly Muslim Arab and Kurdish population of the country. For Britain this background made them a particularly dependable body of soldiers. In addition to these considerations, the British recruited Assyrians because the newly created Iraqi government wanted to enlist Arabs into its own army. Unlike the Iraqi army, which was formed in 1921 and was primarily officered by Arabs, and was at least partly under the control of the Iraqi government, the levies were British imperial troops under the complete control of the British authorities in Iraq.[1]

On numerous occasions in the 1920s the levies engaged in combat against Turkish incursions into northern Iraq and against Kurdish uprisings against the central government in Baghdad. Invariably they fought with distinction, and in this manner did much to preserve the unity and territorial integrity of Iraq.[2]

The good performance of the levies during military operations in the 1920s, coupled with the gradual growth and development of the Iraqi army, enabled the British government to reduce and eventually entirely to withdraw British and Indian troops from Iraq. In this manner Britain saved a considerable amount of money and avoided political difficulties in India. To illustrate the dimensions of the withdrawal, in December 1920 there were 102,000 British and Indian troops in Iraq.[3] By 1930, however, there were no longer any British or Indian troops in Iraq. The Iraqi army of about 9,000 men, mostly under the command of its own officers, now maintained internal security. This force was supplemented by five squadrons of British warplanes, one and one half armored car companies manned by Royal Air Force personnel, and about 2,000 levies under British officers.[4]

The Iraqi government did not want the levies to continue in existence after independence. It believed that the recruitment of Iraqi subjects into a military force under British control was a derogation of national sovereignty and that its continuation would be tantamount to an indefinite prolongation of the British military occupation. In addition, the Iraqi government feared that the levies would pose a rebellious and secessionist threat because they were drawn primarily from the discontented Assyrian community. Indeed, as we have observed in the previous chapter, in the summer of 1932, a few months before Iraq became independent, the Assyrians in the levies did stage a short-lived revolt in an effort to gain an autonomous enclave in northern Iraq. For the Iraqi government the levies were an even greater danger than appeared at first glance because each member retained his modern British rifle and 200 rounds of ammunition after leaving the service. As a result of this arrangement the entire Assyrian community in Iraq was heavily armed.[5] Aside from these considerations, some Iraqi leaders probably opposed the levies also because they calculated that the British airbases would be more vulnerable to Iraqi pressure if they were deprived of a strong force of reliable armed guards under British control.

This question was discussed at some length during the negotiations for the Anglo-Iraqi treaty of 1930.[6] It was finally resolved in article 4 of the annexure of the treaty, which was an integral part of the treaty and was published and ratified by both sides. According to the terms of this article, the Iraqi government was obligated to provide at British request and at British expense special guards from its own forces to protect the British airbases upon mutually agreed conditions and to secure the enactment of any legislation required for the fulfillment of these conditions. In this manner the levies, which were British imperial troops swearing an oath of allegiance to King George, were scheduled to be abolished and replaced by an air defense force from the Iraqi army that would swear an oath of allegiance to King Faysal. Thus article 4 of the annexure apparently safeguarded Iraqi sovereignty and thereby satisfied public opinion in Iraq.

However, the British government would not accept this arrangement without considerable qualification because it wanted a greater degree of security for the airbases. It feared that without the protection of reliable British controlled ground troops the R.A.F. personnel at the airbases would be excessively vulnerable to any form of pressure the Iraqi government might choose to apply.[7] Consequently, at British insistence, on 30 June 1930, the same day that the treaty was signed, Nuri al-Said, the Iraqi prime minister and foreign minister, wrote a secret unpublished letter to Sir Francis Humphrys, the British high commissioner in Iraq, stipulating the mutually agreed conditions under which article 4 of the annexure would be implemented. Nuri's letter letter stated that the air defense force referred to in this article would be entirely under the command of a British officer and any other officers whom he appointed. According to the letter, the commanding officer would have full power over recruitment of personnel, administration, nature of arms and equipment, method of training, rates of pay, and conditions of service. In addition, Nuri promised that all the men in the force would be exempt from the provisions of any Iraqi law requiring compulsory military service. Although these points were major concessions to Britain, Nuri's letter did contain some regard for the Iraqi point of view. For example, it stated that the air defense force would consist of a maximum of only 1,250 troops, that some of the officers would have to be Iraqi, that all of the officers would hold the commission of the king of Iraq, and that, with the exception of its British personnel, the force would be subject to Iraqi military law. Nonetheless, it is clear that while article 4 of the annexure seemingly protected Iraqi sovereignty, Nuri's letter qualified that protection considerably. It is hardly surprising that Iraqi governments, and especially Nuri himself when he was in office, wanted to keep this letter secret for fear of arousing hostile comment and criticism within Iraq.[8]

Britain's unwillingness to allow the Iraqi government to protect the British airbases indicates that as early as 1930, even before Iraq became independent, Britain was mistrustful of its ally.

This mistrust was reciprocated by Iraqi leaders who suspected that Britain was attempting to utilize the airbase guards to prolong its occupation of Iraq. Thus the relationship between the two powers began inauspiciously.

The air defense force mentioned in article 4 of the annexure of the treaty was never established because Britain and Iraq never agreed on the terms under which the force should be established. The dispute centered around the question of the legality of Nuri's secret letter of 30 June 1930. Beginning in June 1934, when Nuri was no longer in office, the Iraqi government maintained that the letter was not legally valid because, unlike most of the other treaty documents, it had not been presented to and ratified by the Iraqi parliament and it had never been approved by the Iraqi council of ministers. In addition, the Iraqi government argued that Nuri's letter was illegal because its terms were inconsistent with both the text and the spirit of article 4 of the annexure of the treaty.[9] Even when Nuri was again foreign minister, for example, in October 1934, he too maintained that the letter in question, although signed by him, was not legally binding.[10]

British officials, on the contrary, always maintained that Nuri's letter was an integral part of the treaty settlement which fully committed the Iraqi government. They emphasized that Nuri was prime minister and foreign minister of Iraq at the time and therefore his letter could not be considered a mere personal assurance. Even if Nuri had exceeded his constitutional powers in this undertaking, British officials believed that the responsibility for that transgression rested upon him and upon the government he represented and not upon the government to whom he gave the assurance. They also pointed out that they had agreed to article 4 of the annexure only on the understanding that Nuri's letter would stand as a qualifying and amplifying document.[11]

However, the British government's legal case in this matter was weakened by the fact that, unlike most of the other treaty documents, it did not register Nuri's letter with the League of Nations at Geneva. Thus it was awkward for Britain to insist upon the legal validity of this letter because article 18 of the covenant stated that all binding international engagements must be registered with the League.[12] During the treaty negotiations in 1930 the foreign office had alerted the colonial office, which conducted the negotiations, to this problem. It had also pointed out that embodying an important item of a treaty settlement in an unpublished note was inconsistent with a long established British policy.[13] But the Iraqi government opposed the inclusion of the provisions of Nuri's letter in the body of the treaty or in a formal letter that would have to be published with the treaty, and the British government was unwilling to insist upon this point.[14] Consequently, the foreign office suggested the use of an informal and unpublished letter which, it believed, would not have to be registered at Geneva but would still be legal.[15] Ultimately the British government adopted this method, but the expedient did nothing to solve the problem. The British government was still uncomfortably vulnerable to the embarrassing accusation either that the letter was not legally binding or that Britain had violated the covenant of the League of Nations.

The British government might have minimized the dimensions of this problem, or possibly even eliminated it entirely, if it had insisted upon specifying in the body of the treaty that all of the notes accompanying the treaty would be regarded as integral parts of the treaty. Indeed, in 1930 it did consider this option. However, G. W. Rendel, a member of the eastern department of the foreign office who soon became head of the department, maintained that "Our experience has been that the validity of notes attached to treaties is not called in question, and that it is unusual to ratify them. If any notes attached to the Treaty are specifically mentioned as being an integral part of the Treaty, the effect might be to cast a doubt on the validity of other exchanges of notes."[16] Rather shortsightedly, the British government adopted Rendel's advice, although neither of his arguments appears particularly strong. As a result, the British government created, or at least failed to ameliorate, a long-standing and serious problem in Anglo-Iraqi relations.

Because the Iraqi government never introduced legislation to legalize an air defense force in accordance with the terms of Nuri's letter, after Iraqi independence in 1932 Britain retained 1,250 levies as British imperial troops functioning as airbase guards. It also continued to recruit Iraqi subjects into the levies in order to replace soldiers who retired from the force. In justification for this behavior, British officials maintained that the levies' status and position could not be changed without British consent because article 4 of the annexure of the treaty stated that the Iraqi government would provide airbase guards from its own forces only at British request and only upon mutually agreed conditions. For Britain the mutually agreed conditions were contained in Nuri's letter, and if the Iraqi government would not accept this proposition then the levies would simply continue in existence.[17] British officials were not entirely displeased with this result because, with their large Assyrian component, the levies were politically reliable, well-disciplined troops.[18] Moreover, British officials feared that the Assyrians would probably be unable to serve in the air defense force because they would refuse to swear an oath of allegiance to the Iraqi king. Thus even if Britain controlled recruitment for the air defense force, as stipulated in Nuri's letter, the troops would probably be composed primarily of Arabs upon whose reliability in a crisis the British government was less confident.[19]

But the Iraqi government had no intention of allowing Britain to control recruitment for the air defense force. Indeed, this point was one of Iraq's major grievances against the levies.[20] Consequently, in April 1936 the Iraqi government proposed to honor its commitment under article 4 of the annexure of the treaty by creating an air defense force composed of men who had completed their military service with the Iraqi army and thus had probably received a considerable amount of anti-British indoctrination.[21] In February 1938 the Iraqi government proposed another scheme under the terms of which the air defense force would be composed of specially detached units of the Iraqi army.[22] Under both plans the commanding officer of the force would have been British but he would have been directly responsible to the Iraqi ministry of defense, and most (under the first plan) or all (under the second plan) of the other officers would have been Iraqi. Thus the Iraqi government would have had a very large measure of control over the air defense force and, from Britain's point of view, the troops would have been quite unreliable. Because of these considerations, on both occasions the British government rejected the Iraqi proposal.[23] Indeed, by the late 1930s, as Arab nationalist sentiment in Iraq grew as a result of events in Palestine and Syria, and as the Iraqi army grew more threatening as a result of its coup d'etat in October 1936 and its subsequent interventions in politics, British officials, and especially those in the R.A.F. in Iraq and in the air ministry in London, became increasingly less willing to contemplate the replacement of the levies by an air defense force because this development would necessarily have resulted in some, and perhaps much, diminution of their control.[24]

However, the foreign office was not happy with the levies because they angered the Iraqi government and thereby damaged relations between the two countries. It was also concerned because the continued existence of the levies was not sanctioned anywhere in the treaty or in the accompanying notes, and it feared that the Iraqi government would not allow the existing situation to last indefinitely.[25] Indeed, the Iraqi government repeatedly contended that the levies were illegal.[26]

In 1937 the foreign office contemplated making the levies more palatable to the Iraqi government by recruiting more Arabs and fewer or no Assyrians but rejected this course of action because it would have made the levies a much less dependable body of soldiers. The foreign office was reluctant to adopt this expedient also because it would have had unfortunate economic consequences for the Assyrians since the entire community in Iraq derived a substantial proportion of its income from the emoluments of those members who served in the levies. Nonetheless, the foreign office believed that in the long term the Assyrians themselves would be injured by service in the levies because it made them objects of suspicion and dislike in Iraq. If the levies ever engaged in military operations against Iraqi Muslims, the foreign office feared that there might be reprisals against Assyrian villages or even another massacre as in 1933. In the opinion of the foreign office, service with the levies also encouraged the Assyrians to look to Britain for protection at a time when Britain had no desire to jeopardize its relations with the Iraqi government by sheltering this small minority group. Indeed, by 1937, after the failure of various schemes for the emigration of the Assyrian community from Iraq, the foreign office was convinced that both British and Assyrian interests would be furthered if the Assyrians assimilated fully into Iraqi society. And the foreign office believed that such assimilation would only occur when the Assyrians stopped serving in the levies.[27]

Thus the foreign office was confronted with the problem of eliminating the levies while still ensuring the security of the British airbases in Iraq. This problem would have been more manageable if Britain had had the right permanently to station British or Indian troops around the airbases. However, in a major concession during the negotiations for the treaty of 1930 the British government had agreed to Iraq's demand that its residual forces in the country would only comprise R.A.F. units together with their ancillary services; and that Britain would not be allowed to station ground troops around the airbases except temporarily in time of emergency and even then only after consultation with the Iraqi government rather than entirely on its own volition.[28]

In November 1937, and again in 1938 and 1939, the foreign office proposed to circumvent this obstacle by raising a special British military force under the authority of the air ministry designed specifically for the protection of the British airbases in Iraq. The foreign office thought that the Iraqi government might be amenable to this scheme because it would lead to the abolition of the levies and thereby end the employment of Iraqi subjects in a purely British military force. In any event, the foreign office believed that Britain had the legal right to create such a force because it could plausibly be described as part of the R.A.F.'s ancillary services. In the opinion of the foreign office, the British government's legal position was further strengthened by the fact that article 4 of the annexure of the treaty was entirely permissive and did not require Britain to ask Iraq for airbase guards.[29]

However, this scheme was never implemented because of the opposition of the air ministry. In April 1938, and twice again in 1939, the air ministry maintained that it would be too expensive to replace the levies with R.A.F. personnel because British airmen would have to be paid more, have improved accommodations and amenities, require special training for the task which the air ministry was not at present equipped to provide, and be rotated frequently due to the inhospitable conditions in Iraq. In addition, the air ministry believed that it would be difficult to recruit the necessary personnel for the force at a time of intensive rearmament in Britain.[30] Basically, the air ministry rejected the plan because it had no desire to alter a long functioning arrangement that was administratively convenient, financially inexpensive, and, at least in normal times, provided adequate security. Thus the foreign office's scheme to replace the levies with a special British military force floundered.

During the Second World War, the British government expanded the levies from 1,250, at which strength they had been since 1933 in accordance with the terms for the air defense force mentioned in Nuri's letter, to a peak of around 10,000. This large-scale expansion occurred with the consent of the Iraqi government, although not until after May 1941 when Iraq passed firmly under British influence. About 3,000 of the additional recruits were Assyrians, including many from the group which had migrated to Syria between 1933 and 1936. During the war the levies were not only stationed in Iraq but also in Iran, Syria, Lebanon, Palestine, and Cyprus. In these places they guarded airbases and other vital installations, thereby freeing British troops for front line duty against the axis powers.[31] However, some of the levies were also involved in combat operations. Indeed, in May 1941 800 levies, most of whom were Assyrian, participated in a distinguished manner in the successful defense of the British airbase at Habbaniya against the Iraqi army.[32] A few weeks later the Assyrians again performed notably against strong Iraqi opposition during the British attack on the town of Falluja which blocked the road to Baghdad.[33] And in September 1944 Assyrian levies specially trained as paratroopers fought bravely against German armored units in the fierce combat at Arnhem in Holland.[34] Whether an alternative military force, such as that mentioned in article 4 of the annexure of the treaty, would have performed so well under such demanding circumstances must remain a matter of conjecture.

When the mandate was terminated, the British government insisted upon keeping airbases in Iraq without providing adequate and definite arrangements for their defense. As a result of this error, the British government was compelled to retain the levies or, in other words, to continue the arrangement that had existed under the mandate. Because Britain had no treaty sanction for the levies, the Iraqi government contended, and not entirely without justification, that Britain was maintaining an illegal military force on Iraqi territory. The British foreign office rejected this accusation, but not with the assurance that normally accompanies a confident legal position. Indeed, it never offered to submit the dispute to arbitration. Because the foreign office was unsure of the strength of its legal position, and because it did not want to endanger the Assyrian community in Iraq, it attempted to replace the levies, first with the air defense force stipulated in article 4 of the annexure of the treaty as qualified by Nuri's letter, and then with a special force of British airmen. These efforts failed because of the unwillingness of the Iraqi government to recognize the legality of Nuri's letter, and because of the reluctance of the air ministry to abandon an arrangement with which it was reasonably content. As a result, the levies remained in existence throughout the 1930s and 1940s: an important factor in the maintenance of British influence in Iraq and a continual reminder to Iraq of its subservient position vis-à-vis Britain.

CHAPTER 6

Arab Independence and Unity

During the First World War Faysal, the future king of Iraq, led a revolt in the Hijaz against the Turks in an attempt to achieve the independence of the Arab districts of the Ottoman empire. At the Paris peace conference in 1919 he again struggled for this objective. Both of these efforts failed, though for a brief period in 1920 Faysal reigned as king of Syria until he was evicted by the French.[1] Because of this background, when Faysal became king of Iraq in 1921 his vistas and ambitions were not limited to the confines of his adopted country. On the contrary, as soon as Iraq became independent in 1932 Faysal wanted to use the power of the state to help secure the independence from British and French rule, and the eventual unity under Iraqi auspices, of all the Arab lands of the fertile crescent. Faysal believed that the implementation of this program would strengthen Iraq and thereby make the country less vulnerable to pressure or aggression from neighboring non-Arab states like Turkey or Iran or from European powers. It would also fulfill an Iraqi desire to gain unfettered access to the Mediterranean Sea and thereby free the country from dependence upon Basra, its only port, which was located dangerously near the Iranian border. For Faysal the unity of the Arab lands of the fertile crescent would have an additional advantage because in Iraq Sunni Arabs, like himself, constituted only about 20 percent of the total population but in the fertile crescent as a whole they were a majority.[2]

In the 1930s and early 1940s most of Iraq's key political and military leaders shared Faysal's views on the question of Arab unity. The majority of these men were former officers in the Ottoman army and thus had recently served a government that had ruled nearly all of the Arab lands in Asia as a single political unit. Many of them were from northern Iraq which traditionally had close commercial links with Syria and suffered economically from the partition of the Arab lands of the Ottoman empire after the First World War. And nearly all of them were Sunni Arabs who, like Faysal, felt kinship for the predominantly Sunni Arab population of Syria, Transjordan, and Palestine.[3]

For various reasons, in the 1930s and early 1940s the British government was not favorably disposed toward any plan for Arab unity or federation. To begin with, Britain did not want to alienate France which was strongly opposed to the idea. France feared that the new state would stimulate nationalist sentiment throughout the Middle East and thereby weaken French control in Syria and Lebanon, even if those countries were not included in the Arab federation. France also suspected that British sympathy for Arab nationalism was merely a tool to oust France from the Levant and bring the entire Middle East under British influence. Because Britain needed good relations with France in order successfully to oppose the threat of German and Italian aggression, it felt that it had to be especially sensitive to French interests and concerns in the Middle East.[4]

In addition to France, the British government feared that support for Arab unity would offend Turkey. For Britain Turkey's friendship was important because that country occupied a vital position blocking Germany's advance into the Middle East. Although Turkey frequently maintained that it did not have any territorial claims except for that part of Syria known as the *sanjak* (district) of Alexandretta, British officials suspected that sooner or later it would also attempt to gain control of Aleppo and Mosul, and that it would regard the formation of a strong united Arab state as an impediment to these aspirations.[5]

The British government was unwilling to support Iraq's scheme for Arab unity also because it did not want to anger Ibn Saud, the king and absolute ruler of Saudi Arabia. For Britain, with millions of Muslim subjects in India and elsewhere, Ibn Saud's friendship was important because he controlled Mecca and Medina, the holy cities of Islam. In addition, his territory bordered that of several states Britain was obligated to defend, like Kuwait, Qatar, and Abu Dhabi, all of which were vulnerable to political subversion and military raids from Saudi Arabia. Because of Ibn Saud's conquest of the Hijaz in 1924–25 and his expulsion of its Hashimite kings, considerable suspicion and enmity existed between him and the Hashimite rulers of Iraq and Transjordan. As a result, Ibn Saud strongly opposed any accretion of Hashimite strength such as might accrue from an Arab federation created under Iraqi leadership. Thus if Britain favored such a scheme it would risk losing Ibn Saud's goodwill.[6]

Actually Britain would risk even more because the Hashimite rulers of Transjordan and Iraq were jealous and suspicious of each other. In particular, they both hankered after the somewhat nebulous throne of Syria, and they both wanted to dominate Palestine. Thus British support for a scheme of Arab unity under Iraqi leadership would alienate the Amir Abdullah of Transjordan who was a close friend and loyal ally of Britain.[7]

Aside from reluctance to offend France, Turkey, Saudi Arabia, and Transjordan, during this period the British government believed that Arab unity would weaken Britain's own position in the Middle East. Under a variety of different arrangements, Britain exercised a considerable degree of influence in Egypt, Palestine, Transjordan, Iraq, the Persian Gulf shaykhdoms, and southern Arabia. In this manner Britain protected its vital interests such as the sea and air routes to India and the important oilfields in Iran and Iraq. Were these small and weak Arab states to unite into a larger and more powerful entity, the British government believed that its influence in the area would inevitably decline.[8]

The British government was especially concerned that Syria would eventually dominate any Arab federation in the fertile crescent because it believed that Syria was more economically and culturally advanced than Iraq. For Britain this prospect was alarming because it thought that France would always retain great influence in Syria and through Syria gain influence in Iraq. Even if this development could be prevented, British officials feared that with part of the Arab federation bound to Britain and part to France, Anglo-French rivalry and discord would rapidly develop over control of the new state.[9]

The British government foresaw other problems too. For example Transjordan was covered by the terms of the League of Nations' mandate for Palestine of which technically it was an integral part. Before Transjordan could become part of a larger entirely independent Arab state, Britain would first have to approach the League to secure its release from the mandate. But British officials did not believe that the League would consent because Transjordan did not fulfill the conditions the League had established for the release of a territory from the mandatory regime.[10]

As far as Palestine itself was concerned, since 1917 the British government had been pledged to promote a Jewish national home in that territory. Obviously, Britain could not continue this policy if it relinquished the mandate and permitted Palestine to become part of a larger Arab state. Nor was there any reason to believe that a larger Arab state would continue to promote a Jewish national home by allowing an appreciable number of Jewish immigrants into Palestine.[11]

Although the British government was not favorably disposed toward Arab unity in the 1930s and early 1940s, it did not want to oppose the movement openly because it realized how popular the idea was among Iraqi leaders. Consequently, during this period the British government said that it would view sympathetically any steps the Arabs took of their own accord to further the cause of Arab unity but that it would not take any initiative of its own in this area. In this manner it hoped to avoid alienating Iraqi leaders and others in the Middle East who were staunch supporters of Arab unity.[12]

But this policy was not entirely successful. For example, in 1932 King Faysal wanted to hold a conference in Baghdad with delegates from various Arab countries, ostensibly to promote closer cultural and economic union in the Arab world. The British government opposed the conference because it believed that the delegates would concentrate mainly on political questions like European control over Palestine and Syria. Consequently, it applied pressure on Iraq to abandon the idea of holding a conference and in July 1933, just before his death, Faysal was obliged to yield.[13]

Another problem developed in the spring of 1936 when Iraq was negotiating with Saudi Arabia for the conclusion of a treaty of brotherhood and alliance. Both Iraq and Saudi Arabia wanted to include provisions in the treaty calling for military and political cooperation to promote Arab interests in Palestine and Syria. However, the British government objected to these provisions because it believed that they might threaten Britain's dominant position in Palestine. As a result of British pressure, Iraq was obliged to eliminate these provisions from the treaty.[14]

Still another problem arose in April 1938 when Britain and Italy concluded an agreement in which each party pledged not to seek a privileged position of a political nature in Saudi Arabia or

Yemen. Britain and Italy further stated that it was in their common interest that no other power should acquire such a position in either of these two countries.[15] In this manner the British government hoped to protect its strategic interests in the Red Sea by preventing Italy from establishing a military base or a sphere of influence in either Saudi Arabia or Yemen. The British government also thought that this agreement was in the interests of both Saudi Arabia and Yemen because it would protect their independence and territorial integrity.[16]

However, the agreement angered the Iraqi government because it was not consulted beforehand, although article 1 of the Anglo-Iraqi treaty of 1930 stated that "there shall be full and frank consultation between them in all matters of foreign policy which may effect their common interests." In addition, the Iraqi government believed that the agreement might diminish the freedom of Saudi Arabia and Yemen in a manner that would impede the closer cooperation and eventual unity of the various Arab countries. For example, it feared that the terms of the agreement might obligate Britain to use its influence to prevent Iraq and Saudi Arabia from exchanging pieces of territory along their common frontier, to prevent Iraq from sending an army officer to Saudi Arabia to advise the king on military matters, to prevent Iraq from sending troops to Saudi Arabia to help crush a rebellion against the regime, or to prevent Iraq from forming a customs union or political federation with Saudi Arabia or Yemen or both. Since Iraq had concluded a treaty of brotherhood and alliance with Saudi Arabia in 1936, to which Yemen had adhered in 1937, for the express purpose of promoting closer relations between these countries, it was especially irritated that Britain had made an agreement that might frustrate the achievement of this objective.[17]

In June 1938 Britain informed the Iraqi government that its fears were unjustified because Iraq was not bound by the Anglo-Italian agreement and its behavior was not restricted by it. Continuing, the British government stated that it was not obligated by the agreement to prevent or in any way interfere with steps toward Arab cooperation and collaboration like Iraqi assistance to Saudi Arabia for the purpose of suppressing a tribal rebellion or the appointment by the Saudi Arabian government of an Iraqi subject as military advisor or an arrangement between Iraq and Saudi Arabia for the exchange of territory along their common frontier. Furthermore, the British government said that it would never oppose any Iraqi measures that were conceived in good faith for the welfare of Saudi Arabia or Yemen.[18] The Iraqi government accepted these assurances and dropped the matter, but the episode did nothing to alleviate Iraqi suspicions that Britain stood in the path of progress toward Arab unity.[19]

It was over Palestine that British and Iraqi differences appeared in the most acute form. In April 1936 the Arab population of Palestine began a general strike in an effort to halt further Jewish immigration and secure an independent Arab state. Soon the general strike turned into a widespread rebellion against British rule in Palestine. In June 1936 Nuri al-Said, the Iraqi foreign minister, proposed to mediate the conflict on the basis of a halt to Jewish immigration and the incorporation of Palestine into an Arab federation controlled by Iraq. Aside from promoting Arab independence and unity, and Iraq's position as leader of the Arab world, the success of this scheme would save Iraq revenue which it was losing as a result of the damage inflicted by Arab rebels in Palestine upon the oil pipeline that ran from Kirkuk in northern Iraq to the port of Haifa in Palestine. It would also reduce the likelihood of riots directed against the Jewish minority in Iraq, which, Iraqi leaders feared, might easily get out of control and turn against foreign residents or even against the government itself. In addition, it would greatly increase the government's prestige and strengthen its position against its opponents within Iraq. However, Nuri's plan came to nothing because the Jews refused to stop immigration, and because Britain was not seriously prepared to contemplate an Arab federation.[20]

In July 1937 a commission established by the British government to investigate the Palestinian question recommended that the territory should be partitioned into an independent Jewish state and an Arab area which would be merged with Transjordan. Iraq immediately rejected the commission's report because the existence of an independent Jewish state would make it impossible to create an Arab federation encompassing the entire fertile crescent; because the Jews, who received the coastal areas of northern Palestine, would be in a position to block Iraqi oil and other exports that moved through Palestine on their way to Europe; because most of Palestine was given to Transjordan while Iraq was not strengthened at all; and because at this time the Iraqi government, which was headed by Hikmat Sulayman, who descended from a Georgian, and was kept in power by General Bakr Sidqi, a Kurd, was widely accused of being insufficiently concerned with pan-Arabism and consequently felt a need to emphasize the strength of its Arab nationalism. In large part because of opposition from Iraq and other Arab states, the British government decided not to implement the commission's recommendations. Iraq approved of this decision, but the Palestinian question continued to trouble Anglo-Iraqi relations.[21]

In May 1939 the British government issued a white paper on Palestine that allowed a maximum of 75,000 more Jewish immigrants over the next five years, placed strict restrictions on land sales to Jews, called for the appointment of Palestinians to head government departments, and said that an independent Palestinian state should be created within ten years provided that there existed "such relations between the Arabs and the Jews as would make good government possible."[22] In this manner Britain essentially abandoned its long established policy of promoting a Jewish national home in Palestine. To a large extent Britain reversed its policy on this question in order to win the friendship and support of Iraq and the other Arab states in the forthcoming struggle against Germany and Italy. But the Higher Arab Committee, the Palestinian Arabs' main political organization, rejected the white paper because it did not provide a sufficiently firm guarantee of independence, and because it did not grant an amnesty to the participants in the Arab rebellion. As a result of this decision, Iraq and the other Arab states except for Transjordan felt bound to reject the white paper also. Thus the white paper, although intended as a major concession to the Arabs, did not significantly ameliorate the dispute between Britain and Iraq over the question of Palestine.[23]

After the outbreak of the Second World War in September 1939 the British government continued to enforce the immigration and land purchase provisions of the white paper. But it did not want to embark upon a major administrative change under war conditions, especially since Palestine was near the area of possible military operations. Therefore, it did not act upon the constitutional provision of the white paper which called for the appointment of Palestinians to head government departments. Since the white paper had stated that these appointments would occur only "As soon as peace and order have been sufficiently restored in Palestine," the British government felt justified in postponing the implementation of this provision.[24] However, the delay in the movement toward self-government angered Iraq. Consequently, in July 1940, when Britain was in a weak position following the fall of France, Nuri, once again foreign minister, pressed Britain to establish a semi-independent government in Palestine (rather like the one Britain had established in Iraq in 1920) which, he said, would temporarily remain under British supervision. Nuri preferred that the government should be a monarchy headed by Prince Abd al-Ilah, the present regent of Iraq. After the establishment of this government in Palestine, Nuri proposed that Britain should take the initiative to form a federation of Arab countries consisting, in the first instance, of Iraq, Transjordan, and Palestine.[25]

But Nuri's scheme foundered because in August 1940 the British government informed Iraq that it would not make any further concessions to the Arabs over Palestine.[26] British officials feared that concessions would be widely interpreted in the Arab world as a sign of weakness at a time when Britain's position in the Middle East depended to a considerable extent on the appearance rather than the actuality of strength. They also believed that more concessions on Palestine would not make any appreciable difference in Arab attitudes or policies because as long as Britain maintained its predominant position in the Middle East it would incur Arab resentment and animosity. In addition, British officials feared that concessions to the Iraqi government and the Higher Arab Committee would jeopardize the cooperation of moderate Arabs in Palestine who might be inclined to accept the policy laid down in the white paper. Finally, the British government did not want to alienate public opinion in the United States, which was generally pro-Zionist, at a time when it desperately needed American support in the war.[27]

Besides remaining firm over Palestine, the British government adhered to its longstanding policy of refusing to take any initiative to form an Arab federation. In the summer of 1940 it was especially reluctant to support an Arab federation, which would probably have increased Iraqi influence in the Middle East, because Anglo-Iraqi relations were quite strained.[28]

In the 1930s and early 1940s most Iraqi leaders felt strongly about the need to end British and French rule in Palestine and Syria and create some form of united Arab state or federation. During this period Iraqi governments took steps to further these aims. However, in 1941 Palestine and Syria were still under British and French control, and the Arab countries were still disunited. Inevitably Iraqi leaders blamed Britain, the dominant European power in the Middle East, for frustrating their objectives.[29] These accusations were not entirely justified. In Syria Britain could do little, while in Palestine Britain made important concessions to the Arabs. Moreover, the disunity of the Arab world was due as much to jealousy and rivalry among the Arab states as to British opposition to Arab unity. Nonetheless, Iraq's perception of Britain as an obstacle to progress toward Arab independence and unity embittered Anglo-Iraqi relations. It also contributed to the belief among many Iraqi leaders that the expulsion of British influence from Iraq and other Arab lands was essential for the achievement of their ambitions and aspirations.

CHAPTER 7

The Struggle for Kuwait

In the late 1930s Kuwait was a quasi-independent shaykhdom of about 70,000 inhabitants covering approximately 5,800 square miles at the head of the Persian Gulf. Most of the population of Kuwait lived in the town by the sea about eighty miles south of Basra. At this time Kuwait was firmly under British influence. According to the terms of various agreements between the British government and the shaykh of Kuwait dating back to 1899, Britain was obligated to protect Kuwait (the entire principality and not just the town) against aggression while, in exchange, the shaykh agreed not to receive the representatives of foreign powers. The shaykh also agreed not to cede or lease any part of his territory, or to give a concession for oil development or pearl fishing, to any foreigner or foreign power without British consent. Thus Britain was responsible, *de facto* if not *de jure,* for managing the shaykh's foreign relations and honor bound to uphold his interests generally. Britain's dominant position in Kuwait was further indicated by the fact that the shaykh was not allowed to levy custom dues in excess of 4 percent on goods imported or exported by British subjects. In addition, the British representative in Kuwait had full judicial authority over all British subjects and protected persons in Kuwait. This representative, whose title was political agent rather than ambassador as in Iraq, was a member of the Indian political service and was responsible to the political resident in the Persian Gulf at Bushire. Unlike the British ambassador in Iraq, the resident was not responsible to the foreign office but rather to the India office and the government of India.[1]

During this period Iraq tried to gain control of Kuwait. Iraqi leaders pursued this objective because, like the leaders of many countries, they sought territorial aggrandizement for the sake of prestige and power. They also believed in Arab unity, especially if it were realized under their auspices. Doubtless too they hankered after the rich oil deposits which, although not yet discovered, were rumored to exist in the shaykhdom.

In addition, Iraqi leaders tried to gain control of Kuwait in order to prevent the smuggling of goods from Kuwait into Iraq. This smuggling cost Iraq a considerable amount of money in lost custom revenues. Indeed, in September 1938 Iraqi officials maintained that the loss was as high as £250,000 per year, plus the cost of preventive measures such as extra police patrols along the frontier. The main reason for this smuggling was that Iraq maintained high tariffs—about 75 percent on such items as tea, coffee, sugar, tobacco, and matches—to raise revenue while Kuwait kept its tariffs low—about 4 percent on most items—to encourage trade. Aside from the loss of revenue from this smuggling, Iraqi leaders were concerned that arms were moving from Kuwait into Iraq and that this illicit traffic increased their difficulty in maintaining firm control in the tribal areas of the country along the Euphrates. However, in spite of repeated Iraqi requests, the shaykh of Kuwait refused to do anything to curb smuggling—for example, raise tariffs, institute a quota system for imports, or take active preventive measures—because Kuwait's economy was heavily dependent upon trade, because he believed that it was Iraq's responsibility to control the illicit movement of goods into its own territory, and because he had major outstanding differences with the Iraqi government concerning the taxation and ownership of certain valuable date gardens in Iraq.[2]

As important as these considerations were for Iraq, probably the main reason why it attempted to gain control over Kuwait was to acquire freer access to the open sea. At this time Basra was Iraq's only port. Basra was a well-developed port but it had the disadvantage, from Iraq's point of view, of being situated over seventy miles up the Shatt al-Arab River from the sea. Although a treaty between Iraq and Iran in 1937 confirmed Iraq's full control of the Shatt al-Arab (except for portions in the vicinity of Khorramshahr and Abadan where the frontier followed the *thalweg* or line of deepest flow), the Iraqi government was concerned about the ease with which Iran from its own territory could impede or block the movement of ships proceeding up the river to Basra.

Consequently, by the spring of 1938 the Iraqi government began to consider seriously the possibility of constructing an additional port in order to secure more satisfactory access to the sea. But the length of Iraq's coastline along the Persian Gulf was less than forty miles, and the topography of this area did not readily lend itself to the development of a port. Kuwait, on the other hand, had a much longer coastline along the Persian Gulf and thus more room for the construction of a port.[3]

Iraq based its legal title to Kuwait on the Anglo-Ottoman convention of 1913. This agreement, which was never ratified, stipulated that Kuwait was an autonomous district of the Ottoman empire and that the shaykh of Kuwait was an Ottoman official. Since Iraq was the successor state to the Ottoman empire in this region, Iraqi leaders believed that they inherited the Ottoman empire's suzerainty over Kuwait.[4]

Britain did not accept Iraq's contention. It pointed out that Turkey had renounced all claims to Kuwait in the treaty of Lausanne of 1923. The British government also noted that when Iraq was admitted to the League of Nations in 1932 it had formally accepted the border with Kuwait that Britain had established in 1923 and which had existed since that time.[5]

Aside from these legal arguments, the British government rejected Iraq's claim to Kuwait because it was determined to maintain its own dominant position in the shaykhdom. There were several reasons for this policy: Kuwait occupied an important location on the British air route to India, and British officials believed that this location might become even more important in the future if an unfriendly government in Baghdad expelled Britain from its airbases in Iraq; British officials envisaged the possibility of moving troops along a motor route from Kuwait to Amman through Saudi Arabian territory if Iraq obstructed transport along the road from Baghdad to Amman; Ibn Saud, the king of Saudi Arabia with whom the British government was eager to maintain good relations, preferred that Britain stay in Kuwait in order to prevent the growth of Iraqi influence in the shaykhdom; by 1938, although Kuwait was not yet exporting oil, prospects for oil development appeared good and the Kuwait Oil Company, which held the concession, was half owned by the British controlled Anglo-Iranian Oil Company; British officials considered the possibility of using Kuwait as a base for defending the large oilfields in southwestern Iran, for which the Anglo-

Iranian Oil Company held the concession, in the event of an emergency; and the British government feared that its prestige in the Persian Gulf region would fall if it sacrificed Kuwait to Iraq.[6]

In the late 1930s Iraq employed several methods in its efforts to gain control of Kuwait. For example, it waged a vigorous propaganda campaign in the press and on the radio against Shaykh Ahmad, the ruler of Kuwait, accusing him of oppressing his subjects and not spending any of his abundant revenues on education, health, or social welfare. These articles and broadcasts constantly referred to Kuwait as an integral part of Iraq and openly advocated Iraqi annexation of the shaykhdom.[7] The propaganda campaign was accompanied by Iraqi support for dissident elements within Kuwait and by incursions of Iraqi police cars into Kuwait.[8] During this period Iraq also tried to gain British permission to take over a large section of northern Kuwait; station police in Kuwait; maintain a political adviser at the shaykh's court; form a customs union with Kuwait; and build a port on the bay of Kuwait and a railway linking that port with Iraq, both of which would remain under Iraqi control.[9] All of these efforts failed be-

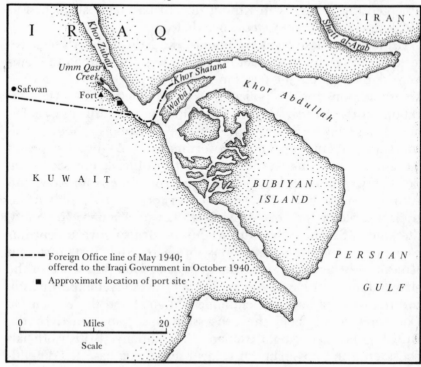

cause Shaykh Ahmad would not yield to Iraqi pressure or accept any Iraqi influence in his country, and because Britain firmly supported him in this matter.[10]

But the British government did not want to alienate Iraq unduly. Although it did not have the same legal and moral obligations toward Iraq that it had toward Kuwait, Iraq was a larger and more influential country and one in which Britain had important military and commercial interests. In addition, British officials were sympathetic with Iraq's desire to develop a port outside of the Shatt al-Arab that would therefore be less vulnerable to Iranian harrassment.[11] Consequently, in October 1938 the British government suggested that Iraq should consider the possibility of building a port on the Khor Abdullah. The Khor Abdullah was a channel of water jutting into the mainland west of the Shatt al-Arab. With its northwest arm, the Khor Shatana, it was bordered on one side by Iraq and on the other side by the Kuwaiti islands of Bubiyan and Warba. The British government believed, and tried to persuade the Iraqis, that the Khor Abdullah was a better location for a port than the bay of Kuwait because the water was deeper, both on the approach and near the shore, and therefore dredging costs would be lower. Indeed, the Khor Abdullah would require relatively little dredging because it was already about nineteen feet in depth at low tide and twenty-nine feet at high tide, which was adequate for most of the ships that used the Persian Gulf. By contrast, the construction of a modern port on the bay of Kuwait would necessitate large-scale dredging and the building of a long breakwater to provide shelter against unfavorable winds. In addition to this factor, the British government argued that the Khor Abdullah was a better location for a port because it lay appreciably closer to the Iraqi railway system than did the bay of Kuwait.[12]

Because of ministerial changes in Baghdad, for over a year the Iraqi government did not reply to the British suggestion regarding the construction of a port on the Khor Abdullah. The Iraqi government delayed its response also because it wanted to await the results of a survey it was making of the area. Finally, in November 1939 it informed Britain that it had decided to build a port near the Umm Qasr creek, which flowed into the Khor Abdullah by way of the Khor Zubair. The mouth of the creek was six miles north of Warba island. Although the border between Iraq and Kuwait in this region had not been delimited on the ground, at the time it appeared to the British government that while the northern side of the creek and the creek itself were in Iraq, the southern side might be in Kuwait. The Iraqi government did not specify where in the vicinity of the Umm Qasr creek it intended to construct the port. However, Kuwaiti ownership of the islands of Bubiyan and Warba meant that Kuwait controlled half of the channel leading to any port site in the area of Umm Qasr. In order to gain complete control of the access route to the envisaged port, in November 1939 the Iraqi government informed Britain that for security and navigational reasons it would like to acquire Bubiyan and Warba. Although these islands constituted a significant proportion of Kuwait's total territory, Iraq did not offer a *quid pro quo* to Kuwait for their cession. In the opinion of the Iraqi government compensation was unnecessary because the islands were barren and nearly uninhabited and therefore valueless to Kuwait. Indeed, at certain times of the year large sections of the islands were under water at high tide.[13]

The British foreign office opposed Iraq's demand for Bubiyan and Warba because it could not envisage a threat to Iraq from a small and weak state like Kuwait which was in close treaty relationship with the British government. However, the foreign office sympathized with Iraq's desire for navigational reasons to control the entire channel leading to Umm Qasr. It also believed that Iraqi possession of undivided control of at least one good means of access to the sea would result in stabler conditions in that region in the future. In addition, the foreign office maintained that ownership of half of the Khor Abdullah was useless to Kuwait. Consequently, in December 1939 the foreign office suggested that the British government should urge Kuwait to cede its rights in the Khor Abdullah in exchange for a monetary payment from Iraq.[14]

The political resident in the Persian Gulf, Lieutenant-Colonel C. G. Prior, who was responsible for protecting Kuwait's interests, strongly objected to the foreign office's proposal. In February 1940 he pointed out that in the future Kuwait might wish to construct its own port on the Khor Abdullah for the purpose of exporting oil and would not want the sea approaches to be completely controlled by Iraq; that Kuwaiti and thereby British control of one bank of the sea approaches to Umm Qasr was desirable because the British government would then possess a useful means of pressure on Iraq; that Ibn Saud would resent any Kuwaiti concession to Iraq on this issue because he strongly opposed an increase in Iraqi territory or privileges at the expense of Kuwait; and that any extension of Iraqi influence at the expense of Kuwait was inherently undesirable because Iraq's policy was ultimately to gain complete control of Kuwait.[15]

Prior's opposition to the foreign office's proposal to encourage the shaykh of Kuwait to yield his rights in the Khor Abdullah to Iraq was supported by the government of India, the India office, and the British ambassador in Iraq.[16] In addition, the Kuwait Oil Company urged the British government to preserve the shaykh's rights in the Khor Abdullah because it wanted to retain the option of exporting Kuwait's oil through that waterway.[17] Finally, in March 1940 the shaykh of Kuwait adamantly refused to concede to Iraq any part of his territory or his territorial waters.[18] As a result of this opposition, in May 1940 the foreign office agreed that Britain should not press the shaykh to surrender his rights in the Khor Abdullah.[19]

By the spring of 1940 it was apparent to the British government that the Iraqis preferred to construct their port immediately south of the Umm Qasr creek at a point on the Khor Zubair that was not clearly in Iraqi territory.[20] The foreign office wanted to obviate the problem of the undemarcated border at this sensitive point and also alleviate the disappointment of the Iraqi government with its failure to secure Bubiyan and Warba or Kuwait's rights in the Khor Abdullah. Consequently, in May 1940 the foreign office suggested that the British government should recommend that Iraq and Kuwait demarcate their common frontier in a manner that would clearly place in Iraq not only the southern side of the Umm Qasr creek but also the entire length of the Khor Zubair including the southernmost section between the Umm Qasr creek and Warba island.[21]

The political resident and the India office supported the foreign office's proposal. They were eager to secure Iraqi agreement to demarcate the frontier because it would connote abandonment of Iraq's claim to the entirety of Kuwait. They also hoped that demarcation would end or at least reduce the considerable number of border violations by Iraqi police cars which had occurred in recent years. In addition, they believed that demarcation was desirable in order to eliminate possibly serious complications if either country discovered oil in the vicinity of the frontier.[22] Consequently, in October 1940 and again in February 1941 the British government asked Iraq to agree to demarcate its frontier with Kuwait on the basis of the foreign office's pro-Iraqi interpretation.[23]

The Iraqi government, while not commenting on the accuracy
or equitableness of the British interpretation, refused to demarcate the border until it had received Bubiyan and Warba which
would give Iraq full control over the Khor Abdullah.[24] Probably
the Iraqi government was also concerned that demarcation would
involve recognizing the legitimacy of Kuwait, thereby making it
more difficult for Iraq later to claim sovereignty over the entire
shaykhdom. In addition, the Iraqi government may have calculated that it could get better terms from Britain in the future if
Germany were successful in the war. Finally, the Iraqi government probably refused demarcation of the frontier because at this
time it lacked the financial resources to build a port at Umm Qasr
and therefore from its perspective there was no pressing need to
establish the exact location of the border.[25]

As a result of Iraqi unwillingness, the Iraqi-Kuwaiti frontier was
not demarcated during the Second World War. For military reasons, during the war the British government built and adminis-
tered a port on the Khor Zubair south of the Umm Qasr creek,
precisely where Iraq had planned to build a port. At the end of
the war Britain dismantled the port, in part in order to prevent
its ownership from becoming a source of dispute between Iraq
and Kuwait.[26] In the early 1960s, after Britain had relinquished
its protectorate over Kuwait, the Iraqi government finally constructed its own port on this spot, although the frontier between
Iraq and Kuwait was still undemarcated. Today the question of
the undemarcated border is dormant, but it still retains the seeds
of a possibly serious quarrel in the future between Iraq and Kuwait.

In the late 1930s and early 1940s Iraq challenged Kuwait's status as an independent shaykhdom under British protection. In
various ways Iraq attempted to chip away at Kuwait's sovereignty
and territorial integrity. All of these efforts failed because of
British opposition. But in the process of thwarting Iraq's designs
on Kuwait and maintaining its own dominant position in the
shaykhdom, Britain alienated Iraq. From Iraq's perspective Britain was depriving Iraq of much needed custom revenues, increasing Iraq's internal security problems, blocking Iraq's path to
the open sea, and impeding the advancement of Arab unity. Thus
Britain failed to reconcile its obligation to uphold the interests of
Kuwait with its desire to maintain the friendship of Iraq. Probably Britain's task was impossible and no policy would have succeeded in achieving both of these objectives. Nonetheless, the fact

remains that the various disputes over Kuwait—Iraq's legal claim to the entire shaykhdom; Iraq's attempt to construct a port under Iraqi control on the bay of Kuwait; Iraq's effort to gain control of Bubiyan and Warba; even Britain's attempt to secure a demarcation of the border, which would have meant the abandonment of Iraq's claim to the entirety of Kuwait—embittered Anglo-Iraqi relations. And, by emphasizing the incompatibility of British and Iraqi interests at the head of the Persian Gulf, these disputes over Kuwait undermined the moral foundations of Britain's imperial position in Iraq.

CHAPTER 8

The Supply of Arms

Throughout the 1930s and early 1940s, all Iraqi governments placed a high priority on purchasing from abroad significant quantities of modern weapons. During this period Iraqi leaders envisaged several possible threats to their security. Some believed that Turkey had never reconciled itself to the loss of the *vilayet* (province) of Mosul during the First World War and would seek to reacquire that oil rich area at the first convenient opportunity. Turkey's strenuous and ultimately successful effort in the late 1930s to repossess from Syria the *sanjak* (district) of Alexandretta intensified their fears that Mosul was next on Ankara's list. In 1939 one Iraqi minister even suspected that Britain had promised Mosul to Turkey in order to win Turkish assistance in the forthcoming struggle against the axis powers.[1]

Generally, Iraqi leaders were even more concerned about the possibility of an attack by Iran.[2] For a long time Iraq (and its predecessor, the Ottoman empire) and Iran had been locked in a bitter dispute over the division of the waters of the Shatt al-Arab. Although the matter was settled by agreement in 1937,[3] the relationship between the two countries remained tense. For Iraq this situation was especially worrisome because Iran was militarily stronger. For example, in early 1935 Iraqi leaders estimated that within five weeks of the declaration of mobilization Iran could concentrate along the Iraqi frontier at least forty-four infantry battalions and four cavalry regiments, while to oppose this force Iraq could place in the field only fifteen infantry battalions and two cavalry regiments.[4] And in late 1936 the British air ministry estimated that Iran had twice as many modern warplanes as Iraq.[5]

Aside from concern over Turkey and Iran, during the 1930s and early 1940s some Iraqi leaders wanted to strengthen the country because they envisaged the possibility of a military clash with Britain.[6] Such a clash might result from government efforts to assert firm control over a minority group like the Assyrians. Or it might come from government attempts to reduce or eliminate Britain's military privileges in Iraq, such as the right to move troops across the country and the right to maintain air-bases with guards under British control. A clash with Britain might also result from Iraqi efforts to oust Britain from Palestine, or from a dispute over the British protected principality of Kuwait, to which Iraq maintained a territorial claim.[7] Even if an armed conflict with Britain were avoided, these leaders probably calculated that increased military power would put them in a better position to exert various forms of pressure on Britain which would ultimately result in a complete British withdrawal from Iraq and elsewhere in the Middle East.

In addition to the need to combat foreign powers, Iraqi governments attempted to acquire arms in order to assert themselves over dissident elements within the country. During the 1930s important groups among the Assyrians, Kurds, Yazidis, and Shiites were not reconciled to the rule of the Sunni Arab dominated government in Baghdad. The government's determination to enforce conscription for the army was especially unpopular among large sections of the population. Since much of the population outside of the urban areas was armed with rifles, Iraqi leaders believed that they needed sophisticated weapons like artillery, tanks, and airplanes in order to overawe and, if necessary, to suppress their internal opponents.[8] This belief was reinforced by the Iraqi army's experience in the spring of 1932, on the eve of independence, when it managed to crush a Kurdish uprising in northern Iraq only after the intervention on its behalf of the Royal Air Force.[9] But after independence Iraqi leaders would no longer be able to rely on British assistance to maintain internal order.

Iraqi governments attempted to purchase modern weapons abroad also because they wanted to appease Iraqi military commanders and thereby reduce the chance of being overthrown by the army. For example, the government of Hikmat Sulayman, which was brought to power by a military coup in October 1936 and which probably feared dismissal in the same manner, immediately formulated an ambitious plan to increase substantially the quantity and quality of equipment available to the armed forces.[10] In December 1938 military leaders clearly demonstrated that their views on the question of arms supply would have to be taken seriously when they overthrew the government of Jamil al-Midfai, in part because they felt that it had not provided them with enough weapons.[11] Apparently taking this lesson to heart, Nuri al-Said, Midfai's successor as prime minister, immediately upon coming to power asked Britain for a large financial credit to facilitate the purchase of armaments.[12]

Assuming that Iraqi leaders were willing to subordinate development projects and social needs, they could afford to buy modern weapons because, beginning in 1931, they derived substantial income from the sale of oil concessions and, three years later, from the export of oil. In 1935, for example, Iraq exported over three and a half million tons of oil, and by 1937 this figure had risen to over four million tons. The Iraq Petroleum Company, a conglomeration of British, French, American, and Dutch interests which operated the oilfields and the pipelines to the Mediterranean, paid the Iraqi government a royalty of four shillings (gold) per ton on oil exported from Iraq. By 1939 these royalties, plus dead rent payments the company paid for the concession for certain areas of the country that were not yet producing oil, amounted to about £2,200,000 annually.[13]

Illustrating the importance Iraq placed on its armed forces, between financial years[14] 1932–33 and 1940–41 the government's military budget (excluding appropriations for the police) rose from 800,000 dinars[15] (22 percent of total expenditure) to 2,100,000 dinars (32 percent of total expenditure). In reality, however, military expenditure in 1940–41 was considerably greater than 2,100,000 dinars because this figure, which was the amount of the government's ordinary military budget (and which was 32 percent of the total ordinary budget), was supplemented by a substantial proportion of a special capital works budget. In 1940–41 the capital works budget, which came from oil revenues and from a loan from the Iraq Petroleum Company, amounted to about 2,650,000 dinars.[16]

The government's military budget was also supplemented by contributions from the Iraq Airplane Society. The society was a quasi-official organization that donated all of its funds to the government to help pay for the purchase of military aircraft. Each year in the middle and late 1930s the government obligated all of its employees to contribute between one-third of a month's salary and an entire month's salary to the society. In addition, the government organized lotteries to raise money for the society.[17]

This rise in outlays for the military was accompanied by a significant growth in the size of the army and air force. For example, in the summer of 1932 there were 10,200 men in the Iraqi armed forces, while by the summer of 1940 this figure had increased to 43,400.[18] Similarly, the number of planes in the Iraqi air force rose from nine in early 1932 to 116 in the spring of 1941.[19]

While the Iraqi government desired to purchase modern weapons and was financially able to do so, its freedom to import armaments was greatly circumscribed by a provision in the Anglo-Iraqi treaty of 1930 which stipulated that Iraqi military equipment "shall not differ in type from those of the forces of His Britannic Majesty." Thus, although Iraq was permitted to buy weapons from any country provided that the weapons were of a sort used by the British armed forces, in reality this clause obligated Iraq to purchase virtually all of its military equipment exclusively from Britain.

In 1930 the British government insisted upon including this provision in the treaty because it believed that the two armies would be able to operate more efficiently together in wartime if they used similar equipment. British officials also calculated that the requirement to use British military equipment would make Iraq dependent upon Britain for spare parts and therefore eager to retain Britain's friendship. In addition, they feared that the importation of non-British weapons into Iraq, possibly accompanied by foreign military instructors, would quickly lead to the growth of foreign political influence in Iraq. Finally, they wanted to preserve the Iraqi market for British arms manufacturers for purely commercial reasons.[20]

In exchange for accepting this clause of the treaty, the Iraqi government received a commitment from Britain to sell "arms, ammunition, equipment, ships and aeroplanes of the latest available pattern." Thus, although the treaty obligated Iraq to purchase nearly all of its weapons from Britain, the treaty also obligated Britain to sell to Iraq unlimited quantities of the most modern armaments that British industry was able to produce.

However, in the middle and late 1930s the British government's ability to honor this pledge was limited because British industry was just beginning to tool up for large-scale military production and, consequently, delays and bottlenecks were common.

In addition, Britain's own military forces were eager to buy most of the output of Britain's armaments industry in order to match the growing strength of potential enemies like Germany, Italy, and Japan. Indicating the British army's desperate need for up-to-date military equipment, in September 1938, at the time of the Munich crisis when war with Germany was a serious possibility, there were only fifty modern anti-aircraft guns in all of Britain.[21] In the summer of 1939, on the eve of the war, the four British divisions earmarked for dispatch to France in the event of hostilities with Germany had only 50 percent of the anti-tank and anti-aircraft weapons they required and only 30 percent of the necessary ammunition.[22] It was only at the beginning of 1940, several months after the war began, that the British army received enough modern medium tanks to equip one battalion.[23] And in 1941 some British artillery units were still using guns manufactured forty years earlier during the Boer War.[24] The Indian army, which the British government expected to play a major role in any new conflict, and which was almost entirely dependent on Britain for its arms and equipment, was also in great need of modern weapons and vehicles. At the beginning of 1939 it consisted almost entirely of horse cavalry, unmechanized infantry, and horse-drawn artillery. There were no anti-tank units, and only eight anti-aircraft guns in all of India.[25]

Compounding the problem, during this period the British government was also confronted with requests for military equipment from the dominions and from various other countries like France, Poland, Romania, Portugal, Greece, Turkey, and Egypt. For example, in the autumn of 1938 South Africa requested enough machine-guns to equip fourteen army battalions.[26] In the opinion of British military leaders, many of these countries were in greater danger of enemy attack or of greater strategic importance to Britain than Iraq was. Indeed, in November 1938 they concluded that Iraq should rank as the sixth foreign country in order of priority for British arms, while in July 1939 they thought that Iraq should rank in the ninth position.[27] As far as the nations of the Middle East were concerned, in the middle and late 1930s the British government consistently ruled that the equipment needs of the Egyptian armed forces must take precedence over those of Iraq because Egypt helped to protect the Suez Canal.[28]

Thus it was often not possible for Britain to fulfill Iraqi orders for military equipment without extensive delays unless it were willing to jeopardize its own security or that of other important allied and friendly nations. Indicating the long waiting period which these considerations sometimes imposed, in January 1937 Iraq wanted to purchase twelve modern medium tanks, but the British government said that it could not deliver them for at least four years.[29] In May 1937 the British government informed Iraq that it needed three years to fulfill a request for thirty 3.7-inch howitzers.[30] In April 1938 the British government said that it could not give Iraq anti-aircraft guns or anti-tank guns until 1941.[31] And in May 1939 the British government informed Iraq that it could not deliver mortars until the spring of 1940.[32]

Other items were delivered only after the scheduled date. For example, fifty machine-guns which were supposed to be shipped to Iraq in November 1935 were not actually sent until five months later, and then in a useless condition because they lacked tripods.[33] In August 1936 the Iraqi government still had not received a batch of artillery shells it had ordered fifteen months previously, while a number of howitzers it had ordered twenty-six months earlier had only just been shipped.[34] In February 1937 the Iraqi government still had not received 50,000 rounds of revolver ammunition it had purchased eighteen months earlier.[35] And in January 1938 some Iraqi orders for range-finders had been outstanding for over two years, while certain gun fuses bought in 1934 had only just arrived.[36]

But not all delays were due to problems on the British end. Some were caused by Iraq's habit of insisting upon newly made rather than old but perfectly serviceable equipment of the same type that was immediately available from British stockpiles. For example, in October 1936 Britain offered Iraq reconditioned parts for the gun carriages for its 6-inch howitzers, but the Iraqi government insisted upon new manufacture which resulted in a six month delay. During the same period Iraq demanded new manufacture for a batch of artillery shells, thereby causing a delay that would have been obviated by taking shells from British stockpiles. Although it had been ready for delivery to Iraq for three months, in May 1937 an order for revolver ammunition remained in Britain because the Iraqi government insisted upon shipping the cargo in newly made cases, which were not yet available, rather than in entirely adequate cases taken from British stockpiles. This same problem affected a shipment of gun-cotton and primers for Iraq's artillery pieces.[37]

Other delays were caused by the Iraqi government's failure to pay a deposit at the time of purchase. For example, an order for rifles, machine-guns, artillery, and artillery shells placed in May 1935 was delayed between eight and ten months for this reason.[38]

Still other delays were due to the fact that in the 1930s Iraqi governments which changed frequently, sometimes cancelled equipment orders placed by their predecessors. Occasionally, after a period for reflection and reconsideration, the same item was reordered. This inability to adhere to a single plan upset production schedules in Britain and made timely deliveries to Iraq extremely difficult. For example, in June 1936 the government of Yasin al-Hashimi decided upon a major program of weapon purchases in Britain which included armored fighting vehicles (light tanks). But in October 1936 Yasin was ousted by a coup d'etat led by General Bakr Sidqi, and the entire program was scrapped and replaced by a different one. After Bakr Sidqi was assassinated in August 1937 the next government, led by Jamil al-Midfai, placed an order in Britain for armored fighting vehicles. However, in December 1938 Midfai was ousted by another military coup and his successor, Nuri al-Said, immediately cancelled the order. Eventually Nuri's government decided that it too wanted armored fighting vehicles. But by this time the war in Europe had begun and Britain was unwilling to deliver the vehicles because they were needed for its own armed forces.[39]

Regardless of the cause, delays in the delivery of military equipment infuriated Iraqi leaders.[40] They were acutely conscious that in 1935 they had been left on their own to combat a serious uprising by Shiite tribes along the Euphrates in southern Iraq when the British government refused their repeated request for assistance from the R.A.F.[41] They were also aware of the fact that in 1936, as a result of a delay in the delivery of military equipment from Britain, their army had suffered from a shortage of machine-guns while engaged in another major military operation against Shiite tribal dissidents.[42] Morover, their assessment of the risk of enemy attack on Iraq was usually greater than that made by British officials.[43] Nor could they understand how a great power like Britain was unable to spare the relatively small quantities of weapons which Iraq, an allied country, wanted to purchase. They suspected that the British government was attempting to keep Iraq weak and perpetually dependent on Britain for its security and therefore unwilling to dispense with the British airbases. Even if the British government had been a reliable and timely supplier of modern military equipment, Iraqi leaders would have chafed at the provision of the treaty that restricted their freedom to buy elsewhere and thereby prevented them from reducing Iraq's dependence on Britain. The British government's frequent inability or unwillingness to deliver weapons without inordinate delays only increased their anger and strengthened their determination to rectify what they considered to be a humiliating and even dangerous situation.

Contrary to the belief of many Iraqi leaders, in the 1930s the British government did not withhold arms in an effort to keep Iraq weak and dependent. True, British officials considered this course of action. Such consideration was extremely likely because British-manufactured arms, rather than being used to defend Iraq against external foes, were often employed for acts of domestic suppression against groups that were not anti-British and with which Britain had no quarrel. Sometimes the arms were also used in a rather indiscriminate or even brutal manner. Aside from the Assyrian affair in 1933 which we have already discussed, in 1935, during the course of a rebellion in northern Iraq by a section of the small Yazidi community against military conscription, the Iraqi army massacred over 200 Yazidis, most of whom had not even participated in the revolt.[44] In 1935–37 the Iraqi army also engaged in extensive military operations against the Shiite tribes along the Euphrates in southern Iraq. To a considerable extent the Shiite rebellions, like the Yazidi uprising, were the result of an intensely felt opposition to military conscription. Sometimes there were additional causes that pointed to maladministration, like the appointment of incompetent local officials and the prohibition of certain Shiite religious processions.[45] Commonly during these military operations in the south the Iraqi air force bombed villages, crops, and date palms, and the Iraqi army summarily executed prisoners and other local inhabitants.[46] More galling for Britain, in October 1936 General Bakr Sidqi, who had led the Iraqi army against the Assyrians in 1933 and almost certainly deserves much of the responsibility for the massacres, and who was very anti-British, used planes and ordnance purchased from Britain to bomb Baghdad in a successful effort to overthrow the established government of Yasin al-Hashimi with which Britain had good relations.[47] After Bakr Sidqi's coup British officials became concerned that a powerful and hostile Iraqi military establishment might one day turn its arms against the virtually defenseless British airbases in Iraq.[48] Nonetheless, in spite of these moral dilemmas and physical risks, throughout the middle and late 1930s the British government deliberately chose to expedite the shipment of weapons to Iraq to the maximum feasible extent, bearing in mind only the equipment needs of the British armed forces and those of other friendly countries.[49]

The British government chose this course of action primarily because it wanted to retain Iraqi friendship, which it considered essential to ensure the security of the British airbases in Iraq and the British supply lines across the country. In particular, the British government wanted to strengthen the position of pro-British elements within Iraq and undermine the position of anti-British elements by clearly demonstrating the value to Iraq of the treaty of 1930. British officials also wanted to discourage Iraq from turning to other countries to fulfill its armament needs. They were especially eager to prevent Iraq from buying German weapons because they feared that German instructors would soon follow and that German political influence in Iraq would grow.[50] Although most arms purchases from other countries would constitute a violation of the Anglo-Iraqi treaty, British officials believed that Iraq would be justified if Britain first infringed the agreement by refusing to make a bona-fide effort to satisfy Iraq's requests.[51] In addition to these considerations, the British government expedited the shipment of weapons to Iraq because it wanted to increase Iraq's ability to withstand an attack by Turkey or Iran and thereby reduce the number of troops which, in the event of such an attack, it would be obligated to send to defend the country.[52]

Illustrating the British government's desire to meet Iraq's demand for up-to-date military equipment, in the middle and late 1930s it continually offered Iraq the most modern British aircraft combined with quite reasonable delivery dates.[53] For example, in February 1937 the British government offered Iraq Gladiator fighters, a new plane that entered service with the R.A.F. that very month, with deliveries commencing only five months later.[54] Alternatively, it offered Iraq Fury fighters, an older plane that entered service in 1931 but was still operational with the R.A.F., with shipment of the entire lot within six weeks.[55] In March 1937 the British government offered Iraq Battle bombers, a new plane not yet in service, with first deliveries scheduled in ten months.[56] In May 1937 it offered Iraq Blenheim bombers, which entered service with the R.A.F. only two months previous, and Hurricane fighters, which were still in the design stage, with deliveries of Blenheims starting in fourteen months and Hurricanes in sixteen months.[57] In May 1939 the British government again offered Iraq Blenheim bombers, this time with deliveries beginning in four months.[58] And in June 1939 it offered Iraq Lysander army cooperation planes, which entered service with the R.A.F. only one year previous, with first deliveries in two months.[59] All of these offers were for a single squadron (usually consisting of between fifteen and twenty aircraft), which was the quantity Iraqi officials expressed interest in purchasing.

The British government offered these planes to Iraq at some risk to its own security. Illustrating the R.A.F.'s great need for the planes, in September 1938, at the time of the Munich crisis, it had only ninety-three modern fighters available for the defense of the entire United Kingdom.[60] The British government also offered these planes to Iraq despite the fact that during this period many of its other friends and allies were demanding military aircraft. For example, in April 1939 Romania and Poland requested 450 and 250 planes, respectively.[61]

Iraq eventually purchased fifteen Gladiators and fifteen Lysanders.[62] However, in the middle and late 1930s Iraqi governments were determined to buy some non-British aircraft in order to reduce their dependence on Britain and, if possible, to secure more rapid delivery times. Probably certain Iraqi leaders also hoped to obtain lucrative sales commissions on these purchases.[63] In any event, in June 1937 Iraq ordered from Italy fifteen Breda fighters and five Savoia bombers with delivery of all aircraft promised within three months.[64] The British government was angered by this clear breach of the treaty, particularly because it involved the importation of Italian instructors and mechanics into Iraq and the sending of Iraqis to Italy for training, but could do nothing.[65] In September 1939 Iraq again bought a non-British aircraft, this time choosing fifteen fighter-bombers from the Northrop corporation in the United States.[66] This purchase too angered the British government, but not as much as the one from Italy because Anglo-American relations were close and Britain did not fear the growth of American influence in Iraq.[67]

It was not only in the area of military aircraft that Iraqi leaders were determined to diversify their source of supply. For example, in June 1935 Iraq purchased 20,000 rifles from Czechoslovakia,[68] and in May 1936 ordered 200 Czech machine-guns.[69] Turning to Germany, in July 1937 the Iraqi government bought eighteen dual purpose anti-aircraft/anti-tank guns,[70] and in March 1939 ordered eighteen more of these guns.[71] From Italy, in the summer of 1937 Iraq purchased fourteen light tanks,[72] in November 1938 5,100 bombs,[73] and in March 1939 another 6,900 bombs.[74]

As another method of reducing its dependence on Britain for war material, in the early 1930s the Iraqi government contracted a British firm to build a factory for the production of small arms ammunition. This factory opened in August 1934 and by 1938 was producing 9,000,000 rounds annually.[75] In the late 1930s Iraq employed the same company to construct a rifle factory, which opened in August 1940.[76]

Continuing its efforts to become self-sufficient, in June 1939 the Iraqi government placed an order in Britain complete with a down payment for the construction of a factory for the manufacture of artillery shells. However, before delivery of the necessary machinery could begin, in September 1939 the war in Europe intervened. Now Britain's own need for this equipment became urgent. In addition, India and South Africa wanted to purchase similar equipment and since they, unlike Iraq, were actually belligerents the British government gave them priority. Consequently, it refused to allow delivery of the machinery to Iraq and, as a result, the shell factory was not built.[77]

Like the machinery for the shell factory, after the outbreak of war Britain could not provide many weapons to Iraq because it had to reserve nearly all of its available supply for itself. In addition, the British government gave priority to countries which, unlike Iraq, were already under attack or which it considered to be in immediate danger of attack.[78] Nonetheless, it continued to deliver limited quantities of arms to Iraq. For example, between September 1939 and June 1940 it shipped a total of forty-five guns and howitzers to Iraq.[79] And until May 1940 it sent significant quantities of artillery ammunition to Iraq, amounting in total to 36,000 rounds.[80] It was only in late 1940, when Anglo-Iraqi relations were very bad, that Britain attempted to apply pressure on Iraq by withholding certain items of military equipment, especially some training aircraft, which otherwise it was willing to deliver.[81] But even this embargo was only partial, and through March 1941 the British government provided spare parts for vehicles and weapons of British manufacture in Iraqi service.[82] It was only in April 1941, when Britain and Iraq were on the brink of war, that the British government halted delivery of all military equipment to Iraq.[83]

After the outbreak of the Second World War, when Britain's ability and willingness to deliver arms were less than ever, the Iraqi government was especially eager to acquire more weapons. Some Iraqi leaders feared that Russia, which was now linked to Germany by the Nazi-Soviet pact of August 1939, might attack and that Britain, preoccupied by the conflict in Europe, would be unable to assist Iraq.[84] Other Iraqi leaders wanted more arms in order to use the opportunity created by Britain's preoccupation with the struggle against Germany to end, if necessary by force, Britain's privileged position in Iraq.[85] Whatever the reason, the Iraqi government now attempted to buy military equipment, and especially anti-aircraft guns, from Italy,[86] France,[87] Hungary,[88] Japan,[89] Germany,[90] and the United States.[91] Nearly all of these efforts were unsuccessful because of transportation difficulties,[92] because Britain was unwilling to give Iraq the foreign exchange needed for purchases outside of the sterling bloc,[93] and because in wartime most nations were inclined to husband their military equipment[94] or, in the case of the United States, sell primarily to Britain. However, in early 1941 the Easter corporation in the United States agreed to sell seventy-five Colt machine-guns suitable for installation on the Northrop fighter-bombers Iraq had recently purchased. These guns were scheduled to arrive at Basra in April 1941 on the American cargo ship *Brooklyn Heights*. But by this time Anglo-Iraqi relations had worsened so badly that the British government was eager to prevent any weapons from reaching Iraq. Consequently, on 19 April, while Britain and Iraq were still at peace, a British warship intercepted the *Brooklyn Heights* in the straits of Hormuz and diverted it to Karachi.[95] As a result of this action, the Iraqi government was unable to use these guns against Britain in the fighting that broke out between the two countries the following month.

From 1932 to 1940 the British government gave Iraq significant quantities of modern weapons like planes, artillery, and machine-guns. The British military mission helped to maintain these weapons and provided instruction and advice to a large number of Iraqi soldiers. Iraqi officers were trained in British staff colleges and other institutions in Britain and India.[96] Nonetheless, many influential Iraqis, especially in the military, remained alienated from Britain. They believed that the British government had given too few weapons too slowly. They hated the very idea of a British military presence in Iraq in the form of airbases, levies, and a military mission.[97] In May 1941 these men used the Iraqi military machine, which the British government had supplied, trained, and nurtured for two decades, to wage war against Britain.[98]

Perhaps if the British government had given more weapons to Iraq more quickly it would have won the friendship and goodwill of virtually the entire ruling class in Iraq, reconciled them to the continued existence of a British military presence, and thereby maintained its dominant position in Iraq without having to fight its way back into the country in 1941. But this policy would have deprived Britain's own armed forces and those of important allied nations of much needed weapons at a time of great danger, and if it had failed to win over the Iraqis it would have increased the threat to the extremely vulnerable British airbases.

Possibly if the British government had given fewer and less sophisticated weapons, Iraqi leaders, aside from being unable to wage war so successfully against their own people, could never have contemplated a military clash with Britain. However, in this case the Iraqi government could have accused Britain of violating the treaty, retaliated by purchasing more weapons from other nations, and thereby strengthened the Iraqi army while also reducing British influence in the country.

Thus the British government's dilemma, which resulted from its decision in 1929–30 to grant Iraq independence while only retaining minimally guarded airbases, was acute. All of its policy options in the matter of arms supply were risky. Perhaps none of them would have succeeded in safeguarding the airbases while also producing an Iraqi government sincerely devoted to friendship with Britain and willing to accept the continuation of Britain's dominant position in the country. In any event, the one chosen did not succeed.

CHAPTER 9

The Supply of Credit

In order to facilitate trade and further economic development, in the middle and late 1930s Iraq invested large sums in railway construction. Most of this money went for a line from Baiji, just north of Baghdad, to Tel Kotchek in Syria. The Iraqi government favored this project because upon completion it would link Basra, Baghdad, and Mosul, Iraq's main three cities, with Syria and Turkey and through those countries to Europe. Construction of the line began in November 1936. However, due to poor planning and hasty development before the completion of a proper survey, costs rose unexpectedly. By early 1939 Iraq had already spent £1,900,000 and still needed £1,500,000 more in order to finish construction. But Iraq could not afford to pay the remaining sums. Indeed, it could not even afford to pay for £550,000 worth of railway equipment it had recently ordered from British manufacturers.[1]

Nor could the Iraqi government afford to pay for other railway lines, roads, flood control and irrigation works, an oil refinery, an automatic telephone exchange, a grain silo, and a port at Umm Qasr it wanted to build.[2] Indeed, largely because of a high level of expenditure on the Baiji-Tel Kotchek extension and on equipment, munitions, and salaries for the armed forces, by the spring of 1939 the Iraqi government was so short of money that in order to pay its bills the minister of finance was forced to draw on the revenue of the municipalities of Baghdad, Basra, and Mosul; and as an economy measure he was contemplating paying civil servants only 50 percent of their salaries in cash and giving them promissory notes for the remainder.[3]

In an effort to improve its financial situation, in January 1939 the Iraqi government asked Britain for £2,000,000 in credits for commercial purchases and £3,000,000 in credits for military purchases.[4] Iraqi leaders were encouraged to ask for money because at this time Britain was giving commercial and military credits to several other countries to help them resist German and Italian enticements and pressure. Iraqi leaders believed they had a better claim on British largesse than most of these countries—Turkey was a much quoted example—because they were a long-standing ally and could give good security in the form of oil royalties.[5]

The British government was favorably disposed toward Iraq's request. It wanted to stay on good terms with Iraq in order to protect the British airbases in Iraq and the British air route to India that passed through Iraq. Equally important, the British government wanted to safeguard its land route from the Persian Gulf through Iraq, Transjordan, and Palestine to the Mediterranean.[6] In the late 1930s this route was especially significant because Italian ships and planes based in Eritrea were well situated to attack British troopships moving through the Red Sea to Egypt. For British military leaders this danger was so worrying that in the event of a war in which Italy was hostile they planned to send all troop reinforcements for Egypt via the land route until the Red Sea had been properly secured.[7]

Aside from these military considerations, the British government wanted to stay on good terms with Iraq in order to preserve its strong economic position in that country. Indicating the strength of this position, in 1938 the total value of Britain's exports to Iraq was nearly £3,000,000. This figure represented 30 percent of Iraq's imports, and was about as much as the total value of Britain's exports to Turkey and Iran combined.[8] However, to a considerable extent Britain's success in exporting to Iraq was the result of Iraq's abidance by a provision of the treaty of 1930 which obligated it to employ British subjects whenever it needed foreign officials. The importance of this provision is illustrated by the fact that in 1934 there were still 242 British subjects working for the Iraqi government. Most of these men were employed in technical and engineering departments of the government such as the railways, the port of Basra, irrigation, and public works. From these positions they were well placed to steer orders for machinery and equipment to British companies. If Iraq began to employ significant numbers of people from other countries, either from pique or from a desire for emancipation from a restrictive provision of the treaty, some British manufacturers would probably suffer considerable losses.[9]

Britain's success in exporting to Iraq was also dependent upon Iraq's continued abidance by the terms of the Anglo-Iraqi railway agreement of March 1936. This agreement transferred ownership of the railways in Iraq from Britain to Iraq. In return, the agreement obligated Iraq to purchase all of its railway material in Britain, provided that suitable material was available on reasonable conditions. Thus if Iraq utilized a pretext, such as high prices, low quality, or extended delivery periods, to evade its commitment to purchase British railway equipment, certain British companies would lose substantial orders.[10]

There were several other reasons why the British government was willing to give credits to Iraq. To begin with, it feared that otherwise Germany would do so and thereby gain political influence in Iraq. Indeed, in early 1939 Iraqi leaders frequently pointed out that Germany had offered to sell large quantities of arms on generous terms that Iraq had rejected only out of loyalty to the alliance.[11] The British government was favorably disposed toward Iraq's request also because virtually all of the money would be spent in Britain and thereby aid British manufacturers. In fact, credits were the only way that British companies could be paid for the £550,000 worth of railway equipment Iraq had already ordered. An additional explanation for Britain's willingness to provide credits was Iraq's revenue from oil, amounting to about £2,200,000 per year, which provided good collateral. Finally, the foreign office justified financial assistance for Iraq by pointing out that as a result of the dangerous international situation the British government was altering its policy in Palestine in order to win the friendship of the Arab states, and that it would be paradoxical and inconsistent if it did not do everything possible to accommodate the Arab states in other areas also.[12]

In March 1939 the war office recommended that Iraq should be obligated to spend a portion of the credits to improve the Iraqi section of the Baghdad-Haifa road. The British government had already spent about £600,000 to improve the Transjordanian section of the road, but the Iraqi section still contained unpaved sections that were regularly closed for about a week each year due to flooding. For the war office this road was important not only because it might be needed to move troops from the Persian Gulf to Egypt but also because under certain circumstances it might be needed to move troops from Palestine to Iraq.[13]

The war office's request that Iraq should be obligated to spend a portion of the credits on the road was not accepted because of the opposition of the foreign office. Since the Iraqis did not place a high priority on the road, the foreign office did not believe that they would willingly accept this condition. If the Iraqis accepted under duress, the foreign office feared that Britain would lose much of the political benefit of the credits. The foreign office also maintained that it was unnecessary to insist upon this condition because the existing road was adequate for all but a few days each year. Finally, the foreign office pointed out that the British government could not easily make this demand because as part of the treaty settlement of 1930 it had promised that Iraq would not have to bear any extra cost as a result of placing its territory and facilities at British disposal in time of war.[14]

In early May 1939 the foreign office recommended that Britain honor Iraq's full request for financial assistance, which now amounted to £3,250,000 in military credits and £2,000,000 in commercial credits. The foreign office also suggested providing an additional £850,000 in commercial credits for two projects for which Iraq had not yet requested money.[15] The export credits guarantee department supported the foreign office's recommendation, providing that an interest rate of 5 percent was charged.[16] However, the treasury, which at this time had to borrow heavily to finance British rearmament, and which was also confronted with requests for financial assistance from numerous other countries, disliked the idea of borrowing additional sums in order to pay for economic development in Iraq. Consequently, it agreed to meet Iraq's full request for military credits but would only provide £650,000 in commercial credits. The treasury chose the figure of £650,000 for commercial credits because it represented the value of purchases for railway equipment and other goods which Iraq had recently made in Britain and was unable to pay for.[17] In spite of appeals by the foreign office and the export credits guarantee department to provide the full amount of commercial credits, the treasury view prevailed.[18]

The Iraqi government was grateful for Britain's offer of credits, but it believed that an interest rate of 5 percent was too high. It pointed out that the previous year Britain had given credits to Turkey at 3 percent interest, although Iraq could offer better security in the form of oil royalties. Aside from the financial cost, considerations of prestige made it difficult for Iraq to accept a higher interest rate than Turkey. Consequently, in June 1939 Iraq rejected Britain's offer of credits unless the interest rate were lowered to 3 percent.[19]

In order to accommodate Iraq, Sir Basil Newton, the British ambassador in Baghdad, recommended lowering the interest rate.[20] However, the export credits guarantee department and the treasury stood firm for an interest rate of 5 percent. They pointed out that the British government had charged 5 percent on credits recently given to Romania and Greece, and that it was asking for 5 percent in credit negotiations currently in progress with Poland and Turkey. If Iraq were offered a lower rate of interest, they feared that other countries would immediately request a similar rate. They were particularly concerned about Greece, which had accepted a rate of 5 percent only when given an assurance that no other government would be charged less.[21]

The export credits guarantee department and the treasury also pointed out that it was not precisely true that Turkey had received credits at 3 percent interest. In May 1938 Britain had given Turkey £6,000,000 in military credits at 3 percent or 1 percent above the bank rate, whichever figure was higher. Since the bank rate had remained at 2 percent since the credits were granted, this meant that in June 1939 Turkey was indeed paying 3 percent. However, under the terms of a complicated procedure, at the beginning of 1943 the interest rate on these credits would probably rise, quite possibly as high as $5\frac{1}{2}$ percent. In addition to the military credits, in May 1938 Britain had given Turkey £10,000,000 in commercial credits at a fixed interest rate of $5\frac{1}{2}$ percent. Thus Turkey was paying an average interest rate of $4\frac{1}{2}$ percent on the total of £16,000,000 of credits, and this figure would probably rise soon. Looked at in this light, and considering that long-term interest rates had risen since these arrangements had been made and that now the British government itself could not borrow money at less than 4 percent, the export credits guarantee department and the treasury did not think that a fixed interest rate of 5 percent on the credits for Iraq was at all unreasonable.[22]

When Britain refused to lower the interest rate to 3 percent, the Iraqi government sought a compromise. In order to finance its most urgent requirements, in early July 1939 it suggested that while negotiations continued Britain should immediately provide £1,500,000 in military credits at an interest rate of 4 percent.[23] The foreign office was willing to accept this proposal but the export credits guarantee department and the treasury would not lower the rate of interest even if the total amount of credits were reduced.[24] Consequently, on 15 August 1939 the Iraqi government finally accepted Britain's offer for £3,250,000 in military credits and £460,000 in commercial credits at an interest rate of 5 percent.[25]

Before the credit agreement could be drawn up and signed by both parties, on 1 September 1939 the Second World War broke out. The British government was now eager to draw Turkey into the conflict on the allied side. Therefore, it offered Turkey £25,000,000 in military credits at an interest rate of only 4 percent, thus breaking its recently established policy of charging foreign countries at least 5 percent. The foreign office was concerned that Iraqi leaders would be angry when they learned that they had to pay a higher rate of interest than Turkey, especially when they had been assured that all countries were now being charged at least 5 percent. Consequently, in October the foreign office recommended that the British government lower the rate of interest on the credits to Iraq to 4 percent.[26] Reluctantly the export credits guarantee department and the treasury agreed, although they feared that the details of the Iraqi credits agreement would eventually become public and provoke demands from other countries for a reduction in their interest rates.[27] Accordingly, in November the British government informed Iraq that it could have the entire amount of credits at an interest rate of 4 percent.[28] The Iraqi government was pleased by this news, and on 1 December 1939 the credit agreement was finally signed.[29]

Although Britain gave Iraq a sizable amount of credits at a low rate of interest it gained little goodwill in return. To begin with, most Iraqis never learned about the agreement because Britain, afraid that other countries would be jealous of the low rate of interest, insisted that the agreement be kept secret.[30] More important, however, because of the outbreak of war in September 1939 and the pressing needs of its own armed forces, the British government refused to deliver most of the weapons and equipment that Iraq wanted to buy with the credits. Consequently, for Iraqi leaders the credits were far less valuable than they had imagined. Indeed, the credits were actually a source of frustration and anger because for the most part Iraq could not utilize them to obtain war material.[31] In an effort to obviate this problem, in October and November 1939 the foreign office recommended that the British government should deliver weapons and equipment to Iraq even at some sacrifice to its own armed forces.[32]

But the war office refused, and its view prevailed.[33] Thus Britain's decision to give a substantial amount of credits on especially favorable terms, which was designed to please Iraq and further to consolidate Britain's dominant position in the country, did not achieve its objective.

CHAPTER 10

The Problem of Oil

The story behind the granting of oil concessions and the subsequent discovery and development of oil in Iraq during the interwar period has been ably recounted in numerous books and articles.[1] It is not my intention to discuss these matters in detail and thereby merely duplicate these works. Rather, I would like to explain some of the ways in which differences over oil-related matters strained Anglo-Iraqi ties during the late 1930s and early 1940s and worsened a relationship which, as we have observed, was already beset with numerous other serious problems.

In March 1925 the Iraqi government granted an oil concession to the Turkish Petroleum Company (T.P.C.). Except for the 5 percent of which was held by a wealthy Armenian investor named C. S. Gulbenkian, the T.P.C. was owned in equal amounts of $23\frac{3}{4}$ percent by four different groups representing four separate nations acting together as a conglomeration. These groups were the Anglo-Iranian Oil Company (British), Royal Dutch-Shell (60 percent Dutch and 40 percent British), Compagnie Française des Pétroles (French), and Near East Development Corporation (an American consortium originally owned by seven different oil companies but by the early 1930s held entirely by Standard Oil of New Jersey and Socony Vacuum). However, at the insistence of the British government, the concession required the T.P.C. to be registered in Britain and always to have a British chairman. These provisions, combined with the substantial degree of British ownership, enabled the British government to exert a considerable amount of control over the company.[2]

The T.P.C.'s concession covered all of Iraq except for the *vi-*

layet of Basra (the old Turkish province covering roughly the southern one-third of Iraq) and a small area near Khaniqin along the border with Iran known as the "transferred territories" (the concession for which was already held by the Anglo-Iranian Oil Company). It was scheduled to last for seventy-five years, and the company was obligated to pay the Iraqi government royalties of four shillings (gold) per ton of oil exported.[3]

In this agreement, as in all of the other oil agreements during the interwar period, Iraq insisted that royalty payments, which were always made in sterling, should be linked to the current price of gold. In this manner it insured itself against a depreciation in the value of sterling. In the late 1930s and early 1940s, when sterling depreciated considerably, Iraq benefited from these provisions.[4]

From the perspective of the Iraq Petroleum Company (as the T.P.C. was known after 1929) the oil concession of 1925 was not entirely satisfactory because the company did not have exclusive exploitation rights throughout the area over which its concession extended. On the contrary, within thirty-two months of the signature of the concession the company was required to select twenty-four rectangular plots, each of an area of eight square miles, in which it wanted to drill. Then the Iraqi government was entitled to offer the remaining territory within the area of the concession for competitive bidding to all interested companies.[5]

This arrangement was not entirely satisfactory to the Iraqi government either because it did not receive any payments until oil was exported. Consequently, in March 1931, after the company had discovered sizable quantities of oil near Kirkuk in northeastern Iraq, the two parties reached a new agreement that gave the company the sole right to exploit all of the land east of the Tigris River (about 32,000 square miles) except for the "transferred territories." In this agreement the company's obligation to pay the Iraqi government royalties of four shillings (gold) per ton of oil exported remained unaltered. However, regardless of the level of oil production, the company was now required to pay the government a minimum of £400,000 (gold) per year beginning immediately, and by the end of 1935 to complete the construction of a pipeline to the Mediterranean Sea with a carrying capacity of at least three million tons of oil per year.[6]

In addition to providing an immediate source of revenue and the likelihood of substantial oil exports within the next few years, the new agreement enabled the Iraqi government to offer a concession for the northwestern part of the country to another oil company. Accordingly, in May 1932 it granted a concession to the British Oil Development Company (B.O.D.) for all the lands of the old Turkish *vilayets* of Mosul and Baghdad west of the Tigris River and north of the 33rd parallel of latitude (about 46,000 square miles). The B.O.D. was a conglomeration of British, Italian, German, Dutch, French, Swiss, and Iraqi interests. The percentage held by each national group altered several times, though by 1935 the Italians had become the majority shareholders with a 52 percent interest. Until production began, the B.O.D. was required to pay a dead rent of £100,000 (gold) in 1933, increasing £25,000 annually up to a total of £200,000. As in the case of the I.P.C., after production began the B.O.D. was obligated to pay royalties of four shillings (gold) per ton.[7]

The B.O.D. began drilling without delay, but its operations were unsuccessful. Soon it had difficulty meeting its dead rent obligations to the Iraqi government. Taking advantage of the B.O.D.'s weak financial situation, in 1937 the I.P.C., acting through a wholly owned subsidiary named the Mosul Holdings Limited, purchased most of the B.O.D.'s shares and thereby gained effective control of the company.[8]

In July 1938 the Iraqi government gave an oil concession for the Basra *vilayet* (about 93,000 square miles in the southern part of Iraq) to the Basra Petroleum Company, a wholly owned subsidiary of the I.P.C. The concession was similar to that given to the B.O.D. for the northwestern part of Iraq in that the company was obligated to pay a dead rent of £200,000 (gold) annually until oil exports began and then to pay a royalty of four shillings (gold) per ton of oil exported.[9]

In this manner the I.P.C. and its two subsidiaries acquired the exclusive right to exploit oil throughout the entire territory of Iraq. For Iraq this situation was undesirable because now it could not easily play off various oil companies in an effort to maximize production levels and royalty payments. Also, the Anglo-Iranian Oil Company, Shell, and Standard Oil of New Jersey all had extensive oil interests elsewhere and thus might be inclined to hold down production levels in Iraq in order to develop their other properties first or to avoid flooding the market. Moreover, Britain's influence over the I.P.C. added to the influence it already had in Iraq as a result of the treaty of 1930. However, Iraq did not have a great choice in this matter because the I.P.C. was probably the only oil company with the desire to work in Iraq and with the technical capability and financial resources necessary to do so.[10]

In accordance with the terms of its concession, between 1932 and 1934 the I.P.C. constructed a pipeline system to the Mediterranean Sea. The system consisted of two parallel lines, each twelve inches in diameter, from Kirkuk in northeastern Iraq to Haditha on the Euphrates River in northwestern Iraq. At that point one line extended through Transjordan to Haifa in Palestine (620 miles in all) and the other through Syria to Tripoli in Lebanon (532 miles in all). Each of these lines was capable of carrying approximately 2,000,000 tons of oil per year.[11]

Iraqi oil production quickly reached the capacity of the pipeline system to the Mediterranean. In 1936, for example, Iraq exported just under 4,000,000 tons of oil, while in 1937 exports were slightly over 4,000,000 tons. But the Iraqi government was not satisfied with this level of production. In order to obtain more money—especially for railway construction and arms purchases—it wanted to increase production as rapidly and as steeply as possible.[12]

Like the Iraqi government, in the second half of the 1930s the Compagnie Française des Pétroles, which was 35 percent owned by the French government and constituted the French interest in the I.P.C., wanted to increase oil production in Iraq. Since the I.P.C. was the only substantial French interest in world oil production, French oil companies elsewhere would not have to reduce production in order to accommodate an increase in production in Iraq. On the contrary, the large French oil refining industry would benefit from an increase in production in Iraq because it would then have a major additional source of crude oil located relatively near France. Moreover, if another pipeline were built from Kirkuk to Tripoli, or the capacity of the existing pipeline enlarged, Syria, which was controlled by France under the terms of a League of Nations' mandate, would benefit from the construction activity and from the greater number of tankers that would then call at Tripoli.[13]

In spite of the wishes of the Iraqi government and the Compagnie Française des Pétroles, for various reasons in the second half of the 1930s the I.P.C. did not make any effort to raise production in Iraq. To begin with, the other companies in the organization feared that the Compagnie Française des Pétroles would use its share of the additional oil either to displace the oil they currently refined and marketed in France or to compete with them for sales in other European countries. They were also reluctant to spend large sums of money to build more refineries to handle additional quantities of crude oil from Iraq, especially since they were uncertain about their ability to market the additional quantities of oil products. Nor were they enthusiastic about allocating substantial funds to construct more pipelines through politically unsettled territories like Syria and Palestine where sovereignty was in dispute and rebellion and civil strife were ever-present dangers. Furthermore, if oil production in Iraq were increased, the Anglo-Iranian Oil Company would have to make room for this new supply by reducing production in Iran where it alone held the concession. Aside from its effects on the Anglo-Iranian Oil Company's profits, a reduction in production would anger the Iranian government and possibly jeopardize the company's concession. Like the Anglo-Iranian Oil Company, Shell and Standard Oil of New Jersey had access to substantial amounts of crude oil elsewhere and did not want more from Iraq at this time. Rather, these two companies, alarmed by the nationalization of their properties in Mexico in 1938 and fearing that other Latin American countries might soon adopt similar policies, preferred to produce as rapidly as possible from their concessions in Venezuela, Columbia, and Peru while leaving Iraq, which they viewed as a relatively safe reserve, for the future.[14]

Although oil production remained at 4,000,000 tons per year, by the end of the 1930s the British, Dutch, and American groups in the I.P.C. were not entirely satisfied with the situation in Iraq. They were particularly concerned because the B.O.D.'s concession for the northwestern part of the country obligated it to maintain nine drilling rigs in service. This operation cost the company £350,000 per year and only yielded small amounts of interior quality oil which it could not market profitably. They were concerned too because the B.O.D.'s concession stipulated that if oil of marketable quality were discovered, by November 1939 (seven and a half years after the signature of the concession) the company had to begin exporting oil at a minimum rate of 1,000,000 tons per year. Although the company believed that under the circumstances it was legally entitled to refuse to begin exports, it feared that the Iraqi government would capitalize on this default by transferring the concession to a German group that had recently expressed interest in the area.[15]

In the late 1930s the Iraqi government was also dissatisfied with the situation because the I.P.C. was not making any effort to increase production even though it had discovered large quantities of high quality oil in northeastern Iraq. Accordingly, in May 1939 the two parties reached an agreement that relieved the B.O.D. from its obligation to maintain nine drilling rigs in operation. Instead, the company was now obligated to drill 12,000 feet per year, which was roughly the capacity of three rigs. As a result of this change, the company estimated that it would save £175,000 per year. The new agreement also extended for seven additional years the B.O.D.'s obligation to begin oil exports by the end of 1939. In return for these concessions, the I.P.C. gave Iraq a £3,000,000 interest-free loan that included the stipulation that the money would only have to be repaid from royalties in excess of £800,000 (gold) per year, which was about the current level of payments. Thus additional royalties, and the repayments on the loan which would follow, could only come from increased production.[16]

As a result of this arrangement, the I.P.C. was under considerable pressure to increase production. Accordingly, in July 1939 the company decided to construct a pipeline with an approximate capacity of 3,000,000 tons per year from Kirkuk to Tripoli that would run parallel to the existing pipeline between those two places. It also planned to increase the capacity of the existing pipeline from Kirkuk to Haifa by about 1,000,000 tons per year. The I.P.C. estimated that this project would cost roughly £8,000,000 and require about two years to complete.[17] If the scheme had been implemented according to plan, Iraqi oil production would have increased from approximately 4,000,000 tons per year to about 8,000,000 tons per year, and Iraqi royalties from oil exports [excluding dead rent payments from the B.O.D. and the B.P.C totalling £400,000 (gold) per year] would have increased from £800,000 (gold) per year to £1,600,000 (gold) per year.[18]

However, in September 1939, two months after the I.P.C. adopted this scheme, the war in Europe broke out. The company was still willing to proceed with construction, but in February 1940 it estimated that the project would now cost £10,000,000 and require three years to complete. Moreover, because most of British and French industry was now occupied with war work, all the materials for the pipeline would have to be purchased in the United States at a cost of about £6,000,000 in dollar exchange.[19]

Instead of the original plan, which would have involved the construction of an entirely new pipeline, in February 1940 the

I.P.C. offered two alternatives. First, it said that in eighteen months to two years it could increase the capacity of the existing pipeline to Tripoli by 1,500,000 to 2,000,000 tons of oil per year at a cost of £5,000,000, £2,750,000 of which would have to be in dollars for materials purchased in the United States. Second, it said that, in the same time period, and for a further outlay of only £800,000 (£400,000 of which would have to be in dollars), as a temporary emergency measure it could increase the capacity of the existing pipeline to Tripoli by as much as 2,500,000 to 3,000,000 tons per year. If either of these alternatives was adopted, the company said that it could arrange construction in such a manner as to secure a substantial part of the increased production—possibly as much as 1,000,000 tons—within one year.[20]

The French government strongly supported the I.P.C.'s proposal to raise the output of the existing pipeline to Tripoli by as much as 3,000,000 tons per year. (It should be recalled that France did not sign an armistice with Germany, and thereby leave the allied coalition, until 22 June 1940.) It pointed out that for Britain and France Iraq was a much nearer source of crude oil than the Persian Gulf or the Gulf of Mexico, the two other main sources of supply. For example, the distance to the French Mediterranean coast from Haifa was approximately 1,700 miles, while the distance from the Persian Gulf was about 4,800 miles and from the Gulf of Mexico around 5,400 miles. Therefore, the use of greater quantities of oil from Iraq would mean a considerable reduction in the number of tankers necessary to transport the same amount of oil. Since tankers were in short supply, this consideration was important. For Britain and France there would also be a savings in foreign currency because they would not have to charter as many tankers from neutral countries. In addition, for the tankers transit through the Mediterranean would be much safer than through the Atlantic because there would be less risk of attack from German submarines.[21] (It should be recalled that Italy did not enter the war on the side of Germany until 10 June 1940.)

The French also argued that for Britain and France the dollars required to purchase materials in the United States to expand the output of the pipeline to Tripoli would soon be recouped because the allies could then import more oil from Iraq, which accepted payment in sterling, rather than from countries like the United States or Venezuela which only accepted payment in dollars. Indeed, according to the French, for every extra

1,000,000 tons of oil imported from Iraq by the British and French groups in the I.P.C. the allies would save $12,000,000,[22] which was roughly the dollar cost of expanding the pipeline to Tripoli to the maximum extent feasible. Nor would the allies have to pay all the costs of expanding the pipeline because the American group in the I.P.C. would pay nearly one-quarter. Finally, the French pointed out that there would be an additional financial benefit from increasing oil production in Iraq because the I.P.C. would then be able to recover the £3,000,000 loan it had made to Iraq in May 1939.[23]

Of course, for France increasing the capacity of the pipeline to Tripoli was not only a matter of promoting the allied war effort. As we have observed, for France, with its nearly one-quarter financial interest in the I.P.C., its lack of substantial oil interests elsewhere, its large domestic oil refining industry, and its control over Syria, the project would also have been an attractive long-term commercial proposition.

For various reasons, during the first half of 1940 the British government was much less enthusiastic about increasing the capacity of the pipeline to Tripoli. To begin with, it pointed out that for the allied powers there was not a shortage either of crude oil or refined oil products. On the contrary, since the war began Iran and Venezuela, two major oil-producing nations, had been forced to reduce production because of a worldwide surplus of oil. Consequently, if the I.P.C. increased production in Iraq, Iran and Venezuela would probably have to reduce their production even further. British leaders feared that this development would damage British relations with both countries and possibly jeopardize the position of the British oil companies in those countries. For Britain Venezuela was an especially important source because it produced large quantities of aviation fuel for the R.A.F., but the production of this fuel was dependent upon maintaining a high level of output of crude oil and refined oil products.[24]

Since the outbreak of the war in September 1939 Britain had made a strong effort to prevent Germany from importing petroleum or petroleum products. Indeed, to a considerable extent Britain's hopes for victory depended upon denying Germany these vital commodities. During the first part of the war Britain focused much of its attention on Romania, a neutral power, which exported sizable quantities of refined oil products. To prevent Germany from obtaining these products, Britain and France purchased most of them for their own economies. For example, in January 1940 Britain and France bought 255,000 tons and 106,000 tons, respectively, of refined oil products from Romania. As a result of this action, and also because of transportation problems, during this month Germany was only able to purchase 10,000 tons. However, British officials feared that if France could buy much more crude oil from Iraq it would be unwilling to continue to purchase such large quantities of refined oil products from Romania. In that event, British officials were concerned that they would have to buy France's share of Romania's oil products. For Britain this would be expensive because, as a result of the avid competition among the great powers for purchases, in the first six months of the war Romania's oil products tripled in price. But for Britain the alternative, which would be to watch the oil go to Germany, would be even more unpalatable.[25]

All the increase in Iraqi oil production was scheduled to go to France for refining. But British officials feared that the French oil refineries might be damaged by enemy bombing raids, and that Italy might enter the war and close the central Mediterranean to allied shipping. If either of these events occurred there would not be any way to market the additional quantities of oil from Iraq, and all the investment in expanding the pipeline to Tripoli would be wasted.[26]

Even if these events did not occur, British officials were unhappy about providing the large amount of precious dollars that would be necessary to pay for the purchase of materials in the United States. They pointed out that if certain ships carrying materials were torpedoed, the completion of the project, and the resultant recouping of the dollars expended, would be seriously delayed.[27]

In addition, British officials were concerned about the fact that all the extra production was scheduled to go through the pipeline to Tripoli rather than through the pipeline to Haifa. They believed that this development would lead to an increase in the prosperity of French-controlled Syria at the expense of British-controlled Palestine; and that an expansion of the pipeline to Tripoli now would preclude a later expansion of the pipeline to Haifa because of the difficulty of marketing still more oil from Iraq.[28]

Nor did British officials accept the proposition that an expansion of the pipeline to Tripoli would substantially reduce the number of tankers the allied powers would require. They believed that the French Mediterranean refineries could not handle any more crude oil, and that all the additional production from Iraq would have to go to the French Atlantic and Channel refineries which were farther away from Tripoli. They also pointed out that importing crude oil was an inefficient use of tankers because 10 percent of the load was lost in the process of refining. Indeed, according to their calculations, by importing more crude oil from Tripoli rather than additional quantities of refined oil products from the Gulf of Mexico France would save only 3¾ tankers for each 1,000,000 tons of oil.[29]

Rather than spend large quantities of dollars on a pipeline that under certain entirely plausible circumstances would not be of any use to the allied war effort, British officials suggested purchasing more tankers from the United States. This would cost fewer dollars, and the tankers could be used to import more oil from Iran which, like Iraq, accepted payment in sterling. Moreover, unlike the pipeline, the tankers would be useful even if Italy entered the war and cut the central Mediterranean. In addition, this expedient would leave open the possibility of expanding the pipeline after the war when British companies, now entirely occupied with war work, would be able to provide many of the necessary materials.[30]

For all these reasons, during the first half of 1940 the British government was unwilling to agree to expand the capacity of the pipeline to Tripoli. On 10 June the entire question became moot because Italy entered the war and closed the central Mediterranean to allied shipping (except for a few heavily protected convoys carrying urgently required munitions and supplies from Britain to Malta and Egypt). The following day the I.P.C., acting on instructions from the British government, closed the pipeline to Tripoli because there was no longer any convenient way to market this large quantity of crude oil. The company also reduced the flow of crude oil through the pipeline to Haifa from 2,000,000 tons per year to 800,000 tons per year because this lower figure was the capacity of the refinery at Haifa which provided fuel for the British fleet in the Mediterranean.[31] As a result of these steps, Iraq's total annual income from oil (including royalties and dead rent payments) decreased from £1,200,000 (gold) to £800,000 (gold). Measured in sterling, Iraq's total annual income from oil decreased from nearly £2,200,000 to about £1,400,000.[32] Since Iraqi leaders had been expecting an increase in production and revenue rather than a decrease, and since recently they had made some important concessions to the I.P.C. to obtain these increases, it is not surprising that they felt aggrieved.[33]

In the second half of 1940 Anglo-Iraqi relations were again strained by an oil-related matter. As we have observed, since 1938 the Basra Petroleum Company (B.P.C.), a wholly owned subsidiary of the Iraq Petroleum Company, had held an oil concession for the southern part of Iraq. According to the terms of the concession, the company was obligated to begin drilling operations by November 1941. In order to meet the deadline, in July 1940 the company asked the British government for permission to start purchasing the necessary equipment and materials. The company calculated that the purchases would cost £436,000 in sterling plus another £264,000 in dollars to be spent in the United States.[34] But in October 1940 the British government, which in wartime exercised especially close control over the activities of the I.P.C. and its subsidiaries, rejected the company's request to raise additional capital in Britain and to exchange its sterling assets for dollars. The British government took this action because it already had ample supplies of crude oil from the Middle East and, therefore, the discovery of additional oil in Iraq would not be of any value to Britain at the present time. Indeed, under certain not entirely implausible circumstances it might be of considerable value to Germany. Moreover, the drilling operations would require substantial quantities of scarce and extremely valuable dollars, steel, and other materials. Like its earlier decisions regarding the pipelines to Tripoli and Haifa, the British government did not take this action to injure Iraq. Nonetheless, Iraqi leaders were angry because from their perspective Britain was compelling the B.P.C. to violate a contractual obligation the fulfillment of which would probably have been of great benefit to Iraq.[35]

Although Iraq's vital interests were involved, in 1940 the British government did not consult Iraq about expanding the capacity of the pipeline to Tripoli, shutting down this pipeline, reducing the through-put of the pipeline to Haifa, or preventing the B.P.C. from drilling. On all of these matters it acted purely out of concern for British commerical interests and for the promotion of the allied war effort. In each instance it treated the Iraqis as outsiders who in due course would be informed of the decisions taken in London and Paris, rather than as trusted allies with a major stake in the proceedings. Of course, these events occurred during a great war when British leaders had to make quick decisions in response to a rapidly changing military situation. Moreover, it was only natural that British leaders would give priority to the interests of their own country rather than to those of Iraq, especially since Iraq was a neutral power that had refused to declare war against Germany. Nor was the situation of the two countries comparable because if the capacity of the pipeline to Tripoli had been expanded and drilling operations had been conducted, Iraq, unlike Britain, would have benefited from the increased production and the construction activity without having to provide any capital, bear any risk, or suffer any inconvenience. Nonetheless, Britain's offhand treatment, its disregard for Iraq's interests, and its unabashed use of the I.P.C. and the B.P.C as instruments of its foreign policy, angered Iraqi leaders and reinforced their determination to reduce British influence in Iraq and gain firmer control of their most precious natural resource.[36] As we shall observe in the following chapters, to facilitate this endeavor by the second half of 1940 many of them were even willing to align themselves with Nazi Germany, Britain's deadliest enemy.

CHAPTER 11

The Deterioration of Anglo-Iraqi Relations:

Phase One
September 1939–October 1940

As a result of Germany's attack on Poland, on 3 September 1939 Britain declared war on Germany. The British government now expected Iraq to declare war on Germany because the two nations were bound by the treaty of alliance of 1930. British officials believed that an Iraqi declaration of war would be a propaganda victory for the allied powers and would encourage other nations to enter the struggle against Germany. They also feared that if Iraq did not declare war Germany would score a propaganda triumph by claiming that an important British ally was reneging on its commitment. In addition, British officials were concerned that without a declaration of war Iraq would not stop trade with Germany or intern German nationals who might otherwise sabotage British installations or communications.[1]

While the British government wanted Iraq to declare war, it had no desire to use Iraqi troops in the fighting against Germany or to send them to Egypt to oppose the Italian threat to the Suez Canal. On the contrary, British officials believed that the Iraqi army could be best employed by maintaining internal order at home and thereby securing Britain's land route from India through Iraq, Transjordan, and Palestine to Egypt.[2] Although at this stage Britain did not need to use the land route, it feared that Italy might enter the war at any time and, from bases in Eritrea and Libya, jeopardize the movement of British ships through the Red Sea and Suez Canal.[3] Aside from this consideration, the British government did not want to send Iraqi troops to the front because it was incapable of equipping and supplying them properly.[4]

When the Second World War broke out, Iraq was not specifically obligated to declare war on Germany or even to break diplomatic relations with Germany. According to the terms of article 4 of the treaty of 1930, in the event of war Iraq was obligated merely to "come to his [Britannic Majesty's] aid in the capacity of an ally." The treaty further stated that this aid would consist of "furnishing to His Britannic Majesty on Iraq territory all facilities and assistance in his power, including the use of railways, rivers, ports, aerodromes and means of communication."

In early September 1939 the Iraqi government decided not to declare war on Germany. At this time most Iraqi leaders did not want to become more deeply involved than necessary in a dispute among the European powers. Taha al-Hashimi, the defense minister, and most leading army officers were especially opposed to a declaration of war. Their views were particularly important because, by intervening or threatening to intervene in the political process, the military exercised great influence on the politicians and frequently made or unmade cabinets. These men feared that war would mean dangerous battles on distant fronts for causes that did not directly concern Iraq. They also thought it incongruous, even obscene, to wage war to liberate Poland while Palestine and Syria were currently occupied by the very nations on whose side Iraq was expected to fight. Instead of fighting Germany, they preferred to use the conflict to extract concessions from Britain and France that would further the cause of Arab independence in Palestine and Syria. Some military leaders even believed that Iraq should capitalize on the war by sending its army into Palestine and Syria to liberate those countries from British and French rule.[5] Aside from pressure from the military, the Iraqi government did not declare war on Germany because it was concerned that its opponents in parliament and elsewhere in the country would strongly oppose any step that went beyond Iraq's treaty obligations.[6] In addition, the Iraqi government was reluctant to declare war when Egypt, which was also bound to Britain in a treaty of alliance, did not do so.[7]

While the Iraqi government did not declare war on Germany, it demonstrated its friendship for Britain in various ways. For example, it facilitated British communications across Iraq, broke diplomatic relations with Germany, stopped trading with Germany, arrested all male German citizens of military age and handed them over to the British military authorities at Habbaniya, expelled other German citizens including some who were employed as teachers, prohibited German radio broadcasts in public places, introduced press censorship and suppressed news from German sources, implemented a scheme to protect the port of Basra by preventing the blocking of the Shatt al-Arab, and occupied major bridges to prevent sabotage.[8]

The Iraqi government took these measures because in the autumn of 1939 it was headed by Nuri al-Said, perhaps the most pro-British of the leading politicians in Iraq. Indeed, Nuri personally wanted to go further and declare war on Germany but was dissuaded by the opposition of his colleagues.[9] The Iraqi government took these measures also because at this time the allied position in the Middle East was quite strong: Germany was confined to central Europe, Italy was still neutral, British and French troops were ensconced in Egypt, Palestine, Transjordan, and Syria, not to mention the British airbases in Iraq itself. Moreover, Iraq was in a weak position economically because all its oil exports, which brought in a substantial proportion of its revenues, went by pipeline to the British- and French-controlled ports of Haifa and Tripoli. Iraq was additionally vulnerable to allied pressure because British warships in the Persian Gulf could easily halt imports to Iraq's only port of Basra.

On 6 September 1939 the Iraqi government informed Britain that it would consider going beyond the measures it had already taken and actually declare war against Germany if it received guarantees that: a declaration of war would not entail any responsibilities, for example, the dispatch of troops to the front, in addition to those which Iraq had assumed in the treaty of 1930; Britain would protect Iraq from enemy retaliation; Britain would provide financial assistance to enable Iraq to strengthen its army for the purpose of resisting enemy attack; Iraq would have a voice in the peace settlement; and Britain and France would take steps toward Arab independence in Palestine and Syria.[10] In this manner the Iraqi government attempted to extract financial and diplomatic compensation from Britain in exchange for entering the war.

Whether the Iraqi government would have actually declared war against Germany if Britain had given the requested guarantees is uncertain because Britain did not give the guarantees, or at least not all of them. Although disappointed and somewhat irritated about Iraq's reluctance to enter the war, by the end of September British officials were reasonably content with the measures Iraq had taken and decided not to press further for a declaration of war. Thus they felt little need to meet Iraq's demands. In addition, they disliked the idea of bargaining for the fulfillment of what they believed was already implicit in the treaty. Nonetheless, on 25 September the British government informed Iraq that it was willing to guarantee that: a declaration of war would not involve Iraq in any additional responsibilities; Britain would protect Iraq from enemy attack; and Iraq would have a voice in the peace settlement. However, the British government was unwilling to give Iraq any financial assistance beyond the credits already promised and was unwilling to give Iraq any commitment regarding Palestine that went beyond the policy established by the white paper of May 1939. Regarding Syria, the British government did not promise anything because the territory was under French control and Britain exercised no authority there. Nor was Britain willing to jeopardize its relations with France, its most important ally in the struggle against Germany, by pressing for changes in French policy in Syria.[11]

Thus at the end of September 1939, just after the outbreak of war in Europe, Anglo-Iraqi relations were reasonably amicable. While Iraq did not declare war on Germany, under Nuri's leadership it adopted a pro-British posture, fulfilled all its obligations under the treaty of 1930, and took various other measures to assist Britain. The British government was content with this situation and, while also wanting a declaration of war, was not so eager or desperate that it was willing to pay a financial or diplomatic price for it. Soon, however, a series of events occurred that significantly weakened British influence and prestige in Iraq and set the stage for the development of a severe crisis in Anglo-Iraqi relations.

In October 1939 Haj Amin al-Husayni, the former mufti of Jerusalem and a leading figure in the Arab rebellion against British rule in Palestine which began in 1936, arrived in Baghdad. As a renowned Arab nationalist Husayni was welcomed in Iraq and voted a large sum of money by the Iraqi parliament for his personal expenses. Husayni was an advocate of close Arab ties with Germany in order to free Palestine and Syria from colonial rule and, not incidentally, to install himself in a position of power. With his abundant financial resources, great prestige, and forceful personality, Husayni did much to increase anti-British and pro-German sentiment within the influential segments of Iraqi society. In this manner Husayni helped to create a political movement in Iraq which, when the propitious moment arrived, was willing and even eager to support a decisive and, if necessary, violent break in Iraq's relations with Britain.[12]

On 31 March 1940 Nuri, a strong advocate of a pro-British foreign policy, resigned as prime minister. Since he had become prime minister in December 1938 he had harassed and persecuted his political opponents, and his government now had little support among the leading politicians in the country. Moreover, his cabinet had been significantly weakened in January 1940 by the assassination of his finance minister and political ally, Rustum Haydar. Nuri, who remained in the new cabinet as foreign minister, apparently believed that in spite of his resignation as prime minister he could still retain significant power and also broaden political support in the country for his pro-British foreign policy.[13] However, as we shall soon observe, contrary to his expectations Nuri was unable to control the foreign policy of the new government.

In accordance with the terms of a prearranged deal, Nuri was replaced as prime minister by Rashid Ali al-Gaylani. Rashid Ali, forty-eight, was a Sunni Arab who descended from a family of distinguished religious scholars in Iraq. He had been a lawyer and a judge and had held several different cabinet positions. Immediately before assuming the prime ministership he was chief of the royal diwan or court chamberlain. Rashid Ali did not share Nuri's deep-rooted conviction that Iraq's interests were best served by maintaining intimate ties with Britain. In 1930 he had opposed the conclusion of the Anglo-Iraqi treaty because it gave Britain a privileged position in Iraq. In September 1939 he had opposed an Iraqi declaration of war against Germany. When Rashid Ali came to power in late March 1940 he may not have been resolved to break with Britain but he was certainly open to any suggestion or opportunity to minimize British influence in Iraq and to advance the cause of Arab independence in Palestine.[14] Thus Nuri's resignation and Rashid Ali's ascendancy to power weakened British influence in Iraq and was an essential ingredient for a serious deterioration in Anglo-Iraqi relations.

The third and probably most important factor that weakened British influence in Iraq and set the stage for the development of a major crisis in Anglo-Iraqi relations was Britain's terrible military and diplomatic defeats in the spring of 1940. On 14 May Holland surrendered to Germany, followed by Belgium on 28 May. On 8 June Germany completed its conquest of Norway. On

10 June Italy entered the war on the side of Germany, thereby opening entirely new fronts for Britain in the Mediterranean, Egypt, and East Africa, and jeopardizing Britain's hitherto secure position in the Middle East. Turkey thereupon announced that it would remain firmly neutral in spite of the treaty of October 1939 which obliged it to enter the war on the side of the allies if Italy declared war on Britain or France. Finally, on 17 June France, Britain's most important ally, sued for peace with Germany. As a result of these blows, by the middle of June 1940 much, perhaps most, of the ruling class in Iraq, and not only in Iraq, thought that Britain would lose the war. Many of these men believed that Iraq should now dissociate itself from Britain and associate itself with Germany to the maximum extent feasible. Far better, they calculated, to ingratiate oneself with the victor, the power that would soon control the destiny of the Middle East, than to remain loyal to a restrictive alliance with a defeated nation which, aside from continuing to occupy Palestine, was unable to defend even its immediate neighbors and major allies, let alone Iraq, a distant country in a secondary theatre of the war.[15]

By the summer of 1940 the combined effect of Husayni's agitation, Rashid Ali's ascendancy to power, and Britain's military defeats, coupled with all the other disagreements and irritants in Anglo-Iraqi relations we have already discussed, created a situation or atmosphere conducive to a severe crisis between Britain and Iraq. The actual crisis that soon developed had several immediate causes. To begin with, after Italy entered the war on 10 June the British government wanted Iraq to break diplomatic relations and intern Italian nationals. Ideally, it preferred a declaration of war, but it would have been content with these steps which were similar to those Iraq took in relation to Germany in September 1939. The British government felt entitled to these measures, not only because of the existence of the treaty of 1930, but also because it believed that Britain was now the only country preventing an Italian conquest and subjugation of the entire Middle East, including Iraq. With its fortunes at a particularly low ebb after its recent military defeats, the British government thought that a conspicuous demonstration of Iraqi solidarity and continued adherence to the alliance would be a valuable boost to British prestige in the Middle East. British officials asked Iraq to break relations and intern Italian nationals also because they wanted to prevent the leakage of important military information through the Italian legation, for example, on British troop movements across Iraq. In addition, they wanted to prevent the Italian community from spreading axis propaganda, intriguing with Iraqi politicians, and possibly sabotaging vulnerable points on the British line of communications across Iraq.[16]

In spite of repeated British requests, the Iraqi government refused to break diplomatic relations with Italy. Iraqi leaders believed that this step was legally unnecessary because it was not explicitly stipulated in the treaty and physically dangerous because it might provoke Italian retaliation. But most important, the Iraqi government refused to break diplomatic relations with Italy because it wanted to be able to negotiate with the axis powers in order to gain their support for the elimination of British influence in Iraq and the liberation of Palestine and Syria from colonial rule. However, to allay British suspicions Rashid Ali, the prime minister, told the British ambassador that the Italian legation was harmless and could not damage British interests in the country. He also argued that a diplomatic break would turn public opinion in Iraq against Britain for demanding it and against the Iraqi government for acquiescing to it. Finally, he assured the ambassador that he remained completely faithful to the Anglo-Iraqi treaty of 1930.[17]

Iraq's persistent refusal to break diplomatic relations with Italy infuriated the British government and was an important cause of the crisis that developed in Anglo-Iraqi relations in the summer of 1940. Indeed, the issue continued to embitter the relationship between the two powers until the outbreak of hostilities between them in May 1941.[18] It should be noted, parenthetically, that Nuri, who was foreign minister in Rashid Ali's government, advocated breaking diplomatic relations with Italy but was overruled by Rashid Ali and a majority of the cabinet.[19] Thus within three months Nuri's belief that he could continue to control Iraq's foreign policy after he resigned as prime minister was disproved.

A second major cause of the crisis in Anglo-Iraqi relations was Rashid Ali's negotiations with Germany and Italy for the purpose of promoting Iraqi and other Arab collaboration with the axis powers in the war. These discussions began, at Iraqi initiative, in July 1940 and continued intermittently until the spring of 1941. They were conducted by Rashid Ali and several trusted comrades, including the former mufti of Jerusalem, without the consent and to some degree without the knowledge of Nuri, the foreign minister. Some of the talks were held in Baghdad with the Italian minister, some in Istanbul with the German ambassador to Turkey, and others in Berlin and Rome with German and Italian foreign ministry officials. In these negotiations Rashid Ali wanted Germany and Italy to recognize and support the complete independence of all the Arab countries of the Middle East and agree not to impede their unification. He also wanted the axis powers to supply Iraq with arms and money. In exchange, Rashid Ali offered a full-scale military and political alliance combined with valuable economic privileges in Iraq. Specifically, Rashid Ali promised to reopen diplomatic relations with Germany; oust Nuri from the foreign ministry and replace him with an individual sympathetic to the axis powers; give Germany and Italy a preferential position in regard to the exploitation of Iraq's mineral resources, including oil; promote and support an Arab rebellion in Palestine to tie down British troops; prevent the movement of British troops across Iraqi territory; defend Iraq by all available means if Britain responded to these measures by force; and admit German military personnel into Iraq immediately in order to help prepare the defense of the country against an expected British attack.[20]

Rashid Ali's overtures to the axis powers did not result in German recognition of Arab independence and unity or a flow of weapons to Iraq or a formal agreement to collaborate in the war. It was difficult for Hitler to promise to support Arab independence and unity for fear of angering Mussolini, his leading ally, who was eager to bring the Arab lands of the Middle East under Italian influence. Nor did Hitler want to alienate important neutral countries like Vichy France, which controlled Syria, and Turkey, which did not want to see a strong united Arab state on its southern border. Hitler also realized that problems of distance, combined with those resulting from British opposition and from French, Turkish, and Russian neutrality, would make it difficult for Germany to give weapons to Iraq and even more difficult for Germany to support a major military operation against Britain in Iraq. In addition, by the autumn of 1940 Hitler was already planning to attack Russia and did not want to become involved in a military campaign in the Middle East that would divert German strength from the main theatre. Because of these considerations, in October 1940 Germany and Italy only gave Rashid Ali a vaguely worded declaration of sympathy with Arab nationalist ambitions.[21]

Although the Iraqi government was unable to consummate a formal alliance with the axis powers, these negotiations indicate that by the summer of 1940 Rashid Ali, supported by other influential political and military leaders in Iraq, was willing to commit himself completely to Hitler's cause and to take enormous risks in the hope of ousting Britain from its dominant position in Iraq and freeing Palestine and Syria from colonial rule. By various means, which included the use of broken enemy codes, the British government learned about these discussions and, while perhaps unaware of all the details, was reasonably able to surmise the general content. Not surprisingly, British officials were furious at what they considered to be Rashid Ali's duplicity and untrustworthiness. Indeed, by the autumn of 1940 they viewed him as hopelessly committed to the axis powers.[22] Thus Rashid Ali's negotiations with Germany and Italy were an important cause of the crisis in Anglo-Iraqi relations.

Other Iraqi actions also angered the British government and thereby deepened the split between the two countries. For example, during the summer and autumn of 1940 most Iraqi newspapers, acting under government inspiration or instruction, advocated a neutral posture in the war. By itself this attitude irritated British officials because it implicitly repudiated the Anglo-Iraqi alliance. However, in their coverage of the war most Iraqi newspapers actually favored Germany and Italy by giving more prominence to axis claims than to the British version of events, and by falsely attributing articles dealing with British setbacks to American and Turkish news agencies when the information really came from axis radio broadcasts. The newspapers also frequently carried articles stressing the wickedness of British imperialism and the broken promises made by Britain to the Arabs during the First Word War. Further angering Britain, the Iraqi government never repudiated anti-British newspaper articles, nor did it issue pro-British statements or declarations. Indeed, the government censor actually banned newspaper articles advocating Iraqi adherence to the allied cause.[23]

Despite all the problems that bedevilled Anglo-Iraqi relations, Rashid Ali frequently said that he would cooperate more wholeheartedly with Britain if the British government were more forthcoming about Arab independence in Palestine.[24] Possibly Rashid Ali was sincere in this matter, although more likely the fulfillment of this demand would have merely led to new demands designed to undermine British paramountcy in the Middle East. In any event, the question was never put to the test because, as we observed in Chapter 6, in August 1940 the British government informed Iraq that it would not begin to implement the constitutional provisions of the white paper of May 1939 or make any further concessions to the Arabs in Palestine.[25]

By the summer of 1940 British officials were very alarmed about the decline in British influence in Iraq and the pro-axis drift of the Iraqi government. They believed that the continued maintenance of British paramountcy in the Middle East was intimately linked with and dependent upon the continued maintenance of British paramountcy in Iraq.[26] Consequently, in an effort to reverse the unfavorable trend of developments in Iraq, in early July the British government decided to send a division of Indian troops to Basra.[27] The British government hoped that it would be able to obtain an invitation for the troops from the Iraqi government but was determined to press ahead with the scheme regardless.[28] British officials believed these troops would serve several useful purposes: put pressure on the Iraqi government to break diplomatic relations with Italy and generally adopt a more pro-British posture in accordance with the spirit of the treaty of 1930;[29] deter the Iraqi government from interfering with the movement of British troops and equipment along the overland route from Basra to Haifa which, although not yet used by British forces, had recently become more important for the purpose of reinforcing Egypt because of Italy's entry into the war and the consequent threat to British communications through the Red Sea;[30] protect the two British airbases in Iraq if the Iraqi government turned completely hostile;[31] generally encourage Britain's friends in Iraq, some of whom had privately asked the British government to send troops, to assert themselves by sustaining their belief in the likelihood of an ultimate British victory in the war;[32] clearly demonstrate to friends and foes alike, both within and outside Iraq, that in spite of military reverses in Europe Britain was determined and able to honor its obligations under the treaty of 1930 to defend Iraq against aggression;[33] and deter an attack by Russia, which at this time was linked to Germany by the Nazi-Soviet pact of August 1939, on the Iranian oilfields and the large oil refinery at Abadan, which were vital for the operations of the British fleet, and protect these installations in the event of such an attack or in the case of any type of interference by the Iranian government or sabotage by members of the large German community in Iran.[34]

Although on 1 July 1940 the British government decided to send a division of Indian troops to Iraq, the troops were never sent. Beginning 6 July the viceroy of India, the commander-in-chief in India, and the commander-in-chief in the Middle East in Egypt all objected to the decision. Haunted by the memory of the enormous troop commitment and terrible casualties of the Mesopotamian campaign during the First World War, these officials feared that in the event of Iraqi resistance Britain would be inexorably sucked into a major new military commitment at a time when its troop strength in the Middle East and East Africa was already markedly inferior to that of Italy. They were specially alarmed about the possibility that some of the Indian troops would be sent to northern Iraq to guard the oilfields at Kirkuk, thereby creating a long and vulnerable line of communications. They pointed out that there were no troops immediately available to reinforce the Indian division if it encountered difficulty, and that a military defeat or withdrawal under pressure would have deplorable political consequences in India. In addition, they were concerned that Russia might retaliate by invading Iran, and that a single division would be inadequate to defend the Iranian oilfields. In this regard they emphasized that the contemplated force was an infantry division without anti-aircraft weapons, and therefore unable to defend the Iranian oilfields against Russian air attack. Nor, they said, did Britain have sufficient numbers of fighter planes in Iraq or elsewhere in the Middle East to assist in the defense of the Iranian oilfields against Russian air attack. These officials were also worried about the possibility that Russia might gain control of the Iranian airfields at Bushire, Bandar Abbas, and elsewhere in southwestern Iran and thereby command the British line of communications to Basra through the Persian Gulf. On another aspect of the matter, they pointed out that Britain did not need to use the overland route from Basra to Haifa, and might never need to use it, because thus far Italy had been unable to halt the movement of British ships through the Red Sea. Finally, the Indian officials were concerned about the possibility of Japanese aggression in southeast Asia and, consequently, reluctant to dissipate their strength by undertaking an entirely new and, in their minds, unessential commitment. Similarly, General Archibald Wavell, the commander-in-chief in the Middle East, believed that the troops could be more profitably employed elsewhere in the area under his command.[35]

As a result of these objections, in late July 1940 the British government reversed its earlier decision and decided to place the Indian division at the disposal of General Wavell for deployment to Egypt or the Sudan.[36] Whether this decision was militarily sound, given all the threats and dangers that confronted Britain at this time, is difficult to judge and, in any case, unnecessary for the historian to decide. It is important to note, however, that the decision had fateful consequences for Anglo-Iraqi relations. It deprived the British government of an important means of pressure on Iraq and thereby enabled the pro-German politicians and military leaders in the country to strengthen their position and continue their negotiations with the axis powers with relative impunity and little fear of reprisal. When, the following year, Britain decided that it must at all costs retrieve its crumbling position in Iraq, it encountered an Iraqi government devoid of any pro-British members or sympathy, firmly determined to oppose a pro-British interpretation of the treaty of 1930 by all means at its disposal, and perfectly willing to invite German military forces into Iraq to assist it to resist any form of British pressure. Whether a British troop commitment in the summer of 1940 would have achieved without bloodshed what a similar British effort at a more inopportune moment in the war in the spring of 1941 could only accomplish after serious fighting must remain imponderable.

CHAPTER 12

The Deterioration of Anglo-Iraqi Relations:

Phase Two
November 1940–May 1941

By the autumn of 1940 the British government was convinced that Rashid Ali was firmly committed to the axis cause and that, as leader of Iraq, he constituted a potentially serious threat to the security of the British position in the Middle East. Consequently, beginning in November it made a determined effort to oust him from power and replace him with a more pro-British leader.[1] This effort greatly angered Rashid Ali and other leading Iraqi officials, who viewed it as blatant interference in Iraqi internal affairs.[2] It reinforced their determination to eliminate all British influence in Iraq, if necessary with German assistance, and thus contributed further to the deterioration of Anglo-Iraqi relations.

Since independence in 1932 the British government had never interfered in Iraqi politics to the extent of attempting to oust a prime minister.[3] Consequently, it now had no precedent to follow. And, since the British government was still unwilling to send troops to Iraq because its forces were fully committed elsewhere,[4] it had few means at its disposal to achieve this ambitious objective.

British officials considered economic pressure. Iraq's most valuable export was oil. All of Iraq's oil went by pipeline to Haifa and Tripoli on the Mediterranean Sea. As we have observed in Chapter 10, in June 1940, when Italy entered the war and made transit by sea through the central Mediterranean extremely hazardous, the British government instructed the Iraq Petroleum Company to close the Tripoli branch of the pipeline because there was no longer any convenient way to market the oil. It also instructed the I.P.C. to reduce the through-put of the Haifa branch of the pipeline to the capacity of the refinery at Haifa, whose products constituted the principal source of fuel for the British fleet in the eastern Mediterranean.[5] Although the British government was not attempting to harm Iraq, nonetheless these steps deprived Iraq of about £800,000 per year in royalties. However, the I.P.C. and its two prospecting but as yet unproducing subsidiaries in Iraq still paid the Iraqi government royalties and rents amounting on an annual basis to about £1,400,000.[6] Because the I.P.C. was registered as a British company with a British chairman, substantial British ownership, and headquarters in London, the British government was in a position to stop these payments to Iraq. This measure would have inflicted severe damage on the Iraqi economy, but British officials hesitated because they feared that Iraq would retaliate by cancelling the I.P.C.'s concession and halting the flow of oil through the pipeline to Haifa. Although Britain could have dispensed with Iraqi oil by relying more on oil from Iran, this adjustment would have required at least seven additional tankers (and possibly as many as eleven) to bring oil from Iran to Egypt at a time when tankers were in short supply and, in any case, could not have reached the Persian Gulf for three months. Moreover, taking these tankers from other routes would have reduced the supply of oil to the United Kingdom by 300,000 tons per year. In view of these factors, the British government did not stop the payment of oil revenues to Iraq.[7]

Iraq's main agricultural export was dates. In 1940, for example, Iraq earned over £1,000,000 from date exports. British officials considered applying economic pressure by reducing their purchases of these dates. However, the Iraqi date harvest was in August and September, and Andrew Weir, a British company, had already bought most of the crop. Therefore, a reduction of British purchases would not damage the Iraqi economy very much. In addition, the ministry of food refused to reduce its purchases of Iraqi dates because it said that it had no alternative source of supply. (This was not surprising since Iraq produced about 80 percent of the world's dates.) The ministry of food also pointed out that Andrew Weir sold Iraqi dates to the United States and thereby earned valuable dollars for the British economy. Because of these considerations the British government did not reduce its purchases of Iraqi dates or force Andrew Weir to withdraw from this market.[8]

During this period most goods bound to and from Iraq travelled on British ships. For example, in the six months between

June and November 1940 fifty-four of the ninety ships that entered Basra were British. British officials considered applying
economic pressure by reducing the shipping facilities that they
made available for Iraqi imports and exports. However, they rejected this option because British shipping facilities from and to
Iraq had already been restricted to the minimum required for
the needs of Britain's own import and export trade, and because
they feared that Japan would move into the gap and thereby increase its influence in Iraq.[9]

As another means of applying economic pressure, British officials considered restricting the export of various commodities
such as oil seed, hides, gunny bags, and cloth from India to Iraq.
However, they did not adopt this measure because it would have
injured Indian merchants, and because they believed that Iraq
would still have been able to obtain the goods eventually after
transshipping in various Persian Gulf ports.[10]

In spite of these difficulties, the British government did apply
some economic pressure on Iraq. Iraq was a member of the sterling bloc and therefore dependent on Britain to make dollars
available for purchases outside the bloc. Beginning in the autumn of 1940, the British government refused to give Iraq dollars for various purchases it wanted to make in the United States,
such as trucks and military equipment.[11] The Iraqis believed that
they were entitled to exchange their sterling reserves for dollars,
and this measure greatly angered them.[12]

Because the British government was unwilling to send troops
to Iraq and unable to apply severe economic pressure on Iraq
without discomforting itself and jeopardizing the I.P.C.'s concession, it mainly used political means to oust Rashid Ali from office. In this effort it relied heavily on two strongly pro-British officials in Iraq: Prince Abd al-Ilah, the regent who succeeded to
the powers of the throne when King Ghazi died in April 1939,
and Nuri, the foreign minister. Both Abd al-Ilah and Nuri were
willing to cooperate with Britain to oust Rashid Ali. However, although the regent had the power to appoint a prime minister,
he was legally unable to dismiss him.[13] Consequently, in November 1940 the British government advised Nuri to resign from office. Since the ministry of the interior was already vacant, British
officials believed that Nuri's resignation, coupled with the regent's refusal to agree to the appointment of any new ministers,
would weaken the government sufficiently to bring about its collapse.[14]

But Nuri was not eager to leave office. He feared for his personal safety if he were no longer a member of the government. He also believed that by itself his resignation would not compel Rashid Ali to quit because there would still be eight ministers in the cabinet, while the legal minimum number of ministers was six. As an alternative method of ousting Rashid Ali, Nuri tried to organize a vote of no confidence against the government in the chamber of deputies.[15] British officials doubted whether this method would work because all Iraqi governments had succeeded in dominating the chamber, and no government had ever fallen as a result of a vote of no confidence.[16] Nonetheless, Nuri persevered in this endeavor and in late January 1941 gained the support of the majority of the chamber. His task was facilitated by the fact that the deputies had been elected in May 1939, when Nuri was still prime minister, and therefore had originally been selected for their loyalty to him. His task was also facilitated by the decisive British victories in December and January in the fighting against Italy in North Africa. When Rashid Ali realized that he might lose a vote of confidence he asked the regent to dissolve the chamber and call new elections. Doubtless Rashid Ali believed that, like all previous prime ministers, he could easily control the elections and pack the new assembly with his own nominees. But the regent refused to dissolve the chamber. Instead he fled Baghdad for the south in order to escape from the overweening pressure of Rashid Ali's military supporters. Knowing that he would soon lose a vote of confidence in the chamber, abandoned by Nuri and most of the other members of the cabinet, and believing that the regent had the support of troops and tribal confederations in the south, on 31 January Rashid Ali resigned.[17]

While the British government was attempting to oust him from power in late 1940 and early 1941, Rashid Ali was supported by a group of four extremely influential, militantly pan-Arab, and very anti-British army officers known collectively as the golden square. The officers constituting the golden square were Colonels Salah al-Din al-Sabbagh, Kamil Shabib, Fahmi Said, and Mahmud Salman. Together they commanded two of the army's four divisions including the two located nearest Baghdad, plus the army's only mechanized brigade and the air force. By early 1940 these officers and their loyal subordinates dominated the military establishment, and neither the regent nor any of the politicians could defy them without great political and personal risk.[18]

Now that Rashid Ali had resigned, the golden square insisted that the regent appoint Taha al-Hashimi in his place. Taha was a leading general who had served as defense minister since December 1938. In his views and opinions he did not differ greatly from Rashid Ali, and as defense minister he had been closely associated with all of Rashid Ali's policies.[19] Rather than Taha, the regent preferred to appoint an established politician who was not so closely linked to Rashid Ali and the golden square. However, confronted with the prospect of civil war and unable to muster sufficient support in the army to resist the golden square, on 1 February 1941 the regent yielded and appointed Taha prime minister.[20] Nuri was not included in the cabinet, although the new foreign minister, Tawfiq al-Suwaydi, was friendly to Britain.[21]

Because of his ties with Rashid Ali and the golden square, British officials were not happy with the choice of Taha as prime minister.[22] Still, they hoped that he would prove more amenable to persuasion and pressure than Rashid Ali. Consequently, all through February and March 1941 they pressed Taha to break diplomatic relations with Italy and curb the political influence of the militantly anti-British army officers.[23] Meanwhile they continued to exert pressure by withholding dollars which the Iraqi government wanted for purchases in the United States and by refusing to send any military equipment to Iraq except small quantities of spare parts for weapons already in the Iraqi inventory.[24]

At first Taha refused to break diplomatic relations with Italy without receiving some form of compensation. He especially wanted dollars, arms, and movement toward Arab independence in Palestine.[25] But the British government would not make any concessions in advance,[26] and gradually Taha decided to yield. In arriving at this conclusion Taha was probably influenced by pressure from the regent and from Tawfiq, his foreign minister.[27] He may also have been affected by a strong statement by Colonel Donovan, a special American envoy to Iraq, which emphasized that the United States was giving full support to Britain and would not give any assistance to Iraq unless it did likewise.[28] In addition, Taha was probably influenced by the string of British military and political victories in early 1941. For example, in North Africa on 8 February British troops captured El Agheila, thereby completing an advance of some 500 miles in only two months that netted a total of 130,000 Italian prisoners, 845 guns, and 400 tanks.[29] In East Africa on 25 February British troops occupied Mogadishu, the capital of Italian Somaliland; on 16 March they recaptured Berbera, the capital of British Somaliland; and on 27 March they seized Keren, a major Italian fortress in Eritrea.[30] In the Balkans Greece, Britain's ally, continued successfully to resist the Italian invasion which had commenced the previous October. And in the United States on 11 March Congress passed the extremely important Lend-Lease Act which promised Britain a vast quantity of American armaments of all sorts without payment for the duration of the war.

The leading army officers were strongly opposed to breaking diplomatic relations with Italy, and they were particularly unwilling to act under British dictation. They still believed in the likelihood and desirability of a German victory. They wanted to continue negotiations with the axis powers with the objective of eliminating British influence in Iraq and liberating Palestine and Syria from colonial rule.[31] Soon Taha realized that he would have to break the power of the golden square before he could embark upon a more pro-British foreign policy. Consequently, toward the end of March 1941 Taha attempted to transfer Kamil Shabib, a member of the golden square, from his command of the 1st army division near Baghdad to a politically less influential position as commander of the 4th army division in southern Iraq. Taha intended to follow this move by transferring Sabbagh, another member of the golden square, from the command of the 3rd army division near Baghdad to the command of the 2nd division in northern Iraq. In this manner Taha hoped to remove the members of the golden square from the most important positions in the army without provoking them to rebellion.[32]

Taha's plan failed. The leading army officers discerned his scheme and on 1 April they revolted. The following day they forced Taha to resign and attempted to make Rashid Ali prime minister again. However, contrary to their plan the regent escaped capture in Baghdad and fled to the safety of the British airbase at Habbaniya. For the army officers the regent's flight was awkward because without a royal *irada* (decree) that he alone could sign neither Taha's resignation as prime minister nor Rashid Ali's appointment to that office would be legal. To cope with this unexpected situation, the army officers instructed Rashid Ali to take power in the name of a temporary government of national defense.[33]

Because Rashid Ali's government resulted from a military coup against the legally established authority, Britain considered it illegal and refused to extend diplomatic recognition. More important, British officials denied recognition because they believed that Rashid Ali and the leading army officers who supported him were anti-British and pro-German. They refused recognition also because it would have entailed formally abandoning the regent and Britain's other friends in Iraq.[34]

Rather than recognize the new regime in Iraq, the British government tried to bring it down by encouraging internal opposition.[35] For example, the British government broadcast statements to Iraq in Arabic saying that the new regime was unconstitutional.[36] It flew the regent from his refuge at the British airbase at Habbaniya to Basra so that he would be better located to rally his supporters.[37] It gave the regent money to use for his political activities[38] and allowed him to stay on a British warship in the Shatt al-Arab to avoid capture.[39] It carried letters from the regent to his friends in Baghdad.[40] It distributed 4,000 copies in Baghdad of a radio broadcast the regent made in Basra appealing for resistance to the new regime.[41] It helped pro-British politicians escape Baghdad and join the regent in Basra.[42]

Despite these activities, Rashid Ali and the army quickly consolidated their authority over the country. Britain's friends in Iraq were afraid to protest for fear of arrest and because the new government appeared to have much popular support.[43] Still Rashid Ali wanted British recognition in order to enhance his legitimacy and to discourage internal opposition. In exchange for recognition, on 7 April 1941 Rashid Ali offered to allow Abd al-Ilah to remain as regent. He also promised to abide by the treaty of alliance with Britain, break diplomatic relations with Italy (though not immediately), publicly deny that his regime was pro-axis, stop all agitation about Palestine, and give British advisers much control over the government's propaganda.[44] The British government quickly rejected this proposal because it had no faith in Rashid Ali's assurances. Even if Rashid Ali were sincere, British officials did not believe that the army would allow him to abide by his pledges.[45]

After Britain rejected his proposal, on 10 April Rashid Ali called both houses of the Iraqi parliament into session. At his instance, the parliament voted to depose Prince Abd al-Ilah and to appoint Sharif Sharaf, a distant relative of the king, as regent. Sharif Sharaf thereupon approved Taha's resignation as prime minister and invited Rashid Ali to form a new cabinet. In this manner the government of national defense came to an end and, at least in the opinion of Rashid Ali and the golden square, a legal government was formed and the political situation in Iraq returned to normal.[46]

Against the background of these events, in early April 1941 British officials again began seriously to consider the possibility of sending troops to Iraq.[47] But General Wavell, the commander-in-chief in the Middle East, said that he could not spare any troops for deployment to Iraq.[48] Wavell's attitude was understandable because in North Africa he was hard-pressed by axis forces that launched a major offensive in late March. In addition, he was obligated to defend Greece which was the victim of a large-scale German assault on 6 April. However, the government of India was able to dispatch a brigade of Indian troops by sea to Iraq almost immediately and two more brigades within two months. It was also able at once to send a battalion of British troops by air to the British airbase at Shaiba near Basra. Accordingly, the Indian brigade departed Karachi on 12 April, only ten days after Rashid Ali assumed power. The British battalion left by air a few days later, its departure being deliberately delayed to enable it to arrive concurrently with the Indian brigade.[49]

The British government's decision to send troops to Iraq was not motivated entirely by the desire to oust Rashid Ali from power and restore the regent to his former position. For the British government the achievement of this objective was not an immediate priority and might never have become one if Iraq had not forced a confrontation. In early and mid-April 1941 British policy was merely to place three Indian brigades at Basra as rapidly as possible. No decision was made regarding their future deployment or even to send any of them northward. And certainly no decision was made to use these troops to launch an unprovoked assault on Rashid Ali's government.[50]

The British government's decision to send troops to Iraq was motivated in large measure by the desire to establish a secure base at Basra for the purpose of assembling military aircraft shipped directly from the United States for the use of British forces in the Middle East.[51] In addition to serving this function, British leaders thought that a base at Basra could be used to supply their forces in Palestine if the Suez Canal were closed and they were driven out of Egypt—a realistic possibility because in April 1941 British troops were being forcibly evicted from Libya and Greece. Now that Germany had air superiority in the Aegean Sea, Britain could also use Basra to supply Turkey and thereby help that country to resist German pressure and enticements. In the event that Rashid Ali moved Iraq entirely into the axis camp, Basra could be used as a base for an operation to gain control of the rich oil-fields in northern Iraq and the oil pipeline to the Mediterranean, or at least to deny these assets to the Germans. In the opinion of British leaders, a base at Basra would also encourage pro-allied sentiment in Iran and, under certain circumstances, help to defend the valuable oilfields in southwestern Iran.[52]

For Britain Basra was a particularly desirable location for all of these purposes because it had a large modern port the British themselves had built during the First World War. The port was so spacious that seven ocean-going vessels could unload simultaneously at its wharves, while at the same time five more big ships could unload in mid-stream onto smaller craft for which ample additional wharf space was available. From Basra a railway proceeded northward to Baghdad and then onward through Mosul to Syria and Turkey, while a branch line connected Baghdad with the oilfields around Kirkuk. For Britain Basra was also a desirable location because it had a modern civil airport and a British seaplane base with onshore maintenance facilities, while about ten miles away at Shaiba there was another British airbase.[53]

The British government feared that Rashid Ali would forcibly oppose the establishment of a major new British base on Iraqi territory not specifically sanctioned in the treaty.[54] In order to avoid resistance to the landing at Basra, it attempted to lull Rashid Ali into a false sense of security and deceive him as to the true purpose of the expedition. For example, on 14 April the British government stopped radio attacks on the new regime in Iraq.[55] On 15 April it removed the regent from Basra, where he was unsuccessfully trying to rally support for his cause, and sent him to Transjordan.[56] On 16 April Sir Kinahan Cornwallis, the British ambassador in Iraq, informed Rashid Ali that British troops would soon arrive in Iraq, but he did not say that they would establish a large more or less permanent base at Basra or that they were the precursors of a substantial number of additional troops that would also remain in Iraq. On the contrary, Cornwallis said the troops were being sent to Basra merely for the purpose of opening the line of communications through Iraq, a privilege clearly given to Britain by the treaty. Thus Cornwallis implied, though he did not explicitly state, that all the troops, and any that followed, would soon pass through Iraq on their way to Palestine. In a further effort to reduce the chance of armed resistance, Cornwallis told Rashid Ali that if he cooperated in this endeavor

Britain would immediately enter into informal relations with his government and probably grant full diplomatic recognition in the near future.[57]

Reassured about Britain's intentions toward his government and gratified by the prospect of diplomatic recognition, on 16 April Rashid Ali agreed to allow the troops to land without opposition.[58] Accordingly, on 17 April the first elements of the British battalion arrived by air at Shaiba and the following day the convoy carrying the Indian brigade docked at Basra.[59] But the leading army officers opposed Rashid Ali's hasty decision to permit the troops to land, and they now imposed their views on the government. Consequently, on 18 April, and again three days later, the Iraqi government informed Cornwallis that the troops at Basra must immediately pass through Iraq to Palestine, that no more troops could land at Basra until the first lot had left Iraq, that at no time could there be more than one brigade of British or imperial troops in Iraq, that all troop movements through Iraq must be in small contingents, and that in future reasonable advance notice should be given before the arrival of troops.[60]

The Iraqi government believed that it was legally entitled to make these demands because the treaty of 1930 did not explicitly state that Britain was permitted on its own initiative to station troops in Iraq even in wartime. In the opinion of Rashid Ali, the only possible justification for Britain's action was article 5 of the treaty, as modified by a secret letter from Sir Francis Humphrys to Nuri al-Said on 15 July 1930, which allowed Britain in an emergency and after prior consultation with the Iraqi government to send troops temporarily to reinforce the British airbases. But Rashid Ali was convinced that article 5 did not apply in this case because the British government was now demanding the right to maintain troops at Basra in unlimited quantities for an unlimited period of time without prior consultation or permission.[61]

British officials would not accept any of the restrictions Rashid Ali attempted to place on their use of Iraqi territory. They believed that their position at Basra was fully covered by article 4 of the treaty which in wartime obligated Iraq immediately to "come to his [Britannic Majesty's] aid in the capacity of an ally," and which stipulated that "The aid of His Majesty the King of Iraq in the event of war or the imminent menace of war will consist in furnishing to His Britannic Majesty on Iraq territory all facilities and assistance in his power, including the use of railways, rivers, ports, aerodromes and means of communication." In their opinion, the phrase "all facilities and assistance in his power" was especially relevant because it was certainly in Iraq's power to allow Britain to establish a base at Basra. They also laid particular emphasis on the word "including" which they believed implied that the assistance Iraq was obligated to provide did not consist merely or exclusively of "the use of railways, rivers, ports, aerodromes and means of communication." Finally, British officials would not accept Rashid Ali's demand that reasonable advance notice should be given before the arrival of additional troops because article 7 of the annexure of the treaty obligated Britain merely to give "prior notification" of the arrival of British ships in Iraqi ports without in any way specifying how much notification was required; and because in wartime they were unwilling to trust the Iraqi government, which was hostile to Britain and in constant contact with the axis powers, with vital information regarding the movement of British troopships.[62]

Because the treaty was imprecise and open to divergent interpretations, honorable men could sincerely differ on the question of whether Britain was legally entitled to establish a large assembly base at Basra. However, neither Britain nor Iraq suggested recourse to arbitration or judicial settlement because the dispute between them was not primarily of a legal nature. For military reasons owing to the eastward extension of the war and German victories in Libya and Greece, in April 1941 the British government was determined to establish a base at Basra, if necessary by force, regardless of the treaty position.[63] Similarly, Rashid Ali and the leading army officers were determined to prevent the establishment of such a base, regardless of the treaty position, because they considered it derogatory of national sovereignty, a threat to the very existence of their government, and possibly even a menace to their personal safety.[64]

In spite of growing Iraqi anger and suspicion, the Indian brigade remained at Basra. Because of the strained atmosphere in Iraq and the general deterioration of Britain's strategic position in the eastern Mediterranean in April as a result of German victories in Libya and Greece, British officials in Iraq became alarmed about the possibility of an attack by German paratroopers on the lightly defended British airbase at Habbaniya, about fifty-five miles west of Baghdad. In addition to fears for the safety of the garrison, they were concerned that if Habbaniya fell German planes based there or at Baghdad could bomb the British forces at Basra and Shaiba. Consequently, after giving notification one day in advance, on 24 April the British military authorities in Iraq began to transport some of the troops from the British battalion at Shaiba by air to Habbaniya.[65] This move further angered Rashid Ali because the treaty stated that Britain could reinforce its air-bases with ground troops only after consultation with the Iraqi government, and because British troops at Habbaniya would be well situated to march rapidly on Baghdad.[66]

On 28 April Cornwallis informed the Iraqi government that three troopships would soon arrive at Basra. These ships carried ancillary formations and various types of equipment for the Indian brigade already at Basra. Because none of the original contingent had passed through Iraq on the way to Palestine, Rashid Ali refused permission for the additional troops to land. If the British government proceeded anyway, Rashid Ali threatened to broadcast a denunciation of the action.[67] In this tense situation, with the very real possibility of mob action against British civilians, Cornwallis ordered the immediate evacuation of all British women and children from Iraq.[68]

On the following day, 29 April, the British troopships docked at Basra and began to disembark.[69] Iraqi leaders may have feared that this move, which was taken against their express wishes and was coupled with the evacuation of British women and children, would be followed by bombing raids on Baghdad from the British airbase at Habbaniya.[70] Their apprehension in this regard was probably increased by reconnaissance flights over Baghdad by British planes based at Habbaniya.[71] In any event, the Iraqi government now began to mass forces around Habbaniya which soon numbered about 9,000 troops and fifty artillery pieces, plus light tanks and armored cars.[72]

Acting on instructions from Baghdad, on 30 April the commander of the Iraqi military forces at Habbaniya threatened to attack any aircraft, vehicle, or person that attempted to leave the base.[73] Now, for the first time, war between the two countries became virtually inevitable. Probably the leading army officers, who dominated the government and controlled most of Rashid Ali's actions,[74] had long believed that eventually they would have to challenge Britain in order to achieve their goal of eliminating British influence in Iraq and liberating Palestine and Syria from colonial rule. They chose this particular moment because they were angered and frightened by the continual build-up of British troops at Basra. Influenced by the recent German victories in Libya and Greece,[75] and encouraged by axis pledges of support, they thought that Germany would immediately come to their assistance in the event of hostilities.[76] Probably the Iraqi leaders were also emboldened by an awareness of Habbaniya's weak defenses—aside from about 1,300 air force personnel only 100 British ground troops recently flown up from Shaiba, 800 native levies (mainly Assyrians), eighteen armored cars, two antiquated artillery pieces, no tanks, and no fortifications beyond a fence designed only to keep out wild animals and marauding bedouin[77]—and believed that they could score an impressive victory.[78] At the least they thought that they could hold out until German help arrived.[79]

The British authorities in Iraq immediately demanded that Rashid Ali withdraw his forces from the vicinity of Habbaniya.[80] He refused but said that he would take no hostile action provided that Britain did likewise.[81] This assurance was not good enough for British leaders. They feared that the Iraqi troops would soon begin to shell Habbaniya and thereby destroy or at least immobilize the British aircraft at the base. They were also concerned that given time Germany would send military forces through Turkey or Syria to aid Rashid Ali.[82] In addition, British leaders, and especially Cornwallis, were resolved to seize the opportunity presented by this provocative action to overthrow Rashid Ali's regime, restore the regent to power, and place a friendly government in office in Baghdad.[83] Consequently, without warning and without first issuing an ultimatum, on 2 May British aircraft from Habbaniya attacked the Iraqi troops surrounding the base. The Iraqi forces immediately retaliated by bombarding Habbaniya.[84] In this manner Britain and Iraq went to war.

Contrary to its expectations, within nine years of the termination of the mandate the British government was no longer able to rely on the provisions of the treaty of 1930 or the goodwill of the Iraqi ruling class. By the spring of 1941 Britain's policy of indirect rule had clearly failed; and now only through the prompt and judicious application of military force could it restore its political influence and strategic position in Iraq.

CHAPTER 13

The Hostilities of May 1941

The fighting in Iraq in May 1941 has been ably discussed in numerous books.[1] It is not my intention to give a blow-by-blow description of the battle and thereby merely duplicate these works. Rather, I would like to explain some of the underlying causes or factors that account for Britain's rapid and complete victory. Such explanation is necessary because at the outset of the campaign the disparity in the military strength and geographic advantages of the participants was not so great as immediately to suggest the outcome which ensued. I would also like to indicate some of the major consequences of the campaign both for Iraq and for the surrounding region.

During the fighting in Iraq in May 1941 Germany did not send strong forces to aid Rashid Ali because it was preoccupied with preparations for the impending assault on Russia; because most of its paratroopers and transport aircraft, and a large number of its fighter and bomber aircraft, were heavily involved in the campaign in Crete;[2] because Turkey, which was firmly neutral, blocked Germany's only reasonably convenient land route to Iraq; and because Germany was reluctant to be sucked into a serious military adventure against considerable British opposition in a distant theatre far from its nearest bases in Greece and the Dodecanese Islands. However, German leaders wanted to maintain their prestige in the east and to tie down British troops in Iraq which might otherwise be employed in areas of greater concern to Germany. Consequently, through Syria, which was controlled by the Vichy French, Germany sent twenty-one fighter and bomber aircraft, with their pilots, to assist Rashid Ali's forces.[3] Following

Germany's lead, Italy sent an additional twelve planes.[4] At German instigation, the French authorities in Syria also sent to Iraq by railway 30,000 grenades, 15,500 rifles, 354 pistols, 200 machine-guns, twelve artillery pieces, large quantities of ammunition, and thirty-two trucks.[5] To help finance Rashid Ali's government, Germany provided £20,000 in gold and an additional £80,000 in gold was en route to Iraq by the end of May.[6]

Besides this assistance, Rashid Ali had certain other advantages. For example, the great majority of Britain's forces in the Middle East were tied down in the defense of Crete and Egypt, and the Indian troops at Basra were unable to advance far because of widespread flooding of the rivers in southern Iraq and because the Iraqis had torn up parts of the railway and withdrawn to the north locomotives and river-going vessels.[7]

In addition, the Iraqi forces themselves were not negligible: 46,000 troops;[8] a large number of former soldiers who were familiar with the use of firearms;[9] over 12,000 police, most of whom were equipped with rifles and some of whom had vehicle mounted machine-guns;[10] and sixty-four serviceable aircraft[11] (out of a total inventory of 116).[12]

Nonetheless, on 6 May, after four days of fighting, the British forces at Habbaniya compelled the Iraqi troops who were besieging the base to withdraw from the vicinity. Twelve days later the garrison at Habbaniya was reinforced by about 2,000 British troops from Palestine and British-led troops from the Arab Legion in Transjordan. These men had hurriedly travelled by road and track across some 500 miles of desert in a makeshift column that included many civilian vehicles.[13] In early May the garrison was also reinforced by about 500 British and Indian troops flown up from Shaiba.[14] (The Iraqi artillery around Habbaniya was never able to prevent flight operations from the base.) This combined force, together with the Assyrian levies stationed at Habbaniya, then moved rapidly eastward, defeating the Iraqi army in several engagements. On 30 May, only four weeks after the start of hostilities, two British columns totalling less than 1,500 men approached the outskirts of Baghdad.[15] This force had only eight guns, ten armored cars, and no tanks,[16] and its supply line was dependent upon vulnerable ferries crossing badly flooded terrain (the Iraqis had opened the banks of the Euphrates in order to impede the advance of the British forces).[17] But at this point the most important Iraqi leaders fled to Iran and the remaining ones sued for an armistice, even though they still had some 20,000 troops available for the defense of Baghdad[18] and another 15,000 in the north for the defense of the Mosul region.[19] Moreover, additional German aircraft were en route to Iraq as reinforcements;[20] while in Athens German commanders were gathering a substantial quantity of armaments, including machine-guns, anti-tank guns, and mortars, for air shipment to Iraq.[21]

To a considerable extent Britain's rapid and complete victory in the campaign was due to Germany's failure to act quicker and in greater strength. For example, the first German aircraft did not enter combat until 13 May, eleven days after the beginning of hostilities.[22] By this time the British had already broken the siege of Habbaniya and taken the offensive against the Iraqis. An earlier commitment of German aircraft, especially if accompanied by a small number of highly trained ground troops to stiffen the Iraqi resistance, might have made a substantial difference in the campaign. It might even have affected the course of the war as a whole, especially if Germany had utilized the airfields in the vicinity of Baghdad to stage bombing raids against the large oil refinery at Abadan in southwestern Iran, the products of which were absolutely vital for the conduct of British military operations in North Africa, the Middle East, and the eastern Mediterranean.

Rashid Ali's failure to open hostilities with an all-out attack on Habbaniya was another major factor in Britain's success. Clearly, Iraq's ability to overrun the base, or at least prevent flight operations, would have been greatly enhanced if it had struck first. Doubtless the Iraqis would have suffered heavy casualties in the endeavor but, given their considerable superiority in numbers of men and artillery pieces, with perseverance they probably would have succeeded. Their prospects would have been particularly good if they had attacked at night when the British aircraft could not bomb or strafe with precision and, without the use of a flare path which would have assisted the Iraqi gunners, could only take off and land with great difficulty and danger.[23] Rashid Ali's hesitation at this decisive moment enabled Britain at the outset to gain control of the air over the battlefield and to maintain it for the duration of the campaign. The British commanders at Habbaniya exploited this advantage to the fullest by bringing up reinforcements and supplies by air from Shaiba, preventing the Iraqi commanders at Habbaniya from bringing up reinforcements and supplies by road from Baghdad, and depositing troops behind Iraqi lines by landing transport aircraft on the desert floor. Most important, however, the British commanders used their air superiority to give close air support to their troops in combat. These British air attacks had a devastating effect on the morale of the Iraqi troops.[24] Thus Britain's control of the air, which contributed mightily to its success in the campaign, and which was absolutely dependent upon the use of the airbase at Habbaniya, flowed directly from Iraq's reluctance to cross the threshold from a diplomatic challenge and a military maneuver into open warfare.

The Iraqis made other important mistakes too. For example, although Anglo-Iraqi relations were extremely tense for a month preceding the actual outbreak of hostilities, they did not stockpile aviation fuel, lubricants, and bombs at Mosul, their main airbase in the north and later the center of the German air operation. Consequently, the Germans had to bring most of their supplies by transport aircraft from Rhodes. This airlift was only partly successful because the distances involved were great, and because the German government did not give it sufficient priority. As a result, the German commanders in Iraq were unable to make maximum use of their aircraft because of a severe shortage of fuel and stores.[25]

Nor did the Iraqis install demolition charges on the vitally located bridge over the Euphrates at Falluja on the road between Habbaniya and Baghdad. As a result of this error, the British were able to capture the bridge intact. Since the river at this point was 300 yards wide, the capture of the bridge greatly facilitated the advance of their forces toward Baghdad.[26]

Internal political and social considerations also explain Iraq's abrupt and overwhelming defeat in the fighting in May 1941. In this connection it is important to emphasize that the movement that Rashid Ali headed was not in favor of fundamental changes in the economy, society, or political structure of Iraq. On the contrary, Rashid Ali and the leading ministers in his government in April–May 1941 had all served extended periods in important cabinet positions and were an integral part—the more nationalistic, anti-British, and pan-Arab part—of the small body of Sunni Arabs who had ruled Iraq since the creation of a quasi-independent government in Baghdad in 1920. For example, Rashid Ali first held ministerial office in 1924 and served as prime minister in 1933 and again in 1940. Naji Suwaydi, his finance minister, first held ministerial office in 1921 and served as prime minister in 1929–30. And Naji Shawkat, his defense minister, first held ministerial office in 1928 and served as prime minister in 1932–33.[27]

True, the other members of the nine-man cabinet (of whom only Rauf al-Bahrani, the minister of social affairs, was a Shiite) were younger men who had not served long periods in ministerial office and who doubtless viewed the Rashid Ali movement as an opportunity for advancement. Yunis al-Sabawi, the minister of economics; Musa Shabandar, the foreign minister; Ali Mahmud, the minister of justice; and Muhammad Ali Mahmud, the minister of transportation and public works, fall into this category. Except for Shabandar, who was a wealthy landowner, these men were lawyers of a more middling income and status who were not part of the ruling elite. But neither were they rank outsiders divorced by past association and ideological conviction from the ruling elite. On the contrary, like the ruling elite, they were primarily nationalists rather than social reformers. Moreover, most of them had occupied important government offices beneath the cabinet level. For example, Musa Shabandar had once been elected to the chamber of deputies, and had held diplomatic posts in Germany, at the League of Nations in Geneva, and at the foreign ministry in Baghdad. Ali Mahmud had twice been elected to the chamber of deputies, and had served as a judge in the court of appeal, *mutasarrif* (governor) of the Basra *liwa* (province), and director-general of customs. And Muhammad Ali Mahmud had thrice been elected to the chamber of deputies, and had served as director-general of the ministry of justice, a judge in the court of appeal, vice-president of the chamber of deputies, and chairman of the finance committee of the chamber of deputies.[28]

Like most of the junior members of Rashid Ali's cabinet, the members of the golden square, who held great power behind the scenes, were Sunni Arabs from middle-class backgrounds. But they were not a new force that had suddenly emerged on the political scene demanding the implementation of a radical or even liberal social agenda. On the contrary, their paramount influence in the country dated from August 1937 when they materially assisted in the overthrow of Hikmat Sulayman's government. Afterwards they closely cooperated with members of the ruling elite. For example, in December 1938 they did much to elevate Nuri al-Said to the premiership, and enjoyed amicable relations with him until his resignation in March 1940. During this entire period they were mainly interested in foreign and defense policy, and never showed much concern for internal policy except as it affected their own status and position.[29]

Thus the split in 1941 between the group led by Rashid Ali and the golden square and that led by Nuri al-Said and the regent was essentially a dispute within Iraq's governing class. As we have observed, it was caused by a strong disagreement on the question of whether Iraq, and the Arabs generally, would benefit by leaning toward Germany or Britain. This disagreement, in turn, was influenced by opposing calculations as to which of the great powers was likely to win the war. The split between the two groups was also caused by personal animosities. For example, in 1930, when Nuri was prime minister, both Sabawi and Ali Mahmud were inprisoned for protesting the conclusion of the Anglo-Iraqi treaty; in April 1939 Nuri, who was again prime minister, dismissed Naji Shawkat from his position as minister of the interior; and in May 1939 both Musa Shabandar and Muhammad Ali Mahmud lost their seats in the chamber of deputies as the result of elections which Nuri controlled.[30] At times the location of an individual's financial assets influenced his decision to side with a particular group. For example, Musa Shabandar owned valuable property in Berlin that obviously would be more secure if he were conspicuously pro-German.[31] Pecuniary self-interest was involved for other politicians too because the occupation of high governmental office usually led to financial enrichment.[32] For example, in October 1940 Rashid Ali used his position as prime minister to make a considerable amount of money by arranging the sale of the Iraqi cotton crop to Japan.[33]

The fact that in composition, internal policy, and dependence on military support Rashid Ali's government did not differ materially from previous administrations in Iraq reduced its ability to mobilize large-scale popular support for the war effort. Since 1920 Iraq's ruling class had never made serious efforts to redistribute the wealth or land of the country in favor of the bulk of the population who lived in poverty.[34] To a considerable extent this failure was due to the fact that through rampant corruption and gross misuse of public revenue most of the leading politicians had become quite wealthy and were disinclined to take measures that would injure themselves financially.[35] Now, in 1941, their history of rapacity and indifference to the problems of the poor made them ill suited for the role of leaders of a truly national resistance.

They were also ill suited for this role because they had not won the allegiance of most Shiites or given these people a sense of Iraqi nationality strong enough to take precedence over their local, tribal, or religious loyalties. In large part this failure was the result of an unwillingness to share power with other groups or to allow a significant amount of decentralization or regional autonomy. For example, in the period 1932–36 no Shiite held the office of prime minister, and Shiites received only 15.8 percent of the other ministerial appointments.[36] And in the elections of 1933, the results of which were typical of elections during this period, Shiites woa only twenty-eight out of eighty-eight seats in the chamber of deputies.[37] It was also due to persistent economic discrimination. Thus in 1936, out of 761,180 dinars allocated for economic development under the terms of a three-year plan, Shiite districts received only 121,500 dinars.[38] In addition, it was because the Iraqi ruling class did not deal gently with dissidence or self-assertion from disadvantaged groups. For example, in 1935–36 the government of Yasin al-Hashimi, in which Rashid Ali served as interior minister, brutally suppressed a series of uprisings by Shiite tribes along the Euphrates.[39]

In early April 1941 Rashid Ali's government further alienated the Shiites by arresting Salih Jabr and Abdul Mahdi, two leading figures in the Shiite community, for aiding the fugitive regent. At this time Salih Jabr was *mutasarrif* of the Basra *liwa*, which was predominantly Shiite, while Abdul Mahdi was a member of the chamber of deputies. Both men were former cabinet ministers, and their arrest did nothing to convince Shiites that this government would differ from its predecessors by being especially solicitous about their interests.[40]

For all these reasons, in 1941 there was not a huge outpouring of loyalty and willingness for self-sacrifice from the Shiite community for Rashid Ali's government. And certainly there was little from the Shiite tribes which, in the circumstances, represented a potentially formidable military asset. Indeed, in late April, and again after the fighting began in May, important Shiite tribal leaders in southern Iraq offered their services to the British.[41]

Just as the Iraqi ruling class had failed to win the loyalty of most Shiites, it had failed to win the allegiance of most Kurds. Among these people too there was a strong feeling, not unjustified, of suffering discrimination. For example, Kurdish districts did not get their fair share of social services, particularly education, or of development projects.[42] In the spring of 1941, in the senate, the upper house of Iraq's parliament whose members were appointed by the king on the recommendation of the government, only one out of nineteen members was a Kurd.[43] And by appointing an Arab rather than a Kurd to the position of *mutasarrif* of the predominantly Kurdish inhabited *liwa* of Sulaimani, Rashid Ali did nothing to convince the Kurds that his administration would be more favorably disposed toward their interests than its predecessors.[44] As a result, this large community in northern Iraq, which could have been a great source of strength for Rashid Ali, showed little inclination to defend his government. On the contrary, for Rashid Ali the Kurds were a source of weakness because after the fighting began an important section of the community under the leadership of Shaykh Mahmud in the area near the town of Sulaimani capitalized on the upheaval in Iraq by repudiating the government's authority and offering friendship to Britain.[45]

In this context it is worth recalling that Rashid Ali was prime minister in 1933 at the time of the Assyrian massacres. Undoubtedly, the memory of his role in these tragic events did nothing to encourage the Assyrians who were serving in the levies, and who composed the largest element in that organization, to waver in their loyalty to Britain. Since the levies played a vital role in the defense of Habbaniya and the subsequent battles against the Iraqi army, this point is of some significance.[46]

Nor did the Jews have reason voluntarily to support Rashid Ali because he was in open alliance with Nazi Germany, the most notorious anti-Jewish government in the world. In addition, they probably feared the introduction of anti-Jewish measures.[47] The fact that in Rashid Ali's previous government (March 1940–January 1941) Umar Nazmi, the minister of transportation and public works, had removed Iraqi Jews who were employed by the state railway in order to replace them with Muslims was an inauspicious omen.[48]

Iraq was also handicapped in the fighting because, with the exception of Yunis al-Sabawi, Rashid Ali and his leading associates were not very inspiring or resolute leaders. For example, during the conflict none of them ventured near the front. Nor did they make any serious effort to defend Baghdad or retreat to Mosul to carry on the struggle from the north. And at the first sign of real danger all of them fled to the safety of foreign lands. For all these reasons, in May 1941 most Iraqis outside of the army, while not welcoming a British invasion, were unwilling to risk their lives to defend Rashid Ali's government. Even in the army there were widespread desertions,[49] while some 200 of those taken prisoner near Habbaniya readily switched to the side of the regent.[50]

The Iraqi government's hasty capitulation, coupled with all its other mistakes and deficiencies already discussed, suggests that, whatever the shortcomings of their armaments (about which there is room for dispute),[51] Rashid Ali and his military supporters lacked the boldness, determination, and competence to wage an all-out struggle against Britain with a reasonable chance of success. From their perspective, to challenge Britain militarily at the most convenient opportunity for Iraq was morally and politically permissible, perhaps even incumbent. But their challenge was poorly prepared, halfheartedly executed, and quickly abandoned.

The British response, on the other hand, was forceful and resolute. Once Iraq placed restrictions on the landing of Indian troops at Basra and began to threaten Habbaniya, the British rejected all possibility of negotiations with Rashid Ali. They feared that a compromise settlement at this point would be injurious to their prestige and would allow Germany time to send substantial forces to Iraq.[52] Instead, British commanders initiated hostilities, diverted troops and aircraft to Iraq that were badly needed in Palestine and Egypt, and without hesitation repeatedly attacked numerically superior enemy forces. In the process they risked not only military defeat and the interruption of oil deliveries through the pipeline to Haifa[53] but also the death of some 500 British subjects confined in Baghdad in the British embassy and the American legation.[54] Ultimately, this determination, combined with the skill and resourcefulness with which they conducted the campaign—especially in moving troops, supplies, and vehicles rapidly across numerous water obstacles—rather than any numerical or material superiority, proved decisive.

After the armistice Britain quickly reinstalled the regent, placed a pro-British government in power in Baghdad, and occupied strategic locations throughout the country. In this manner, and with fewer than 200 casualties including those suffered by Assyrian, Arab Legion, and Indian personnel,[55] Britain restored its dominant position in Iraq.

Britain's reconquest of Iraq in May 1941 had important military and political consequences in the Middle East. Because the Vichy French authorities conspired with Germany and Italy to aid Rashid Ali, the British government now became concerned about a danger to its position in the region emanating from Syria and Lebanon. To eliminate this threat, in June 1941 British forces attacked Syria and Lebanon and quickly overran both countries. As a result of this campaign and the subsequent British occupation, French power and prestige in the Levant declined while that of local nationalists increased. By 1946 these developments led to the complete independence of Syria and Lebanon and the expulsion of all French military forces from the Middle East.

Britain's reconquest of Iraq had another important consequence. From their bases in Iraq, in August 1941 British military forces invaded Iran. Simultaneously, Russia attacked Iran from the north. The main objective of this campaign was to install a compliant government in Tehran that would eliminate German influence in the country and permit the opening of a route across Iran for the supply of British and American war material to the Soviet Union. With relatively little fighting Britain and Russia achieved this objective, the result of which may have been significant for the outcome of the war.

As far as Iraq was concerned, after the end of the Second World War—which was soon followed by the withdrawal of all British ground troops from the country—the regent, Nuri, and Britain's other friends maintained their authority in Baghdad. But because they had returned to power on the back of the British army, they were now so closely identified with Britain that they were cut off from the mainstream of Arab nationalist sentiment in Iraq. The disfavor in which Britain was held by most Arab nationalists in Iraq—especially in the army upon which Britain had inflicted some 1,200 casualties during the fighting in May 1941[56]—reflected upon these pro-British elements. Their execution of the members of the golden square, coupled with their policy of cashiering and often imprisoning cabinet ministers, army officers, and civil servants who actively participated in the anti-British movement in 1941, added to their unpopularity.[57] So did their unrelenting grasp on the reins of power, the widespread corruption of their regime, and their neglect of social programs for the poor. Their pro-western foreign policy, culminating in the formation of the Baghdad Pact in 1955 which isolated Iraq from most of the other Arab countries, also alienated many. Gradually, their position became untenable, especially after they were linked, through their close association with Britain, with the tripartite attack on Egypt in 1956. Eventually, with relative ease in 1958 they were overthrown by the army.[58] The new military government adopted a neutralist foreign policy and quickly eliminated all remaining British influence in Iraq. In this manner it achieved many of the objectives sought by the members of the golden square. And thus finally ended in failure Britain's efforts, begun originally in 1920, to create an independent but friendly regime in Iraq that would willingly cooperate in the protection of Britain's vital interests in the Middle East.

CHAPTER 14

Conclusion

During the 1930s the British government believed that Iraqi friendship was necessary in order to secure important British strategic and economic interests in the Middle East. In particular, Britain wanted to protect its airbases in Iraq, its line of communications from the Persian Gulf across Iraq to the Mediterranean Sea, its preponderant share of the Iraqi import market, the Iraq Petroleum Company's large oilfield in northern Iraq and oil pipeline across Iraq to the Mediterranean, and the Anglo-Iranian Oil Company's large oilfield in southwestern Iran and oil refinery at Abadan. Consequently, in various ways during this period Britain accommodated and appeased the different Iraqi governments in an effort to acquire and maintain their friendship. For example, Britain terminated the mandate long before it was legally obligated to do so; withdrew all of its ground troops in Iraq; withdrew from its airbases at Mosul and Hinaidi; reduced the number of levies to a very low figure and agreed to convert them into an air defense force that would be, at least nominally, part of the Iraqi army; provided Iraq with modern military equipment and sizable financial credits; discouraged Kurdish efforts to achieve independence or autonomy and in 1932 actively participated together with the Iraqi army in military operations against Kurdish dissidents; refused to support Assyrian attempts to establish an autonomous enclave in northern Iraq and in 1933 refused to intervene with armed force to protect the Assyrians when they were under attack from the Iraqi army; and in 1939 greatly curbed Jewish immigration into Palestine and agreed to create an independent Palestinian state within ten years.

Initially, Britain's efforts were reasonably successful. True, in

1933 Britain could not prevent the massacre of the Assyrians; in 1936 it could not prevent the anti-British General Bakr Sidqi from overthrowing the pro-British Prime Minister Yasin al-Hashimi; in 1937 it could not prevent Hikmat Sulayman's government from purchasing substantial quantities of German and Italian armaments; and in 1938–39 it could not prevent King Ghazi from waging a violent propaganda campaign against the shaykh of Kuwait. These setbacks clearly demonstrate the limited nature of British influence in Iraq after independence. Nonetheless, at the end of the decade Britain still retained its dominant strategic and economic position in Iraq and thereby protected its vital interests in the Middle East.

During the 1930s Britain was successful because no outside power seriously threatened its position in Iraq. Moreover, during this period there was a sizable group of leading Iraqis who were basically pro-British in orientation and willing to implement the Anglo-Iraqi treaty of 1930. In addition to King Faysal and Prince Abd al-Ilah, this body included influential politicians like Nuri al-Said, Jafar al-Askari, Jamil al-Midfai, Ali Jawdat, Tawfiq al-Suwaydi, Rustum Haydar, and Salih Jabr.[1] It would be untrue to say that these men were not real Arab nationalists or that they were British puppets. Some of them had fought against Britain in the rebellion of 1920.[2] All of them had opposed the mandate and pressed for its earliest possible termination. After independence they still had important differences with Britain; for example, they wanted to end British rule in Palestine, eliminate British influence in Kuwait and annex all or part of that nation's territory, promote the unity of the countries of the fertile crescent under Iraqi leadership, abolish the levies while ensuring that their replacement was firmly under Iraqi control, and procure more arms more rapidly for the Iraqi army. But despite these differences with Britain, these men—perhaps we could describe them as moderate nationalists—believed that Iraqi and Arab interests would be best served by a policy of close cooperation with Britain. In this manner they thought that they could gradually achieve most of their main objectives while simultaneously deterring Turkish or Iranian aggression and also preventing the growth of German or Italian influence in the Arab lands.

However, by 1940 the authority of these pro-British figures was declining as a result of the growing power of the army led by four officers known collectively as the golden square. These officers, and their associates among the civilian politicians, were extreme nationalists. While they shared most of the same goals as the moderate nationalists—and generally showed a similar lack of concern for land reform or social programs designed to benefit the great mass of the population—they were more impatient and believed that their objectives could only be secured through a radical break with Britain. Perhaps because many of them were military leaders, they were more aggrieved than the moderates at what they thought were Britain's attempts to keep Iraq weak by withholding arms. They were also more offended by the residual British presence in Iraq in the form of airbases, levies, and a military mission, which they viewed as a derogation of sovereignty; and by continued British rule in Palestine, which they considered a denial of the elemental right of self-determination and an impediment to the sacred cause of Arab unity. Doubtless too they hungered for the high government offices—and the accompanying means of financial enrichment—which were usually occupied by the leading pro-British politicians. Unlike the moderate nationalists, the members of this group were willing to align themselves with Germany to achieve their aims. This willingness reflected the extent of their hatred of Britain. It also reflected the extent of Hitler's military victories which for the first time made a pro-German policy a reasonable option.

Thus, despite Britain's many concessions to Iraqi sensibilities, by 1940, only eight years after the termination of the mandate, Britain was no longer able to influence the Iraqi government even on matters affecting Britain's most vital interests in the Middle East. At this time, precisely when Britain most needed a friendly government in Iraq because it was harried and harassed by powerful enemies on numerous fronts, it encountered a regime dedicated to the complete elimination of Britain's presence in Iraq and elsewhere in the region and willing to align itself with Britain's deadliest enemy in order to achieve its aims.

Possibly if Britain had followed a firmer policy, for example, by retaining the mandate (as in Palestine and Transjordan) or at least by keeping British ground troops in Iraq (as in Egypt and India), it would have preserved its influence in the country and thereby protected its vital interests in the Middle East. Of course, in the final analysis this policy could have succeeded only if Britain had been willing to use force in order to maintain itself in Iraq. But in the late 1920s British leaders lacked the will for such a policy. Even if they had had the will, they might not have had enough domestic support to implement a policy that would probably have involved increased expenditure and a certain amount of repression within Iraq. Perhaps most important, however, they did not think that the continuation of the mandate or the stationing of British ground troops in Iraq was necessary in order to protect vital British interests in the region. On the contrary, British leaders believed that these interests could be protected more cheaply and, in the long run, more effectively by forging a close alliance with the Iraqi ruling class. That they overestimated the possibility of achieving such an alliance without sacrificing the very interests the alliance was designed to safeguard, we have already observed.

As an alternative to a firmer policy, in the late 1920s Britain could have completely withdrawn from Iraq, including the airbases and the levies, in the hope that Iraqi leaders would respond with gratitude and goodwill. But the British government was not willing to abandon all of the strategic gains it had secured at great cost during the First World War. Nor was it willing entirely to rely on the benevolence and capability of the Iraqi government to protect Britain's vital interests in the region. Consequently, to the consternation of most leading Iraqis, it insisted upon retaining two airbases and a protective screen of levies and in various other ways restricting Iraqi sovereignty. But even if Britain had completely withdrawn from Iraq, Iraqi leaders might not have responded with gratitude and goodwill unless Britain had also been willing to make greater concessions to the Palestinian Arabs, further Iraq's leadership ambitions in the fertile crescent, compromise the interests of the shaykh of Kuwait, and grant Iraq a higher priority in the matter of arms supplies.

Ultimately, however, speculation on the imagined consequences of rejected policies is fruitless. It is sufficient simply to note that a policy of indirect rule was tried and, after a brief period of relative success, in 1940–41 it failed. In 1941 Britain reestablished its dominant position in Iraq, but only after a major military operation. After a subsequent period of military occupation, Britain again withdrew all of its ground troops from Iraq and once more reverted to a policy of indirect rule. This policy then worked reasonably well until it irretrievably collapsed in 1958. Still, from 1932 until 1958—a quarter of a century even discounting the rather unpleasant interval in 1940–41—perhaps not such a bad run for a geographically distant, militarily weakened, economically declining, and grievously overextended European power in the midst of the nationalist passions of the Middle East.

In any event, whether an alternative policy involving either greater or lesser British involvement would have succeeded in preserving essential British interests in Iraq at a tolerable cost for a longer period of time, or at least in avoiding Iraq's alignment with Germany in 1941 and its shift into neutralism after 1958, cannot be known.

Notes

Notes for Chapter 1—Introduction

1. The fighting in Iraq during the First World War is discussed in Brigadier-General F. J. Moberly, *History of the Great War Based on Official Documents: The Campaign in Mesopotamia 1914–1918*, 4 vols. (London, 1923–27); and A. J. Barker, *The Neglected War: Mesopotamia 1914–1918* (London, 1967).

2. Memoranda by Hugh Trenchard (chief of the air staff) and the Middle East department of the colonial office, 11 Dec. 1922, CAB 27/206; Robin Higham, *Britain's Imperial Air Routes 1918 to 1939: The Story of Britain's Overseas Airlines* (London, 1960), pp. 110, 122; H. Montgomery Hyde, *British Air Policy between the Wars 1918–1939* (London, 1976), pp. 91–92, 95, 122.

3. Memoranda by the Middle East department of the colonial office, 11 Dec. 1922, the foreign office, 15 Dec. 1922, and L. S. Amery (first lord of the admiralty), 16 Dec. 1922, CAB 27/206; report of the cabinet committee on Iraq, 23 March 1923, CAB 27/206.

4. Memoranda by the Middle East department of the colonial office, 11 Dec. 1922, and Amery, 16 Dec. 1922, CAB 27/206; Stephen H. Longrigg, *Oil in the Middle East: Its Discovery and Development*, 3rd ed. (London, 1968), p. 71; Benjamin Shwadran, *The Middle East, Oil and the Great Powers*, 3rd ed. (New York, 1973), p. 240; Helmut Mejcher, *Imperial Quest for Oil: Iraq 1910–1928* (London, 1976), pp. 105–75; Marian Kent, *Oil and Empire: British Policy and Mesopotamian Oil 1900–1920* (London, 1976), pp. 155–157; William Stivers, "International Politics and Iraqi Oil, 1918–1928: A Study in Anglo-American Diplomacy," *Business History Review*, Vol. 55 (1981), pp. 519–21.

5. Memorandum by the Middle East department of the colonial office, 11 Dec. 1922, CAB 27/206.

6. Report of the cabinet committee on Iraq, 23 March 1923, CAB 27/206.

7. Memorandum by the Middle East department of the colonial office, 11 Dec. 1922, CAB 27/206.

8. Memoranda by the Middle East department of the colonial office, 11 Dec. 1922 and 16 Feb. 1923, CAB 27/206.

9. Moberly, *The Campaign in Mesopotamia*, IV, pp. i, 331; Philip W. Ireland, *Iraq: A Study in Political Development* (London, 1937), p. 60.

10. George Antonius, *The Arab Awakening: The Story of the Arab Nationalist Movement* (London, 1938), pp. 164–83; Elie Kedourie, *In the Anglo-Arab Labyrinth: The McMahon-Husayn Correspondence and its Interpretations 1914–1939* (Cambridge, 1976), pp. 65–137.

11. Ireland, *Iraq*, pp. 98–99, 457–58; Ghassan R. Atiyyah, *Iraq: 1908–1921, A Socio-Political Study* (Beirut, 1973), pp. 151–52.

12. A. J. P. Taylor, *English History 1914–1945* (London, 1965), p. 160; John Darwin, *Britain, Egypt and the Middle East: Imperial Policy in the Aftermath of War 1918–1922* (London, 1981), pp. 155–56.

13. Taylor, *English History*, pp. 153–54, 163–64.

14. Ireland, *Iraq*, pp. 136–37, 151, 459–60; Atiyyah, *Iraq*, pp. 172–73.

15. Aaron M. Margalith, *The International Mandates* (Baltimore, 1930), pp. 18–34; Quincy Wright, *Mandates under the League of Nations* (Chicago, 1930), pp. 24–63. The text of article 22 is in J. C. Hurewitz (ed.), *The Middle East and North Africa in World Politics: A Documentary Record*, Vol. II: *British-French Supremacy 1914–1945* (New Haven, Conn., 1979), pp. 179–80.

16. Atiyyah, *Iraq*, p. 193.

17. Ireland, *Iraq*, pp. 178, 273, 278, 311–13; Elie Kedourie, *England and the Middle East: The Destruction of the Ottoman Empire 1914–1921* (London, 1956), pp. 197–98, 204; John Marlowe, *Late Victorian: The Life of Sir Arnold Talbot Wilson* (London, 1967), pp. 207, 254; Aaron S. Klieman, *Foundations of British Policy in the Arab World: The Cairo Conference of 1921* (Baltimore, 1970), pp. 83–85, 136; Atiyyah, *Iraq*, pp. 193–211.

18. Lieutenant-General Sir Aylmer L. Haldane, *The Insurrection in Mesopotamia, 1920* (Edinburgh, 1922), pp. 19–34; Ireland, *Iraq*, pp. 145–46, 169, 174, 193–94, 241–43, 246–49, 258, 261–66, 272–73; Stephen H. Longrigg, *Iraq 1900 to 1950: A Political, Social, and Economic History* (London, 1953), pp. 113–21; Kedourie, *England and the Middle East*, pp. 181–93; Marlowe, *Late Victorian*, pp. 153–54, 189–90, 212–13; Atiyyah, *Iraq*, pp. 261–354.

19. Haldane, *Insurrection*, p. 64; Atiyyah, *Iraq*, pp. 339, 344.

20. Haldane, *Insurrection*, p. 331.

21. Ireland, *Iraq*, pp. 220–21, 274–75, 277, 313; Longrigg, *Iraq*, pp. 122–23.

22. Ireland, *Iraq*, pp. 277–87, 363; Longrigg, *Iraq*, pp. 126–28; Atiyyah, *Iraq*, pp. 360–62.

23. Ireland, *Iraq*, pp. 303–18; Longrigg, *Iraq*, pp. 130–31; Klieman, *Foundations of British Policy*, pp. 96–102; Atiyyah, *Iraq*, pp. 362–67.

24. Ireland, *Iraq*, pp. 338–40, 350–62; Peter Sluglett, *Britain in Iraq 1914–1932* (London, 1976), pp. 67–78.

25. The text of the treaty is in Hurewitz, *The Middle East and North Africa in World Politics*, II, pp. 310–12.

26. The text of the military agreement is in FO 371/12260, E4432/86/65.

27. Ireland, *Iraq*, pp. 366–67; Hanna Batatu, *The Old Social Classes and the Revolutionary Movements of Iraq: A Study of Iraq's Old Landed and Commercial Classes and of its Communists, Bathists, and Free Officers* (Princeton, N.J., 1978), p. 89.

28. The last British army battalion left Iraq in March 1927, and the last Indian army battalion was withdrawn in November 1928. Jafna L. Cox, "A Splendid Training Ground: The Importance to the Royal Air Force of its Role in Iraq, 1919–32," *The Journal of Imperial and Commonwealth History*, Vol. 13 (1985), p. 175.

Notes for Chapter 2—The End of the Mandate

1. Cabinet conclusion, 9 Sept. 1929, CAB 23/61; colonial office to Sir Gilbert Clayton (British high commissioner in Iraq), 11 Sept. 1929, CO 730/148, file 68444, part 1.
2. Minute by J. H. Hall (Middle East department of the colonial office), 18 March 1930, CO 730/151, file 78025, part 2.
3. Ireland, *Iraq*, pp. 377–78, 406, 470–71; Sluglett, *Britain in Iraq*, pp. 79–80.
4. Arnold J. Toynbee, *Survey of International Affairs 1925*, Vol. I: *The Islamic World since the Peace Settlement* (London, 1927), pp. 471–528; Ireland, *Iraq*, pp. 406–09; John Joseph, *The Nestorians and their Muslim Neighbors: A Study of Western Influence on their Relations* (Princeton, N.J., 1961), pp. 175–83; Sluglett, *Britain in Iraq*, pp. 103–25.
5. Minute by G. W. Rendel (eastern department of the foreign office), 4 Sept. 1929, FO 371/13758, E4466/6/93; minute by A. M. Cadogan (foreign office adviser on League of Nations affairs), 6 Sept. 1929, FO 371/13758, E4385/6/93.
6. Memorandum by the Middle East department of the colonial office, "New treaty with Iraq," 10 Feb. 1930, CO 730/151, file 78025, part 1.
7. At this time British goods accounted for nearly 35 percent of Iraq's imports. Memorandum by the Middle East department of the colonial office, "New treaty with Iraq," 10 Feb. 1930, CO 730/151, file 78025, part 1.
8. The subject of the British airbases in Iraq is discussed in detail in the following chapter.
9. Atiyyah, *Iraq*, p. 33; Batatu, *The Old Social Classes*, p. 40.
10. Batatu, *The Old Social Classes*, pp. 200, 293–97.
11. Atiyyah, *Iraq*, p. 33; Batatu, *The Old Social Classes*, p. 40.
12. Note by Sir Henry Dobbs (British high commissioner in Iraq), "The Internal Situation in Iraq," 27 June 1927, FO 371/12259, E3220/86/65; note by C. J. Edmonds (acting adviser to the Iraqi ministry of the interior), 27 Sept. 1927, CO 730/123, file 40465; Air Vice-Marshal Sir Edward Ellington (air officer commanding in Iraq) to Sir Hugh Trenchard (chief of the air staff), 4 Oct. 1927, CO 730/123, file 40465; memorandum by Dobbs, 18 Oct. 1927, CO 730/123, file 40465; Elie Kedourie, *The Chatham House Version and Other Middle-Eastern Studies* (New York, 1970), pp. 283–85; Sluglett, *Britain in Iraq*, pp. 310–13.
13. Batatu, *The Old Social Classes*, p. 47.
14. Longrigg, *Iraq*, p. 180.
15. Ireland, *Iraq*, p. 298.
16. Kedourie, *England and the Middle East*, p. 212.
17. Sluglett, *Britain in Iraq*, pp. 142–47, 150–53.
18. Mohammad A. Tarbush, *The Role of the Military in Politics: A Case Study of Iraq to 1941* (London, 1982), pp. 78–79.
19. Batatu, *The Old Social Classes*, p. 423.
20. Dobbs to L. S. Amery (colonial secretary), 4 Dec. 1928, FO 406/63; Ireland, *Iraq*, pp. 76, 85–86, 89, 94, 132; Sluglett, *Britain in Iraq*, pp. 239–53; Batatu, *The Old Social Classes*, pp. 24, 86–100.
21. Batatu, *The Old Social Classes*, p. 40.
22. Toynbee, *Survey 1925*, p. 507.

23. *Ibid.*, pp. 520–21.
24. Great Britain, colonial office, *Special Report by His Majesty's Government in the United Kingdom of Great Britain and Northern Ireland to the Council of the League of Nations on the Progress of Iraq during the Period 1920–1931* (hereafter referred to as *Special Report on Iraq*) (London, 1931), pp. 258–64; Arnold J. Toynbee, *Survey of International Affairs 1934* (London, 1935), pp. 125–32; Longrigg, *Iraq*, pp. 183, 185, 194–96; Joseph, *Nestorians*, pp. 181–82, 189–90; Hassan Arfa, *The Kurds: An Historical and Political Study* (London, 1966), p. 117; Sluglett, *Britain in Iraq*, pp. 118–25, 182–94.
25. Batatu, *The Old Social Classes*, pp. 39–40.
26. *Ibid.*, pp. 40, 247, 311; Kedourie, *Chatham House Version*, pp. 300–01; Atiyyah, *Iraq*, pp. 95, 223, 282.
27. The Assyrian question is discussed in more detail in Chapter 4.
28. John Darwin, "Imperialism in Decline? Tendencies in British Imperial Policy Between the Wars," *The Historical Journal*, Vol 23 (1980), pp. 657–79; Darwin, *Britain, Egypt and the Middle East*, passim; John Gallagher, *The Decline, Revival and Fall of the British Empire: The Ford Lectures and other Essays* (Cambridge, 1982), pp. 97, 109–10, 126.
29. William Ashworth, *An Economic History of England 1870–1939* (London, 1960), pp. 285–91.
30. Alan S. Milward, *The Economic Effects of the Two World Wars on Britain* (London, 1970), p. 50.
31. *Ibid.*, p. 50.
32. Sidney Pollard, *The Development of the British Economy 1914–1967* (London, 1969), p. 188.
33. Paul Kennedy, *The Realities Behind Diplomacy: Background Influences on British External Policy 1865–1980* (London, 1981), pp. 147, 228.
34. Paul Kennedy, *The Rise and Fall of British Naval Mastery* (London, 1976), pp. 270–72; Kennedy, *Realities*, pp. 238–39.
35. Kennedy, *Naval Mastery*, p. 271.
36. Robin Higham, *Armed Forces in Peacetime: Britain 1918–1940, A Case Study* (London, 1962), pp. 326–27.
37. *Ibid.*, pp. 326–27.
38. A. P. Thornton, *The Imperial Idea and its Enemies: A Study in British Power* (London, 1959), pp. 184, 303–07, 313–14; Max Beloff, *Imperial Sunset*, Vol. I: *Britain's Liberal Empire 1897–1921* (London, 1969), pp. 347–48, 361; Kennedy, *Naval Mastery*, p. 272; Kennedy, *Realities*, pp. 238, 241.
39. Lieutenant-Colonel R. S. Stafford, *The Tragedy of the Assyrians* (London, 1935), pp. 6, 97; Toynbee, *Survey 1934*, p. 113; Ireland, *Iraq*, pp. 154, 355, 377; Marlowe, *Late Victorian*, pp. 162–64; Sluglett, *Britain in Iraq*, pp. 79, 264.
40. Memorandum by Viscount Cecil (chancellor of the duchy of Lancaster), 17 June 1927, CO 730/120, file 40299, part 2.
41. S. R. Mehrotra, *India and the Commonwealth 1885–1929* (London, 1965), pp. 208–53; H. H. Dodwell (ed.), *The Cambridge History of India*, Vol. VI: *The Indian Empire 1858–1969* (Delhi, n.d.), pp. 587–616; Toynbee, *Survey 1925*, pp. 189–230, 361–63; Arnold J. Toynbee, *Survey of International Affairs 1928* (London, 1929), pp. 321–28; Kennedy, *Realities*, p. 242; Darwin "Imperialism in Decline?," pp. 657–79; Darwin, *Britain, Egypt and the Middle East*, passim; Gallagher, *British Empire*, pp. 97, 109–10, 126.
42. Margalith, *International Mandates*, pp. 46, 165–67, 197; Wright, *Mandates*,

pp. 231, 324–27, 339, 445–47, 503, 530, 537; Norman Bentwich, *The Mandates System* (London, 1930), pp. 4–5, 16–20.

43. B. H. Bourdillon (acting British high commissioner in Iraq) to Faysal, 22 July 1927, CO 730/120, file 40299, part 2.

44. The text of this treaty is in CO 730/125, file 40626B. However, because the two parties failed to agree on the terms of certain subsidiary documents, the treaty was not ratified and never entered into effect.

45. Minute by Hall, 16 Aug. 1929, CO 730/148, file 68444, part 1; memorandum by the colonial office, "Future Policy in Iraq," 31 Aug. 1929, CO 730/151, file 78025, part 1.

46. The text of this agreement is in FO 371/12260, E4432/86/65.

47. Dobbs to colonial office, 16 Oct. 1928, CO 730/134, file 58400, part 1.

48. Colonial office to Dobbs, 25 Oct. 1928, CO 730/134, file 58400, part 1; minute by Hall, 30 Oct. 1928, CO 730/134, file 58400, part 1; memorandum by Amery, 7 Nov. 1928, CO 730/134, file 58400, part 3; colonial office to Dobbs, 17 Dec. 1928, CO 730/134, file 58400, part 2.

49. Dobbs to colonial office, 6 June 1928, CO 730/134, file 58400, part 1; note by the colonial office, "The position of the Forces in Iraq in the event of the expiry of the Military Agreement," 22 Aug. 1928, CO 730/134, file 58400, part 1.

50. Colonial office to Dobbs, 25 Oct. 1928, CO 730/134, file 58400, part 1; Dobbs to colonial office, 31 Dec. 1928, CO 730/134, file 58400, part 2.

51. Dobbs to colonial office, 6 June 1928 and 14 Aug. 1928, CO 730/134, file 58400, part 1; colonial office to treasury, 20 Aug. 1928, FO 371/13034, E4161/133/65.

52. Opinion of the law officers of the crown, 3 Aug. 1928, FO 371/13034, E4047/133/65; minute by Rendel, 9 Jan. 1929, FO 371/13757, E169/6/93; minute by Hall, 9 May 1929, CO 730/139, file 68015, part 2.

53. Clayton to colonial office, 13 May 1929, CO 730/139, file 68015, part 2; memorandum by the colonial office, "Future Policy in Iraq," 31 Aug. 1929, CO 730/151, file 78025, part 1.

54. Dobbs to colonial office, 24 March 1927, CO 730/151, file 78025, part 1; Clayton to colonial office, 22 July 1929 and 1 Sept. 1929, CO 730/151, file 78025, part 1.

55. Memorandum by the colonial office, "Iraq: Suggested Treaty Revision," 28 Sept. 1927, CO 730/120, file 40299A, part 1; memorandum by Lord Passfield (colonial secretary), 3 Sept. 1929, CO 730/151, file 78025, part 1.

56. Briton C. Busch, *Britain, India, and the Arabs, 1914–1921* (Berkeley, Calif., 1971), p. 448.

57. Air ministry paper for the senior division at Camberley, 1930, AIR 9/14, folio 51.

58. Minute by Hall, 6 Sept. 1929, CO 730/148, file 68444, part 1.

59. That is, so long as Iraq continued to abide by the terms of the Anglo-Iraqi military agreement which expired in December 1928.

60. Air ministry to colonial office, 18 Oct. 1928, CO 730/134, file 58400, part 1; minute by Hall, 30 Oct. 1928, CO 730/134, file 58400, part 1.

61. Prasad, Sri Nandan, *Official History of the Indian Armed Forces in the Second World War 1939–1945: Expansion of the Armed Forces and Defence Organisation 1939–1945* (Calcutta, 1956), pp. xx, 8–9, Beloff, *Imperial Sunset*, I, p. 311, B. R. Tomlinson, "India and the British Empire, 1880–1935," *The In-*

dian Economic and Social History Review, Vol. 12 (1975), pp. 358–62; Brian Bond, *British Military Policy between the Two World Wars* (Oxford, 1980), pp. 102–3, 109–12; Gallagher, *British Empire,* pp. 99, 102; David Fraser, *And We Shall Shock Them: The British Army in the Second World War* (London, 1983), p. 12.

62. Prasad, *Expansion of the Armed Forces,* p. 8.
63. Colonel G. M. Orr, "The Military Forces in India," *Army Quarterly,* Vol. 18 (1929), p. 395.
64. Prasad, *Expansion of the Armed Forces,* p. 9.
65. Arnold J. Toynbee, *Survey of International Affairs 1930* (London, 1931), pp. 274–83; Bond, *British Military Policy,* pp. 87–88.
66. Clayton to colonial office, 4 Sept. 1929, CO 730/151, file 78025, part 1.
67. Hayyim J. Cohen, "The Anti-Jewish *Farhud* in Baghdad, 1941," *Middle Eastern Studies,* Vol. 3 (1966), p. 5.
68. Clayton to colonial office, 1 Sept. 1929, CO 730/151, file 78025, part 1; minute by Rendel, 2 Sept. 1929, FO 371/13758, E4385/6/93; memorandum by Passfield, 3 Sept. 1929, CO 730/151, file 78025, part 1.
69. Dobbs to colonial office, 24 March 1927, CO 730/151, file 78025, part 1; Clayton to colonial office, 22 July 1929, CO 730/151, file 78025, part 1.
70. The text of this treaty, together with the annexure and all the published and unpublished letters that accompanied it, is in FO 371/27092, E1576/146/93. It is reprinted in Tarbush, *The Role of the Military in Politics,* pp. 198–222. However, Tarbush inadvertently omitted article 4 of the annexure and, as a result, incorrectly numbered the remaining articles. Thus in his account articles 5, 6, and 7 of the annexure are wrongly labeled as articles 4, 5, and 6.

Notes for Chapter 3—The British Airbases

1. Comments by Sir Hugh Trenchard (chief of the air staff) at an interdepartmental conference, 3 Sept. 1929, FO 371/13758, E4385/6/93; memorandum by the air ministry, Nov. 1929, AIR 9/14, folio 40; memorandum by the air staff, 7 Jan. 1930, CO 730/151, file 78025, part 1.
2. Memorandum by the air ministry, Nov. 1929, AIR 9/14, folio 40; note by the air staff, undated but probably late 1929, AIR 9/15, folio 16; memorandum by the air staff, 7 Jan. 1930, CO 730/151, file 78025, part 1.
3. Memorandum by the air ministry, Nov. 1929, AIR 9/14, folio 40.
4. Note by the air staff, 10 Oct. 1929, AIR 9/14, folio 41; memorandum by the air ministry, Nov. 1929, AIR 9/14, folio 40; memorandum by the air ministry, 12 Dec. 1929, AIR 9/14, folio 45; note by the air staff, 2 Jan. 1930, CO 730/151, file 78025, part 1.
5. Memorandum by the air ministry, Nov. 1929, AIR 9/14, folio 40; memorandum by the air staff, 7 Jan. 1930, CO 730/151, file 78025, part 1.
6. Memorandum by the air staff, 7 Jan. 1930, CO 730/151, file 78025, part 1.
7. Comment by Jafar in minute by J. H. Hall (Middle East department of the colonial office), 18 March 1930, CO 730/151, file 78025, part 2; comments by Faysal and Nuri, 17 and 29 April 1930, "Record of Proceedings of Meetings of the British and Iraqi Delegations in Baghdad, April–June 1930, Concerning the Proposed New Anglo-Iraqi Treaty" (hereafter referred to as "Record of Proceedings"), CO 730/151, file 78025, part 11; Nuri to Sir

Francis Humphrys (British high commissioner in Iraq), 6 May 1930, CO 730/151, file 78025, part 6; Humphrys to colonial office, 10 June 1930, CO 730/151, file 78025, part 8.

8. Comment by Nuri, 17 April 1930, 'Record of Proceedings'.

9. Comments by Faysal and Nuri, 3 April 1930, "Record of Proceedings." British officials doubted that the League of Nations would agree to terminate the mandate unless Iraq first concluded a treaty of alliance with Britain. Memorandum by the secretary of state for the colonies, 17 May 1930, CO 730/151, file 78025, part 6; memorandum by the colonial office, 14 June 1930, CO 730/151, file 78025, part 8.

10. Comments by Faysal and Nuri, 29 April 1930, "Record of Proceedings."

11. Comment by Faysal, 1 May 1930, "Record of Proceedings."

12. Note by the air staff, 2 May 1930, AIR 9/14, folio 50.

13. Memorandum by the air staff, 29 April 1930, AIR 9/14, folio 49.

14. Memorandum by the air ministry, Nov. 1929, AIR 9/14, folio 40; memorandum by the air staff, 29 April 1930, AIR 9/14, folio 49; interdepartmental conference, 30 April 1930, CO 730/151, file 78025, part 3.

15. Minute by Hall, 28 April 1930, CO 730/151, file 78025, part 3; memorandum by the secretary of state for the colonies, 17 May 1930, CO 730/151, file 78025, part 6; colonial office to Humphrys, 23 May 1930, CO 730/151, file 78025, part 6.

16. Interdepartmental conference, 30 April 1930, CO 730/151, file 78025, part 3; minute by Hall, 15 May 1930, CO 730/151, file 78025, part 6; memorandum by the secretary of state for the colonies, 17 May 1930, CO 730/151, file 78025, part 6.

17. Humphrys to colonial office, 25 April 1930 and 2 May 1930, CO 730/151, file 78025, part 3; Humphrys to colonial office, 14 May 1930, CO 730/151, file 78025, part 6.

18. Memorandum by the air staff, 29 April 1930, AIR 9/14, folio 49; interdepartmental conference, 30 April 1930, CO 730/151, file 78025, part 3 and FO 371/14504, E2144/41/93; note by the air staff, 2 May 1930, AIR 9/14, folio 50.

19. Memorandum by the chief of the air staff, 15 May 1930, CO 730/151, file 78025, part 6.

20. Brooke-Popham to air ministry, 12 May 1930, CO 730/151, file 78025, part 6.

21. Comment by Faysal, 9 June 1930, "Record of Proceedings"; Humphrys to colonial office, 10 June 1930, CO 730/151, file 78025, part 8.

22. Sir Archibald Clark Kerr (British ambassador in Iraq) to foreign office, 12 Dec. 1936, FO 371/20000, E8034/45/93; British embassy in Iraq, "Annual Report on Iraq for 1937," 25 Jan. 1938, FO 371/21856, E794/794/93.

23. Air Commodore F. W. Walker to Sir Charles Portal (chief of air staff), 11 Nov. 1941, AIR 8/549; Major-General I. S. O. Playfair, *History of the Second World War, United Kingdom Military Series: The Mediterranean and Middle East,* Vol. II: *The Germans come to the Help of their Ally* (London, 1956), pp. 177–97.

24. Khadduri, *Independent Iraq,* pp. 223, 237, 312; Longrigg, *Iraq,* pp. 183, 189; Eliezer Berri, *Army Officers in Arab Politics and Society* (New York, 1970), pp. 367–68; Ayad al-Qazzaz, "The Iraqi-British War of 1941: A Review Article," *International Journal of Middle Eastern Studies,* Vol. 7 (1976), p. 595; Paul

P. J. Hemphill, "The Formation of the Iraqi Army, 1921–33," in Abbas Kelidar (ed.), *The Integration of Modern Iraq* (London, 1979), p. 104; Khaldun S. Husry, "The Political Ideas of Yunis al-Sabawi," in Marwan R. Buheiry (ed.), *Intellectual Life in the Arab East, 1890–1939* (Beirut, 1981), pp. 172, 175.

25. The question of the levies is discussed in Chapter 5.

Notes for Chapter 4—The Assyrian Minority

1. Stafford, *Assyrians*, pp. 11–25; Joseph, *Nestorians*, pp. 3–39.
2. Stafford, *Assyrians*, pp. 26–30; Joseph, *Nestorians*, pp. 131–35; Reverend W. A. Wigram, *Our Smallest Ally: A Brief Account of the Assyrian Nation in the Great War* (London, 1920), pp. iv–v, 7–26.
3. Stafford, *Assyrians*, pp. 30–35; Joseph, *Nestorians*, pp. 137–44; Wigram, *Our Smallest Ally*, pp. v, 45–55.
4. Stafford, *Assyians*, pp. 36–37.
5. Stafford, *Assyrians*, pp. 39–49, 74–88; Joseph, *Nestorians*, pp. 152–83.
6. Minute by J. H. Hall (Middle East department of the colonial office), 26 July 1930, CO 730/152, file 78058; Stafford, *Assyrians*, pp. 44–62.
7. Stafford, *Assyrians*, pp. 47–62.
8. Report by Lieutenant-Colonel R. Meinertzhagen (military adviser to the Middle East department of the colonial office), "The Iraq Army and Levies," March 1923, CO 935/1; note by Squadrom Leader G. S. Reed, "The Iraq Levies," 18 July 1932, AIR 5/1255; Brigadier J. Gilbert Browne, *The Iraq Levies 1915–1932* (London, 1932), pp. 6–7, 14–15, 23; Stafford, *Assyrians*, pp. 42, 45, 47, 63–68.
9. Browne, *Iraq Levies*, pp. 34–37; Stafford, *Assyrians*, pp. 47, 67–71, 88; Joseph, *Nestorians*, pp. 195–97.
   The British authorities in Iraq allowed the Assyrians to retain their rifles and ammunition after leaving the levies because most of the Kurdish population of northern Iraq was also armed. Stafford, *Assyrians*, pp. 71–72.
10. Minute by Hall, 26 July 1930, CO 730/152, file 78058; Arthur Henderson (foreign secretary) to Gilbert Murray (chairman, executive committee, League of Nations union), 20 Jan. 1931, FO 371/15314, E385/75/93; minute by Hall, 4 June 1931, CO 730/162, file 88058, part 1; memorandum by J. C. Sterndale Bennett (eastern department of the foreign office), 8 Dec. 1931, FO 371/15317, E6091/75/93; Joseph, *Nestorians*, p. 192.
11. Memorandum by the foreign office, 21 Jan. 1932, FO 371/16028, E369/9/93; Iraqi declaration of guarantees for the protection of minorities, 30 May 1932, FO 371/16031, E4872/9/93; Stafford, *Assyrians*, pp. 92–97; Toynbee *Survey 1934*, pp. 148–49, 194–211; Ireland, *Iraq*, pp. 417–18.
12. Colonial office, *Special Report on Iraq*, p. 277; memorandum by Air Vice-Marshal E. R. Ludlow-Hewitt (air officer commanding in Iraq), 3 Aug. 1932, CO 730/178, file 96602, part 5; Stafford, *Assyrians*, pp. 89–96, 112; Longrigg, *Iraq*, pp. 183, 185, 198.
13. Manifesto of the Assyrian levies, 1 June 1932, FO 371/16035, E4531/23/93; petition of the Assyrian leaders to Humphrys, 17 June 1932, FO 371/16035, E4531/23/93; petition of the Mar Shimun to the League of Nations, 22 Sept. 1932, FO 371/16037, E6023/23/93; Stafford, *Assyrians*, pp. 107–12; Joseph, *Nestorians*, pp. 180–94.

14. Minute by Hall, 15 Aug. 1932, CO 730/178, file 96602, part 4; memorandum by the foreign office, 17 Sept. 1932, FO 371/16036, E4736/23/93; colonial office, *Special Report on Iraq*, pp. 271–72, 275; Joseph, *Nestorians*, pp. 177, 183–84.

15. A. Hormuzd Rassam (Assyrian representative) to the chairman of the permanent mandates commission of the League of Nations, 12 May 1931, FO 371/15316, E4414/75/93; petition of the Mar Shimun to the League of Nations, 22 Sept. 1932, FO 371/16037, E6023/23/93.

16. Opinion of the permanent mandates commission of the League of Nations, 14 Nov. 1932, FO 371/16037, E6023/23/93; Toynbee, *Survey 1934*, p. 148.

17. Memorandum by the colonial office, 23 Feb. 1932, FO 371/16033, E944/23/93; memorandum by the foreign office, 17 Sept. 1932, FO 371/16036, E4736/23/93; Toynbee, *Survey 1934*, pp. 141–42.

18. Ludlow-Hewitt to air ministry, 8 June 1932, FO 371/16033, E3235/23/93; petition of the Assyrian leaders to Humphrys, 17 June 1932. FO 371/16035, E4531/23/93; memorandum by Ludlow-Hewitt, 3 Aug. 1932, CO 730/178, file 96602, part 5; Stafford, *Assyrians*, pp. 114–18.

19. Minute by Hall, 15 Aug. 1932, CO 730/178, file 96602, part 4; colonial office, *Special Report on Iraq*, pp. 271–72, 275.

20. Conference of leading British and Iraqi officials in Baghdad, 3 July 1932, CO 730/177, file 96602, part 3; Nuri al-Said (Iraqi prime minister) to Humphrys, 2 Aug. 1932, FO 371/16035, E4531/23/93.

21. Humphrys to colonial office, 11 June 1932, CO 730/177 file 96602, part 1; minute by Hall, 14 June 1932, CO 730/177, file 96602, part 1.

22. Memorandum by Ludlow-Hewitt, 3 Aug. 1932, CO 730/178, file 96602, part 5; Stafford, *Assyrians*, pp. 115–16.

23. Stafford, *Assyrians*, pp. 113–25.

24. C. J. Edmonds (acting adviser to the Iraqi ministry of the interior) to G. A. D. Ogilvie-Forbes (British charge d'affaires in Iraq), 25 July 1933, FO 371/16884, E4479/7/93; Stafford, *Assyrians*, pp. 101–04, 124–31, 140–41; Joseph, *Nestorians*, pp. 199–201.

25. Ogilvie-Forbes to foreign office, 2 Aug. 1933, FO 371/16884, E4479/7/93; report by Air Vice-Marshal C. S. Burnett (air officer commanding in Iraq), 14 Dec. 1933, FO 371/17834, E946/1/93; Stafford, *Assyrians*, pp. 145–58.

26. Memorandum by Ogilvie-Forbes, 4 Sept. 1933, FO 371/16889, E5190/7/93; comments by Yasin al-Hashimi (Iraqi minister of finance) at the League of Nations, 14 Oct. 1933, FO 371/16894, E6289/7/93; Stafford, *Assyrians*, pp. 151, 159–67, 180; Khadduri, *Independent Iraq*, p. 42; Khaldun S. Husry, "The Assyrian Affair of 1933," *International Journal of Middle Eastern Studies*, Vol. 5 (1974), pp. 164, 176, 349–50, 357.

27. Report by Brigadier-General Hugo Headlam (acting inspector-general of the Iraqi army and head of the British advisory military mission), 6 Sept. 1933, FO 371/16891, E5685/7/93; Stafford, *Assyrians*, pp. 158–65; Khadduri, *Independent Iraq*, pp. 39, 42; Kedourie, *Chatham House Version*, p. 246.

28. G. A. D. Ogilvie-Forbes, the British charge d'affaires in Iraq, suspected that King Faysal himself issued the order for the pogrom. With greater assurance, this view was also held by Nuri al-Said, the Iraqi foreign minister, and by C. J. Edmonds, an Englishman who served as the acting adviser to the Iraqi ministry of the interior. Without accusing Faysal directly, R. S. Stafford, an Englishman who served as administrative inspector of the Mo-

sul and Arbil *liwas* (provinces) in northern Iraq, maintained that the highest political circles in Iraq gave unofficial and verbal instructions to the army for a massacre. Only Sir Francis Humphrys, the British ambassador in Iraq, who was usually inclined to think well of Iraqi political leaders, believed that the entire responsibility lay with the army. Memorandum by Ogilvie-Forbes, 4 Sept. 1933, FO 371/16889, E5190/7/93; views of Nuri and Edmonds in Sir Archibald Clark Kerr (British ambassador in Iraq) to foreign office, 15 Dec. 1936, FO 371/20015, E8113/1419/93; Stafford, *Assyrians*, p. 162; Humphrys to foreign office, 11 Sept. 1933, FO 371/16889, E5331/7/93.

29. Memorandum by G. W. Rendel (head of the eastern department of the foreign office), 6 Oct. 1933, FO 371/16892, E5968/7/93; report by Burnett, 14 Dec. 1933, FO 371/17834, E946/1/93; Stafford, *Assyrians*, pp. 158–92; Khadduri, *Independent Iraq*, p. 42.

Since 1933 Zionists have frequently used the massacre of the Assyrians to bolster their argument that the Jews would not be secure if Palestine became an Arab-ruled state or even a binational state. Walter Laqueur, *A History of Zionism* (New York, 1972), p. 262.

30. Memorandum by General Rowan-Robinson (inspector-general of the Iraqi army and head of the British advisory military mission), 6 Sept. 1933, FO 371/16922, E5555/3118/93; Stafford, *Assyrians*, pp. 151, 159, 193, 199, 203; Husry, "Assyrian Affair," p. 350.

31. Foreign office to Ogilvie-Forbes, 8 Aug. 1933, FO 371/16884, E4402/7/93; minute by Sterndale Bennett, 30 Aug. 1933, FO 371/16888, E5064/7/93; air ministry to foreign office, 14 Sept. 1933, FO 371/16890, E5516/7/93; foreign office to air ministry, 2 Oct. 1933, FO 371/16890, E5516/7/93.

32. Burnett to air ministry, 8 Aug. 1933, FO 371/16884, E4429/7/93.

33. Foreign office to Oligvie-Forbes, 8 Aug. 1933, FO 371/16884, E4402/7/93.

34. Minute by Rendel, 7 Aug. 1933, FO 371/16884, E4402/7/93; Sir Robert Vansittart (permanent undersecretary of state for foreign affairs) to MacDonald, 7 Aug. 1933, FO 371/16884, E4402/7/93; note by MacDonald, 8 Aug. 1933, FO 371/16884, E4439/7/93.

35. In a somewhat similar situation, in 1962, when France withdrew from Algeria, it failed to evacuate most of the Algerian Muslims who had fought on its side during the insurrection. As a result, immediately after independence the Algerian authorities killed between 30,000 and 150,000 of these people, often after torture. Alistair Horne, *A Savage War of Peace: Algeria 1954–1962* (London, 1977), pp. 537–38.

36. Memorandum by Ogilvie-Forbes, 4 Sept. 1933, FO 371/16889, E5190/7/93; comments by Major C. W. Allfrey (British advisory military mission in Iraq), 25 Sept. 1933, FO 371/16891, E5693/7/93; report by Burnett, 14 Dec. 1933, FO 371/17834, E946/1/93; Stafford, *Assyrians*, pp. 165, 193–207; Ernest Main, *Iraq: From Mandate to Independence* (London, 1935), pp. 153–54; Longrigg, *Iraq*, pp. 234, 236; Husry, "Assyrian Affair," pp. 162, 350, 357; Hemphill, "The Formation of the Iraqi Army," p. 107.

37. Memorandum by Sterndale Bennett, 22 Sept. 1933, FO 371/16891, E5653/7/93; memorandum by Sir Samuel Hoare (foreign secretary), 3 Sept. 1935, FO 371/18933, E5266/2/93; memorandum by the foreign office, 25 Jan. 1937, FO 371/20788, E601/1/93.

38. Memorandum by Rendel, 25 July 1934, FO 371/17843, E4945/1/93; con-

clusions of the cabinet committee on the Assyrians, 27 Jan. 1937, CAB 27/629.

39. Government of India to India office, 4 July 1934, L/P&S/12/2874, P.Z. 4454/34.

40. Minute by Sterndale Bennett, 9 Nov. 1933, FO 371/16893, E6101/7/93; memorandum by W. Ormsby-Gore (colonial secretary), 23 Jan. 1937, FO 371/20788, E600/1/93.

41. Memorandum by Rendel, 25 July 1934, FO 371/17843, E4945/1/93; memorandum by the foreign office, 25 Jan. 1937, FO 371/20788, E601/1/93.

42. Report by Major D. A. Thompson (land settlement expert), 28 Sept. 1933, FO 371/16894, E6279/7/93; Stafford to the British adviser to the Iraqi ministry of the interior, 10 Oct. 1933, FO 371/16894, E6231/7/93.

43. Report by the R.A.F. in Iraq, 7 Feb. 1935, FO 371/18927, E1178/2/93; memorandum by J. G. Ward (eastern department of the foreign office), 30 Dec. 1937, FO 371/21840, E98/3/93; memorandum by the foreign office, 14 Jan. 1938, FO 371/21840, E299/3/93; information from the League of Nations on the Assyrians in Syria, 9 April 1938, FO 371/21841, E2281/3/93.

44. Minute by Rendel, 17 Sept. 1937, FO 371/20792, E5502/1/93; minute by Rendel, 12 Oct. 1937, FO 371/20796, E5937/14/93; foreign office to air ministry, 2 Nov. 1937, FO 371/20791, E4471/1/93.

45. This question is discussed in more detail in the following chapter.

46. Air Vice-Marshal J. H. D'Albiac (air officer commanding in Iraq) to air officer commanding-in-chief in Egypt, 28 July 1941, FO 371/52470, E8720/8720/93; memorandum by General A. P. Wavell (commander-in-chief in India), "Operations in Iraq, Syria and Persia May 1941–January 1942," 18 Oct. 1942, FO 371/52341, E2219/2219/65.

47. Foreign office to air ministry, 19 Nov. 1941, FO 371/27084, E5012/22/93; memorandum by Anthony Eden (foreign secretary), 2 June 1945, FO 371/52419, E7425/589/93; memorandym by the secretary of state for the colonies, 12 Aug. 1946, FO 371/52420, E7900/589/93.

48. Joseph, *Nestorians,* pp. 217–18.

Notes for Chapter 5—The Levies

1. Report by Lieutenant-Colonel R. Meinertzhagen (military adviser to the Middle East department of the colonial office), "The Iraq Army and Levies," March 1923, CO 935/1; note by Squadron Leader G. S. Reed, "The Iraq Levies," 18 July 1932, AIR 5/1255; Browne, *Iraq Levies,* pp. 1–15, 23; Stafford, *Assyrians,* pp. 45, 47, 63–68.

   In Syria during the 1920s and 1930s the French raised a military force under firm French control known as the *Troupes Speciales du Levant.* Like the British administrators in Iraq who created the levies, the French authorities in Syria recruited primarily minority group members because they assumed that these people would be less nationalistic and more favorably disposed toward France's presence in the Levant. From France's perspective, during the interwar period this policy worked well. It should be noted, parenthetically, that unlike the British in Iraq, in Syria the French never permitted the creation of a national army in any way outside of their strict control. Stephen H. Longrigg, *Syria and Lebanon under French Mandate*

(London, 1958), pp. 137–38, 182, 268–70; Beeri *Army Officers in Arab Politics and Society*, pp. 33–35.

2. Note by Reed, "The Iraq Levies," 18 July 1932, AIR 5/1255; Browne, *Iraq Levies*, pp. 18–73; Stafford, *Assyrians*, pp. 65–71.

3. Busch, *Britian, India, and the Arabs*, p. 448.

4. Note by the air staff, "The Military Aspects of the Treaty with Iraq," 2 Jan. 1930, CO 730/151, file 78025, part 1; air ministry paper for senior division Camberley, 1930, AIR 9/14, folio 51; address by the chief of the air staff to the imperial defence college, "Air Policy in Imperial Defence," Dec. 1930, AIR 5/173.

5. Comments by King Faysal and Nuri al-Said (Iraqi prime minister), 17 April 1930, "Record of Proceedings," CO 730/151, file 78025, part 11; Sir Francis Humphrys (British high commissioner in Iraq) to colonial office, 25 April 1930, CO 730/151, file 78025, part 3; Stafford, *Assyrians*, pp. 71–72.

   Of course, other sections of the Iraqi population like the Kurds and the Shiite tribes were also heavily armed.

6. Meetings on 17 April and 20 June 1930, "Record of Proceedings."

7. Colonial office to Humphrys, 5 March 1930, CO 730/151, file 78025, part 2; minute by J. H. Hall (Middle East department of the colonial office), 28 April 1930, CO 730/151, file 78025, part 3.

8. Humphrys to foreign office, 23 Jan. 1935, FO 371/18950, E759/759/93.

9. Iraqi ministry of foreign affairs to British embassy in Baghdad, 25 June 1934, FO 371/17867, E4792/665/93; Yasin al-Hashimi (Iraqi prime minister) to Sir Archibald Clark Kerr (British ambassador in Iraq), 25 March 1936, FO 371/20000, E2202/45/93; Tawfiq al-Suwaydi (Iraqi foreign minister) to the British delegation at the League of Nations in Geneva, 27 Sept. 1938, FO 371/21851, E5707/298/93.

10. G. A. D. Ogilvie-Forbes (British charge d'affaires in Iraq) to foreign office, 16 Oct. 1934, FO 371/17867, E6591/665/93.

11. Minutes by W. E. Beckett (legal adviser at the foreign office), 13 Aug. 1934, and J. C. Sterndale Bennett (eastern department of the foreign office), 22 Nov. 1934, FO 371/17867, E4792/E6591/665/93.

12. Minute by Beckett, 13 Aug. 1934, FO 371/17867, E4792/665/93; minute by R. D. J. Scott-Fox (eastern department of the foreign office), 16 March 1936, FO 371/20000, E1018/45/93; comment by Beckett at interdepartmental conference, 11 May 1936, FO 371/20000, E2856/45/93.

13. Foreign office to colonial office, 9 April 1930, FO 371/14503, E1679/41/93; minutes by Lord Monteagle (head of the eastern department of the foreign office) and Beckett, 28 May 1930, FO 371/14505, E2706/41/93.

14. Meeting on 20 June 1930, "Record of Proceedings."

15. Colonial office to Humphrys, 21 June 1930, CO 730/151, file 78025, part 8.

16. Minute by Rendel, 28 June 1930, FO 371/14507, E3464/41/93.

17. Humphrys to Air Vice-Marshal E. R. Ludlow-Hewitt (air officer commanding in Iraq), 14 July 1932, FO 371/16048, E3963/3308/93; Humphrys to foreign office, 16 May 1933, FO 371/16914, E2825/620/93; foreign office to Ogilvie-Forbes, 29 June 1933, FO 371/16914, E3394/620/93; minute by Sterndale Bennett, 22 Nov. 1934, FO 371/17867, E6591/665/93.

18. Air ministry to foreign office, 29 Aug. 1934, FO 371/17867, E5513/665/93; Ogilvie-Forbes to foreign office, 16 Oct. 1934, FO 371/17867, E6591/665/93;

note by J. G. Ward (eastern department of the foreign office), 28 July 1936, FO 371/20000, E4830/45/93.

19. Humphrys to foreign office, 23 Jan. 1935, FO 371/18950, E759/759/93; Air Vice-Marshal W. G. S. Mitchell (air officer commanding in Iraq) to chief of the air staff, 11 March 1936, AIR 40/1419.

20. Comment by Jafar al-Askari (Iraqi defense minister) in Mitchell to chief of the air staff, 11 March 1936 AIR 40/1419; Yasin al-Hashimi to Clerk Kerr, 25 March, 1936 FO 371/20000, E2202/45/93.

21. Proposal of Taha al-Hashimi (chief of the Iraqi general staff) and Nuri al-Said (Iraqi foreign minister) at a meeting with British officials in Baghdad, 16 April 1936, FO 371/20000, E2590/45/93.

22. Tawfiq al-Suwaydi to James Morgan (British charge d'affaires in Iraq), 22 Feb. 1938, FO 371/21850, E1224/298/93.

23. Interdepartmental conference, 11 May 1936, FO 371/20000, E2856/45/93; Morgan to foreign office, 26 Feb. 1938, FO 371/21850, E1224/298/93; air ministry to foreign office, 14 April 1938, FO 371/21850, E2176/298/93.

24. Memorandum by the air officer commanding in Iraq, 9 Dec. 1936, AIR 23/653; air ministry to foreign office, 14 April 1938, FO 371/21850, E2176/298/93; foreign office to air ministry, 2 June 1939, FO 371/23204, E3896/79/93; air ministry to foreign office, 12 July 1939, FO 371/23205, E5010/79/93.

25. Foreign office to air ministry, 24 May 1938, FO 371/21850, E2176/298/93; interdepartmental conference, 24 Jan. 1939, FO 371/23204, E899/79/93; foreign office to air ministry, 2 June 1939, FO 371/23204, E3896/79/93.

26. Iraqi ministry of foreign affairs to British embassy in Baghdad, 25 June 1934, FO 371/17867, E4792/665/93; Yasin al-Hashimi to Clark Kerr, 25 March 1936, FO 371/20000, E2202/45/93; Tawfiq al-Suwaydi to the British delegation at the League of Nations in Geneva, 27 Sept. 1938, FO 371/21851, E5707/298/93.

27. Minute by Ward, 26 June 1937, FO 371/20790, E3372/1/93; minutes by Ward, 19 Aug. 1937, and Rendel, 14 Oct. 1937, FO 371/20791, E4471/1/93; foreign office to air ministry, 2 Nov. 1937, FO 371/20791, E4471/1/93; comments by Rendel at interdepartmental conference, 26 Nov. 1937, FO 371/20793, E7223/1/93.

28. These conditions were incorporated in a letter from Humphrys to Nuri on 15 July 1930 that accompanied the treaty. For Nuri's intransigent demand on this question, see also Humphrys to foreign office, 15 Dec. 1932, FO 371/16052, E6843/5666/93.

29. Comments by Rendel at interdepartmental conference, 26 Nov. 1937, FO 371/20793, E7223/1/93; foreign office to air ministry, 24 May 1938, FO 371/21850, E2176/298/93; foreign office to air ministry, 2 June 1939, FO 371/23204, E3896/79/93.

30. Air ministry to foreign office, 14 April 1938, FO 371/21850, E2176/298/93; comments by Air Vice-Marshal Peirse at interdepartmental conference, 24 Jan. 1939, FO 371/23204, E899/79/93; air ministry to foreign office, 12 July 1939, FO 371/23205, E5010/79/93.

31. British military forces in Iraq weekly intelligence summary, 21 Oct. 1941, AIR 40/1419; interdepartmental conference, 11 Sept. 1944, FO 371/40065, E5922/322/93; memorandum by the office of the resident minister in Cairo, 31 Aug. 1945, FO 371/45289, E6719/78/93.

32. Air Vice-Marshal J. H. D'Albiac (air officer commanding in Iraq) to air officer commanding-in-chief in Egypt, 28 July 1941, FO 371/52470, E8720/8720/93; air ministry to foreign office, 25 Aug. 1941, FO 371/27084, E5012/22/93.

    At one point during this operation the Assyrian troops stormed and captured a strongly defended Iraqi position, in the process seizing sixty machine-guns. Note by Air Chief-Marshal Sir Edgar Ludlow-Hewitt, 10 Oct. 1941, FO 371/27084, E6585/22/93.

33. According to the British air officer commanding in Iraq, "The determination of the Assyrians' at Fallujah when a weak company defied an Iraqi Brigade, supported by tanks, and one platoon counter-attacked and cleared the town when full of Iraqi soldiers was one of the most important factors in breaking the morale of the Iraqi army which certainly was broken at Fallujah." D'Albiac to Sir Kinahan Cornwallis (British ambassador to Iraq), 26 June 1941, FO 624/25, file 506.

34. L. S. Amery, *My Political Life,* Vol. II: *War and Peace 1914–1929* (London, 1953), pp. 312–13.

Notes for Chapter 6—Arab Independence and Unity

1. Antonius, *The Arab Awakening,* Chapters 10–14; Kedourie, *England and the Middle East,* pp. 142–74.

2. Sir Francis Humphrys (British ambassador in Iraq) to foreign office, 21 Dec. 1932, FO 371/16011, E6888/4478/65; Ireland, *Iraq,* p. 356; Khaldun S. Husry, "King Faysal I and Arab Unity, 1930–33," *Journal of Contemporary History,* Vol. 10 (1975), pp. 323–25, 331–33, 337.

3. Khadduri, *Independent Iraq,* pp. 307–09; Longrigg, *Iraq,* pp. 228, 264; Batatu, *The Old Social Classes,* pp. 29, 293–94, 298, 319.

4. Note by J. C. Sterndale Bennett (eastern department of the foreign office), 13 July 1933, FO 371/16855, E4336/347/65; foreign office to F. H. W. Stonehewer-Bird (British minister in Saudi Arabia), 10 May 1939, FO 371/24548, E1759/953/65; memorandum by the eastern department of the foreign office, "Memorandum respecting Arab Federation" (hereafter simply memorandum by the foreign office), 28 Sept. 1939, FO 371/27045, E6357/6/31; foreign office to war office, 16 Dec. 1939, FO 371/23212, E7532/474/93; Y. Porath, "Nuri al-Said's Arab Unity Programme," *Middle Eastern Sutides,* Vol. 20 (1984), p. 87.

5. Memorandum by the foreign office, 28 Sept. 1939, FO 371/27045, E6357/6/31.

6. Memorandum by G. W. Rendel (head of the eastern department of the foreign office), "Attitude of His Majesty's Government towards the Question of Arab Unity" (hereafter simply memorandum by Rendel), 13 June 1933, FO 371/16855, E3119/347/65; memorandum by the foreign office, 28 Sept. 1939, FO 371/27045, E6357/6/31; foreign office to Stonehewer-Bird, 22 Aug. 1940, FO 371/24548, E2432/953/65.

7. Sir Basil Newton (British ambassador in Iraq) to foreign office, 23 Aug. 1939, FO 371/23199, E6118/54/93; memorandum by the foreign office, 28 Sept. 1939, FO 371/27045, E6357/6/31; Husry, "King Faysal I and Arab Unity," p. 327; Y. Porath, "Abdallah's Greater Syria Programme," *Middle*

eastern Studies, Vol. 20 (1984), pp. 172–89; Porath, "Nuri al-Said's Arab Unity Programme," pp. 83–84.

8. Memorandum by Rendel, 13 June 1933, FO 371/16855, E3119/347/65; memorandum by the foreign office, 28 Sept. 1939, FO 371/27045, E6357/6/31.

9. Memorandum by Rendel, 13 June 1933, FO 371/16855, E3119/347/65.

10. *Ibid.*

11. *Ibid.*

12. *Ibid.;* memorandum by the foreign office, 28 Sept. 1939, FO 371/27045, E6357/6/31; foreign office to Newton, 4 Aug. 1940, FO 371/24548, E2027/953/65; Winston S. Churchill (prime minister) to Sir K. Cornwallis (British ambassador in Iraq), 11 March 1941, FO 371/27061, E694/1/93.

13. Humphrys to foreign office, 21 Dec. 1932, FO 371/16011, E6888/4478/65; memorandum by the eastern department of the foreign office, "Proposed Arab Congress," 14 June 1933, FO 371/16855, E3120/347/65; Humphrys to foreign office, 15 July 1933, FO 371/16855, E6221/374/65.

14. Y. Porath, "Britain and Arab Unity," *Jerusalem Quarterly,* Vol. 15 (1980), p. 39.

   The treaty between Iraq and Saudi Arabia in 1936 is discussed in Arnold J. Toynbee, *Survey of International Affairs 1936* (London, 1937), pp. 788–90.

15. The text of this agreement is in Hurewitz, *The Middle East and North Africa in World Politics,* II, pp. 522–27.

16. Foreign office to Sir Maurice Peterson (British ambassador in Iraq), 29 June 1938, FO 371/21907, E2698/1573/25.

17. Iraqi ministry of foreign affairs to British embassy in Baghdad, 3 May 1938, FO 371/21907, E2698/1573/25; Peterson to foreign office, 4 May 1938, FO 371/21907, E2698/1573/25.

18. Foreign office to Peterson, 29 June 1938, FO 371/21907, E2698/1573/25.

19. Peterson to foreign office, 19 July 1938, FO 371/21907, E4643/1573/25.

20. Y. Porath, *The Palestinian Arab National Movement: From Riots to Rebellion,* Vol. II: *1929–1939* (London, 1977), pp. 204, 208; Gabriel Sheffer, "The Involvement of Arab States in the Palestine Conflict and British-Arab Relationship before World War II," *Asian and African Studies,* Vol. 10 (1974), pp. 64, 68; Y. Taggar, "The Iraqi Reaction to the Partition Plan for Palestine, 1937," in Gabriel Ben-Dor (ed.), *The Palestinians and the Middle East Conflict* (Ramat Gan, Israel, 1978), pp. 199, 205–06.

21. Khadduri, *Independent Iraq,* pp. 95–96, 98–99, 107, 110; Batatu, *The Old Social Classes,* p. 182; Porath, *The Palestinian Arab National Movement,* II, pp. 228–31; Sheffer, "The Involvement of Arab States in the Palestine Conflict," pp. 74–77; Taggar, "The Iraqi Reaction to the Partition Plan for Palestine," pp. 196–99, 206–07.

22. The text of the white paper in in Hurewitz, *The Middle East and North Africa in World Politics,* II, pp. 531–38.

23. Porath, *The Palestinian Arab National Movement,* II, pp. 288–93. For Britain's fear in the late 1930s of alienating the Arab states over the Palestinnean question, see also Elie Kedourie, *Islam in the Modern World and Other Studies* (London, 1980), Chapter 8.

24. Memorandum by the colonial office, "The Implementation of the White

Paper Policy," undated but probably March 1942, FO 371/31337, E1850/49/65; Porath, *The Palestinian Arab National Movement,* II, pp. 290–91; Michael J. Cohen, *Palestine: Retreat from the Mandate, The Making of British Policy, 1936–45* (New York, 1978), pp. 89–94.

25. Memorandum by C. J. Edmonds (adviser to the Iraqi ministry of the interior), "Present Pan-Arab Activity in Iraq," 31 July 1940, FO 371/24549, E2283/2029/65; Newton to foreign office, 3 Aug. 1940, FO 371/24549, E2283/2029/65.

26. Newton to foreign office, 31 Aug. 1940, FO 371/24548, E2572/953/65.

27. Minutes by H. M. Eyres (eastern department of the foreign office), 16 July 1940, and H. L. Baggallay (eastern department of the foreign office), 17 July 1940, FO 371/24549, E2283/2029/65; foreign office to Newton, 20 Aug. 1940, FO 371/24549, E2283/2029/65; Cohen, *Palestine,* pp. 91–94.

28. Foreign office to Newton, 4 Aug. 1940, FO 371/24548, E2027/953/65; foreign office to Stonehewer-Bird, 22 Aug. 1940, FO 371/24548, E2432/953/65.

The question of Anglo-Iraqi relations during the summer of 1940 is discussed in more detail in Chapter 11.

29. W. E. Houstoun-Boswall (British charge d'affaires in Iraq) to foreign office, 10 April 1939, FO 371/23201, E2628/72/93; Khadduri, *Independent Iraq,* p. 169; Hemphill, "The Formation of the Iraqi Army," p. 103.

Notes for Chapter 7—The Struggle for Kuwait

1. Memorandum by the India office, "Koweit 1908–1928," 1 Oct. 1928, L/P&S/18/B. 395; interdepartmental conference (including appendixes and enclosures), 5 Oct. 1933, L/P&S/12/3732, P.Z. 1384/34; Great Britain, admiralty, naval intelligence division, *Iraq and the Persian Gulf* (London, 1944), p. 149.

2. Memorandum by J. G. Ward (eastern department of the foreign office), "Smuggling from Koweit into Iraq," 10 May 1935, L/P&S/12/2878, P.Z. 3346/35; W. E. Houstoun-Boswall (British charge d'affaires in Iraq) to foreign office, 10 Sept. 1938, L/P&S/12/2879, P.Z. 7409/38; Tawfiq al-Suwaydi (Iraqi foreign minister) to R. A. Butler (parliamentary undersecretary of state for foreign affairs), 28 Sept. 1938, FO 371/21858, E5688/1982/93; conversation in London between Tawfiq al-Suwaydi and British foreign office officials, 4 Oct. 1938, FO 371/21859, E5841/1982/93; Hurewitz, *The Middle East and North Africa in World Politics,* II, pp. 477–79.

3. Sir Maurice Peterson (British ambassador in Iraq) to foreign office, 30 March 1938, R/15/1/541, ff. 13–14; Tawfiq al-Suwaydi to Butler, 28 Sept. 1938, FO 371/21858, E5688/1982/93; conversation in London between Tawfiq al-Suwaydi and British foreign office officials, 4 Oct. 1938, FO 371/21859, E5841/1982/93; admiralty, *Iraq and the Persian Gulf,* pp. 150–51; Tareq Y. Ismael, *Iraq and Iran: Roots of Conflict* (Syracuse, N.Y., 1982), pp. 54, 57.

4. Peterson to foreign office, 19 April 1938, R/15/1/541, ff. 4–5; Tawfiq al-Suwaydi to Butler, 28 Sept. 1938, FO 371/21858, E5688/1982/93.

5. Peterson to foreign office, 19 April 1938, R/15/1/541, ff. 4–5; memorandum by C. H. Fone (foreign office library), 21 May 1938, R/15/1/541, ff. 38–41; note by W. E. Beckett (legal adviser at the foreign office), 30 May 1938, R/15/5/207, ff. 30–33.

6. Interdepartmental conference, 5 Oct. 1933, L/P&S/12/3732, P.Z. 1384/34;

memorandum by G. W. Rendel (head of the eastern department of the foreign office), "Koweit," 10 May 1937, L/P&S/12/3784, P.Z. 3212/37; interdepartmental conference, 18 May 1937, L/P&S/12/3784, P.Z. 3470/37; Lord Linlithgow (viceroy of India) to Lord Zetland (secretary of state for India), 19 May 1938, L/P&S/12/2892, P.Z. 3836/38; Lieutenant-Colonel T. C. Fowle (political resident in the Persian Gulf) to India office, 31 Oct. 1938, L/P&S/12/3864, P.Z. 7742/38; G. S. De Gaury (political agent in Kuwait) to political resident, 20 Nov. 1938, R/15/1/541, ff. 104–05.

7. R.A.F. intelligence summary for Iraq for May 1938, FO 371/21832, E4042/1642/91; R.A.F. intelligence summary for Iraq for Feb. 1939, R/15/1/549, f. 110; De Gaury, intelligence summary for Kuwait for 16–28 Feb. 1939, L/P&S/12/2864, P.Z. 1744/39.

8. Political resident in the Persian Gulf to British embassy in Baghdad, 21 March 1939, L/P&S/12/2884, P.Z. 1807/39; Houstoun-Boswall to Iraqi ministry of foreign affairs, 25 March 1939, L/P&S/12/2884, P.Z. 2381/39; Houstoun-Boswall to foreign office, 20 April 1939, R/15/5/127, ff. 89–96.

9. Peterson to foreign office, 30 March 1938, R/15/1/541, ff. 13–14; Tawfiq al-Suwaydi to Butler, 28 Sept. 1938, FO 371/21858, E5688/1982/93; Houstoun-Boswall to foreign office, 25 March 1939, R/15/5/127, ff. 35–37.

10. Houstoun-Boswall to foreign office, 7 Sept. 1938, R/15/1/541, f. 84; conversation in London between Tawfiq al-Suwaydi and British foreign office officials, 4 Oct. 1938, FO 371/21859, E5841/1982/93; Houstoun-Boswall to foreign office, 25 March 1939, R/15/5/127, ff. 35–37.

11. Foreign office to India office, 26 Aug. 1938, R/15/1/541, ff. 68–74; minutes of the committee of imperial defence's standing official subcommittee for questions concerning the Middle East, 28 Sept. 1938, L/P&S/12/2892, P.Z. 7136/38.

12. Conversation in London between Tawfiq al-Suwaydi and British foreign office officials, 4 Oct. 1938, FO 371/21859, E5841/1982/93; foreign office to admirality, 5 Aug. 1939, R/15/1/541, ff. 123–32; J. G. Lorimer, *Gazetteer of the Persian Gulf, Oman, and Central Arabia,* Vol. II (Calcutta, 1908), pp. 15–16.

13. Houstoun-Boswall to foreign office, 14 Nov. 1939, R/15/1/541, ff. 141–43; foreign office to admiralty, 5 Aug. 1939, R/15/1/541, ff. 123–32; Lorimer, *Gazetteer,* II, pp. 324, 1503–05, 1927.

14. Minute by P. M. Crosthwaite (eastern department of the foreign office), 30 Nov. 1939, FO 371/23200, E7601/58/93; foreign office to India office, 16 Dec. 1939, R/15/1/541, ff. 146–49.

15. Prior to India office, 8 Feb. 1940, R/15/1/541, ff. 155–60.

16. Government of India to India office, 18 March 1940, L/P&S/12/2892, P.Z. 1624/40; India office to foreign office, 19 April 1940, R/15/5/208, ff. 152–54; Sir Basil Newton (British ambassador in Iraq) to foreign office, 16 Feb. 1940, R/15/1/541, ff. 162–63.

17. Prior to India office, 21 March 1940, R/15/1/541, ff. 179–80.

18. Prior to India office, 22 March 1940, L/P&S/12/2892, P.Z. 1715/40.

19. Foreign office to India office, 4 May 1940, R/15/5/208, ff. 156–57.

20. Newton to foreign office, 15 April 1940, R/15/5/185, ff. 181–85.

21. Foreign office to India office, 5 May 1940, L/P&S/12/2884, P.Z. 2631/40.

22. Political resident to India office, 22 Feb. 1939, R/15/5/184, f. 245; political resident to British charge d'affaires in Iraq, 22 April 1939, R/15/5/184, f.

275; India office to foreign office, 26 March 1940, FO 371/24545, E1326/309/91; India office to political resident, 15 May 1940, FO 371/24545, E1758/309/91.

23. Newton to Nuri al-Said (Iraqi foreign minister), 7 Oct. 1940, R/15/1/525, ff. 126–28; British embassy in Baghdad to Iraqi ministry of foreign affairs, 17 Feb. 1941, L/P&S/12/2884, P.Z. 1501/41.

24. Newton to foreign office, 29 Nov. 1940, R/15/5/184, ff. 108–09; Newton to foreign office, 29 March 1941, R/15/5/208, ff. 164–65.

25. Newton to foreign office, 26 April 1940, L/P&S/12/2892, P.Z. 2596/40.

26. The dispute over the Iraqi-Kuwaiti border and the story behind the construction and eventual dismantling of the British port at Umm Qasr are discussed in more detail in Daniel Silverfarb, "The British Government and the Question of Umm Qasr 1938–45," *Asian and African Studies*, Vol. 16 (1982).

Notes for Chapter 8—The Supply of Arms

1. Sir Basil Newton (British ambassador in Iraq) to foreign office, 30 May 1939 and 19 June 1939, FO 371/23210, E4083/E4611/474/93; Newton to foreign office, 3 July 1939, FO 371/23273, E4625/1809/25; Newton to foreign office, 21 June 1940, FO 371/24556,E2173/220/93.

2. Comments by Hikmat Sulayman (Iraqi prime minister) and General Bakr Sidqi (chief of the Iraqi general staff) in Sir Archibald Clark Kerr (British ambassador in Iraq) to foreign office, 22 Dec. 1936, FO 371/20796, E44/19/93; comment by Muhammad Ali Jawad (head of the Iraqi air force) at a meeting in London with officials of the British air ministry, 11 May 1937, FO 371/20794, E3104/2/93; comment by Nuri al-Said (Iraqi prime minister) in C. W. Baxter (head of the eastern department of the foreign office) to Sir Maurice Peterson (British ambassador in Iraq), 24 Feb. 1939, FO 371/23207, E1502/374/93; comment by Husayn Fauzi (chief of the Iraqi general staff) at a conference in Baghdad between British and Iraqi military officers, 25 Feb. 1939, FO 371/23211, E4705/474/93.

3. Khadduri, *Independent Iraq*, pp. 324–30; Longrigg, *Iraq*, p. 267.

4. Major-General Bruce Hay (inspector-general of the Iraqi army and head of the British advisory military mission) to war office, 9 March 1935, FO 371/18954, E1965/1965/93.

5. Comment by air ministry official at interdepartmental conference, 30 Dec. 1936, FO 371/20794, E2/2/93.

6. Some of the most notable members of this group were General Bakr Sidqi, chief of the general staff in 1936–37; Rashid Ali al-Gaylani, prime minister in 1940–41; and Colonels Salah al-Din al-Sabbagh, Fahmi Said, Mahmud Salman, and Kamil Shabib, all of whom were very influential military commanders in the late 1930s, and early 1940s. Khadduri, *Independent Iraq*, pp. 78, 125, 162–63, 169, 172–73, 181, 192, 223; Beeri, *Army Officers in Arab Politics*, pp. 37, 367–72; Tarbush, *The Role of the Military in Politics*, p. 165.

7. Ghazi, the king of Iraq between 1933 and 1939, was particularly prominent in the agitation for Iraqi annexation of Kuwait. Khadduri, *Independent Iraq*, p. 141; Tarbush, *The Role of the Military in Politics*, p. 248.

8. Khadduri, *Independent Iraq*, pp. 34–35, 61–62, 115–16; Iraqi legation in

London to British foreign office, 7 April 1937, FO 371/20797, E1925/19/93.
In 1932 the Iraqi people possessed in all well over 100,000 rifles, while the government owned only 15,000. Khadduri, *Independent Iraq*, p. 34.

9. Great Britain, colonial office, *Report by His Majesty's Government in the United Kingdom of Great Britain and Northern Ireland to the Council of the League of Nations on the Administration of Iraq for the period January to October, 1932* (London, 1933), pp. 2–4; Toynbee, *Survey 1934*, p. 129; Sluglett, *Britain in Iraq*, pp. 213–14.

10. Clark Kerr to foreign office, 22 Dec. 1936 and 22 March 1937, FO 371/20796, E44/E1660/19/93; Khadduri, *Independent Iraq*, p. 118.

11. Khadduri, *Independent Iraq*, p. 132.

12. This question is discussed in more detail in Chapter 9.

13. Longrigg, *Oil*, pp. 76–79; Shwadran, *Oil*, pp. 240–42; memorandum by the export credits guarantee department, "Export Credits for Iraq," 8 May 1939, FO 371/23208, E3440/374/93. The oil question in Iraq is discussed in more detail in Chapter 10.

14. The Iraqi financial year began on 1 April and ended on 31 March. British embassy in Iraq, "Annual Report on Iraq for 1933," 28 March 1934, FO 371/17871, E2204/2204/93.

15. From 1932 the Iraqi dinar was linked to the British pound sterling and had the same value. British embassy in Iraq, "Annual Report on Iraq for 1932," 18 May 1933, FO 371/16922, E2831/2831/93.

16. British embassy in Iraq, "Annual Report on Iraq for 1933," 28 March 1934, FO 371/17871, E2204/2204/93; Newton to foreign office, 10 June 1940 and 19 Oct. 1940, FO 371/24556, E2198/E2913/203/93.

17. Inspector of the Iraqi air force, "Quarterly Report on the Iraqi Air Force," 15 June 1937, FO 371/20794, E4111/2/93.

18. Note by air ministry, "Forces in the Middle East," 18 June 1932, AIR 9/14, folio 76; Major–General G. G. Waterhouse (inspector-general of the Iraqi army and head of the British advisory military mission), "Quarterly Report on the Iraqi Army and Air Force," 31 Aug. 1940, FO 371/24551, E1235/15/93.

19. British embassy in Iraq, "Annual Report on Iraq for 1933," 28 March 1934, FO 371/17871, E2204/2204/93; British advisory military mission, "Quarterly Report on the Iraqi Air Force," 30 Nov. 1941, FO 371/31366, E1108/101/93.

20. Note by the air staff, 10 Oct. 1929, AIR 9/14, folio 41; comment by Sir Francis Humphrys (British high commissioner in Iraq), 17 April 1930, "Record of Proceedings," CO 730/151, file 78025, part 11; interdepartmental conference, 30 Dec. 1936, FO 371/20794, E2/2/93; minute by J. G. Ward (eastern department of the foreign office), 7 May 1937, FO 371/20797, E2432/19/93.

21. Basil Collier, *History of the Second World War, United Kingdom Military Series: The Defence of the United Kingdom* (London, 1957), p. 65.

22. Fraser, *And We Shall Shock Them*, p. 22.

23. *Ibid.*, p. 22.

24. M. M. Postan et al, *History of the Second World War, United Kingdom Civil Series: Design and Development of Weapons: Studies in Government and Industrial Organisation* (London, 1964), p. 263.

25. Compton Mackenzie, *Eastern Epic,* Vol I: *September 1939–March 1943 Defence* (London, 1951), p. 9; Prasad, *Expansion of the Armed Forces,* pp. xx–xxii, 4–6.
26. Minutes of the committee of imperial defence, 1 Dec. 1938, CAB 2/8.
27. Memorandum by the chiefs of staff, 28 Nov. 1938, CAB 4/29, paper 1488; report by the deputy chiefs of staff, 5 July 1939, CAB 16/219, paper 28.
28. Minute by Ward, 17 Feb. 1937, FO 371/20796, E896/19/93; memorandum by the foreign office, 20 June 1939, CAB 16/219, paper 4.
29. Iraqi ministry of foreign affairs to Clark Kerr, 21 Jan. 1937, FO 371/20796, E692/19/93; memorandum by Ward, 2 April 1937, FO 371/20797, E1835/19/93.
30. War office to foreign office, 19 May 1937, FO 371/20797, E2753/19/93.
31. War office to foreign office, 30 April 1938, FO 371/21853, E2525/448/93.
32. War office to Waterhouse, 12 May 1939, FO 371/23206, E3568/178/93.
33. Iraqi ministry of defence to Iraqi legation in London, 15 Feb. 1936, FO 371/20005, E1433/375/93; war office to foreign office, 7 May 1936, FO 371/20005, E2599/375/93.
34. British embassy in Baghdad to foreign office, 13 Aug. 1936, FO 371/20006, E5396/375/93.
35. Clark Kerr to foreign office, 20 Feb. 1937, FO 371/20796, E1450/19/93.
36. Major-General H. W. M. Watson (inspector-general of the Iraqi army and head of the British advisory military mission), "Quarterly Report on the Iraqi Army and Air Force," 2 Jan. 1938, FO 371/21853, E448/448/93.
37. War office to foreign office, 5 May 1937, FO 371/20797, E2530/19/93.
38. Hay to the chief of the Iraqi general staff, 17 June 1936, FO 371/20006, E4174/375/93.
39. Waterhouse to the Iraqi minister of defence, 26 Oct. 1940, FO 371/24552, E3016/47/93.
40. Jafar al-Askari (Iraqi defense minister) to the Iraqi legation in London, 15 Feb. 1936, FO 371/20005, E1433/375/93; Yasin al-Hashimi (Iraqi prime minister) to Clark Kerr, 9 May 1936, FO 371/20005, E2789/375/93; comment by Rashid Ali (Iraqi minister of the interior) in British embassy in Baghdad to foreign office, 3 Aug. 1936, FO 371/20006, E5337/375/93; comment by Tawfiq al-Suwaydi (Iraqi foreign minister) in Oswald Scott (British charge d'affaires in Iraq) to foreign office, 5 Nov. 1937, FO 371/20798, E6855/19/93; comments by Taha al-Hashimi (Iraqi defence minister) in Waterhouse to W. E. Houstoun-Boswall (British charge d'affaires in Iraq), 20 April 1939, FO 371/23206, E3208/178/93, and in C. J. Edmonds (adviser to the Iraqi ministry of the interior) to Newton, 3 Jan. 1941, Edmonds' papers, box 2, file 3; Taha al-Hashimi, *Mudhakkirat Taha al-Hashimi* (Memoirs of Taha al-Hashimi), Vol. I: *1919–1943* (Beirut, 1967), pp. 198, 365, 400, 411.
41. Clark Kerr to foreign office, 15 May 1935 and 16 May 1935, FO 371/18953, E3287/E3042/1583/93.
42. Yasin al-Hashimi to Clark Kerr, 9 May 1936, FO 371/20005, E2789/375/93.
43. Conference in Baghdad between British and Iraqi military officers, 25 Feb. 1939, FO 371/23211, E4705/474/93; similar conferences on 30 Sept. 1939 and 13 May 1940, AIR 23/667.
44. Memorandum by Ward, "Recrudescence of Moslem Agitation against Re-

ligious Minorities in Northern Iraq," 19 Feb. 1936, FO 371/20002, E968/147/93.

45. Clark Kerr to foreign office, 22 May 1936, FO 371/20015, E3062/1575/93; note by Edmonds, 1 June 1936, FO 371/20015, E3560/1575/93; Khadduri, *Independent Iraq*, pp. 57, 61–62, 115–16; Longrigg, *Iraq*, pp. 242–43.

46. Acting inspector of the Iraqi air force, "Quarterly Report on the Iraqi Air Force," 30 Sept. 1935, FO 371/18951, E6537/759/93; British embassy in Iraq, "Annual Report on Iraq for 1936," 30 Jan. 1937, FO 371/20803, E1055/1055/93; inspector of the Iraqi air force, "Quarterly Report on the Iraqi Air Force," 15 June 1937, FO 371/20794, E4111/2/93; Longrigg, *Iraq*, pp. 242–43.
    In 1935 alone the Iraqi air force dropped 5,678 bombs on rebellious subjects. Tarbush, *The Role of the Military in Politics*, p. 112.

47. Stafford, *Assyrians*, pp. 165, 177; Khadduri, *Independent Iraq*, pp. 42, 87, 108, 125; Longrigg, *Iraq*, pp. 235, 245, 250; minute by Ward, 29 Oct. 1936, FO 371/20013, E6784/1419/93.

48. Memorandum by Air Vice-Marshal W. G. S. Mitchell (air officer commanding in Iraq), 3 Nov. 1936, AIR 20/596; minute by J. C. Sterndale Bennett (eastern department of the foreign office), 19 Nov. 1936, FO 371/20014, E7147/1419/93; minute by the deputy director of operations at the air ministry, 30 Nov. 1936, AIR 20/596.

49. Air ministry to Mitchell, 4 Dec. 1936, AIR 23/653; minute by Ward, 6 Jan. 1937, FO 371/20796, E45/19/93; air ministry to foreign office, 4 May 1938, FO 371/21853, E2611/448/93; war office to foreign office, 12 April 1939, FO 371/23206, E2727/178/93.

50. Minute by G. W. Rendel (head of the eastern department of the foreign office), 18 Sept. 1936, FO 371/20006, E5961/375/93; minute by Ward, 6 Nov. 1936, FO 371/20013, E6940/1419/93; war office to foreign office, 21 July 1937, FO 371/20797, E4201/19/93.

51. Minute by Ward, 15 Feb. 1937, FO 371/20794, E859/2/93; foreign office to war office, 10 Nov. 1939, FO 371/23207, E7423/178/93.

52. Report by the chiefs of staff, "Military Co-operation Between the United Kingdom and Iraq in Time of War," 20 July 1938, CAB 53/40, paper 749.

53. During this period Britain was usually able to supply the Iraqi air force more quickly and completely than the Iraqi army because those sections of British industry responsible for the manufacture of aircraft were, generally speaking, in better condition than those responsible for the manufacture of army equipment. The main reason for the healthier state of the British aircraft industry was that from the beginning of rearmament in Britain in the mid-1930s the equipment needs of the Royal Air Force were given precedence over those of the British army. Correlli Barnett, *The Collapse of British Power* (London, 1972), pp. 494, 504.

54. Air ministry to R.A.F. headquarters in Iraq, 25 Feb. 1937, FO 371/20794, E1222/2/93; Chaz Bowyer, *The Encyclopedia of British Military Aircraft* (London, 1982), p. 117.

55. Air ministry to R.A.F. headquarters in Iraq, 5 March 1937, FO 371/20794, E1410/2/93; Bowyer, *British Military Aircraft*, p. 77.

56. Air ministry to R.A.F. headquarters in Iraq, 9 March 1937, FO 371/20794, E1410/2/93; Bowyer, *British Military Aircraft*, p. 113.

57. Meeting in London between Major Muhammad Ali Jawad (head of the Iraqi air force) and officials from the British air ministry, 24 May 1937, FO 371/20794, E3104/2/93; Bowyer, *British Military Aircraft*, pp. 100, 125.
58. Air ministry to Waterhouse, 17 May 1939, FO 371/23204, E3345/79/93.
59. Air ministry to Waterhouse, 7 June 1939, FO 371/23204, E4162/79/93; Bowyer, *British Military Aircraft*, p. 144.
60. These ninety-three planes were Hurricanes and were grouped together in five squadrons. The Royal Air Force also had five squadrons of Gladiators available for home defense but these planes, while capable of engaging German bombers, were considered unsuitable for operations against the latest German fighters. Collier, *The Defence of the United Kingdom*, p. 65; Higham, *Armed Forces in Peacetime*, p. 186.
61. Minutes of the committee of imperial defence, 20 April 1939, CAB 2/8.
62. Iraq ordered the Gladiators in April 1937 and deliveries began the following September. Iraq ordered the Lysanders in January 1940 with deliveries scheduled to begin the following June. However, as a result of Germany's attack on western Europe in May 1940 and Italy's entry into the war the following month, Britain needed the Lysanders for its own forces and they were not, in fact, delivered to Iraq. Wing Commander S. D. Culley (inspector of the Iraqi air force), "Quarterly Report on the Iraqi Air Force," 21 Sept. 1937, FO 371/20794, E6060/2/93; Waterhouse to Newton, 3 July 1940, FO 624/21, file 484; foreign office to Newton, 12 July 1940, FO 624/21, file 484.
63. All the leading British officials in Iraq were convinced that Iraqi arms purchases from non-British sources were affected by bribery. See, for example, Clark Kerr to foreign office, 9 July 1937, FO 371/20797, E3887/19/93; Houstoun-Boswall to foreign office, 27 April 1939, FO 371/23206, E3208/178/93; Newton to foreign office, 22 Aug. 1939, FO 371/23205, E6154/79/93; Waterhouse to Iraqi minister of defence, 26 Oct. 1940, FO 371/24552, E3016/47/93; and Edmonds to Newton, 14 Dec. 1940, Edmonds' papers, box 2, file 3.
64. British embassy in Baghdad to foreign office, 19 June 1937, FO 371/20794, E3398/2/93.

    The Italian government did not, in fact, meet these delivery dates: the Bredas arrived in Iraq in April 1938 and most of the Savoias the following October. Culley, "Quarterly Report on the Iraqi Air Force," 31 May 1938, FO 371/21850, E3781/298/93; Culley, "Quarterly Report on the Iraqi Air Force," 30 Nov. 1938, FO 371/21851, E7617/298/93.
65. Foreign office to air ministry, 14 March 1938, FO 371/21850, E1297/298/93; foreign office to air ministry, 30 Dec. 1938, FO 371/21851, E7812/298/93.
66. Newton to foreign office, 17 Oct. 1939, FO 371/23205, E7025/79/93.
67. Foreign office to air ministry, 1 Aug. 1939, FO 371/23205, E5072/79/93; air ministry to foreign office, 25 Aug. 1939, FO 371/23205, E6050/79/93.
68. War office to foreign office, 10 Oct. 1935, FO 371/18944, E6101/192/93.
69. Clark Kerr to foreign office, 26 May 1936, FO 371/20005, E3013/375/93.
70. Colonel D. O. W. Lamb (acting inspector-general of the Iraqi army and head of the British advisory military mission), "Quarterly Report on the Iraqi Armed Forces," 31 March 1938, FO 371/21853, E2355/448/93.
71. Waterhouse to Houstoun-Boswall, 20 April 1939, FO 371/23206, E3208/178/93.

72. Waterhouse to Iraqi defence minister, 26 Oct. 1940, FO 371/24552, E3016/47/93.
73. Culley, "Quarterly Report on the Iraqi Air Force," 28 Feb. 1939, FO 371/23204, E2373/79/93.
74. Culley, "Quarterly Report on the Iraqi Air Force," 31 May 1939, FO 371/23204, E4283/79/93.
75. Hay, "Quarterly Report on the Iraqi Army and Air Force," 30 Sept. 1934, FO 371/17850, E6359/10/93; British embassy in Iraq, "Annual Report on Iraq for 1938," 21 Jan. 1939, FO 371/23214, E932/932/93.
76. Waterhouse, "Quarterly Report on the Iraqi Army and Air Force," 31 Aug. 1940, FO 371/24551, E1235/15/93.
77. Newton to foreign office, 15 June 1939, FO 371/23216, E4475/2010/93; minutes of the allied demands supply committee of the war cabinet, 12 March 1940, CAB 92/21.
78. War office to foreign office, 24 Nov. 1939, FO 371/23207, E7738/178/93; war office to foreign office, 15 Jan. 1940, FO 371/24551, E246/47/93.
79. Waterhouse, "Quarterly Report on the Iraqi Army and Air Force," 30 Nov. 1939, FO 371/24551, E15/15/93; Waterhouse, "Quarterly Report on the Iraqi Army and Air Force," 31 May 1940, FO 371/24551, E1235/15/93; foreign office to Newton, 25 June 1940, FO 371/24552, E1948/47/93.
80. Waterhouse, "Quarterly Report on the Iraqi Army and Air Force," 31 May 1940, FO 371/24551, E1235/15/93.
81. Foreign office to Newton, 13 Feb. 1941, FO 371/27061, E405/1/93; minute by M. J. R. Talbot (eastern department of the foreign office), 18 March 1941, FO 371/27062, E874/1/93.
82. War office to foreign office, 19 Jan. 1941 and 25 Feb. 1941, FO 371/27090, E714/E219/133/93; foreign office to war office, 13 March 1941, FO 371/27090, E714/133/93.
83. War office to foreign office, 9 April 1941, FO 371/27090, E1398/133/93; India office to government of India, 16 April 1941, FO 371/27090, E1510/133/93.
84. Paul Knabenshue (United States minister in Iraq) to state department, 19 Sept. 1939, 890G.00/486; conferences in Baghdad between British and Iraqi military officers, 30 Sept. 1939 and 13 May 1940, AIR 23/667; Newton to foreign office, 27 May 1940, FO 371/24561, E2095/2022/93.

   This apprehension was partly based on the experience of the First World War when the Russian army had seized portions of what was now northeastern Iraq around Rawanduz, Panjwin, and Khaniqin. Memorandum by Edmonds, "Russia and the Kurds," 15 Feb. 1940, FO 371/24560, E1360/848/93.
85. Khadduri, *Independent Iraq*, p. 181.
86. Newton to foreign office, 29 Feb. 1940, FO 371/24552, E968/47/93; Lukasz Hirszowicz, *The Third Reich and the Arab East* (London, 1966), p. 108.
87. Houstoun-Boswall to foreign office, 16 March 1940, FO 371/24552, E1340/47/93.
88. Newton to foreign office, 30 March 1940, FO 371/24552, E1430/47/93.
89. Newton to foreign office, 19 June 1940, FO 371/24552, E1658/47/93; Hirszowicz, *The Third Reich and the Arab East*, pp. 108,115.
90. Khadduri, *Independent Iraq*, pp. 184, 189; Hirszowicz, *The Third Reich and the Arab East*, p. 108.

91. Waterhouse to British embassy in Baghdad, 2 Sept. 1940, FO 371/24552, E2703/47/93; Knabenshue to state department, 8 Jan. 1941, United States, department of state, *Foreign Relations of the United States* (hereafter referred to as *F.R.U.S.*): *Diplomatic Papers 1941,* Vol. III (Washington, 1959), p. 488; Al-Hashimi, *Mudhakkirat,* pp. 365–66, 410–11.

92. Khadduri, *Independent Iraq,* p. 181; Hirszowicz, *The Third Reich and the Arab East,* pp. 115–16; Geoffrey Warner, *Iraq and Syria 1941* (London, 1974), p. 83.

93. Treasury to foreign office, 15 Feb. 1940, FO 371/24552, E702/47/93; war office to C.-in-C. Middle East, 14 Dec. 1940, FO 371/24552, E2999/47/93; Knabenshue to state department, 8 Jan. 1941, *F.R.U.S. 1941,* III, p. 488; Al-Hashimi, *Mudhakkirat,* pp. 365–66, 410–11.

94. Frank G. Weber, *The Evasive Neutral: Germany, Britain and the Quest for a Turkish Alliance in the Second World War* (Columbia, Missouri, 1979), pp. 75, 77.

95. Sir Kinahan Cornwallis (British ambassador in Iraq) to flag officer commanding royal Indian navy, 11 April 1941, FO 371/27090, E1405/133/93; Cornwallis to C.-in-C. East Indies, 13 April 1941, FO 371/27090, E1469/133/93; submarine observation force Persian Gulf to C.-in-C. East Indies, 20 April 1941, FO 371/27090, E1469/133/93.

96. In the period 1932–36 an average of twenty-five Iraqi officers went to Britain or India each year for military training. Tarbush, *The Role of the Military in Politics,* p. 78.

97. Khadduri, *Independent Iraq,* pp. 223, 237, 312; Longrigg, *Iraq,* pp. 183, 189; Beeri, *Army Officers in the Arab Politics,* pp. 367–68; Ayad al-Qazzaz, review of *Memoirs of Taha al-Hashimi,* by Taha al-Hashimi, *Middle East Forum,* Vol. 45 (1969), p. 78; Al-Qazzaz, "The Iraqi-British War of 1941," p. 595; Hemphill, "The Formation of the Iraqi Army," p. 104; Husry, "The Political Ideas of Yunis al-Sabawi," pp. 172, 175.

98. During this conflict Iraqi planes strafed the British airbase at Habbaniya. Because the Iraqi air force flew many British manufactured aircraft, the British forces at Habbaniya sometimes had difficulty rapidly distinguishing friend from foe. In combat this inability is a serious disadvantage. Thus the British government's demand that Iraq use British-supplied military equipment had, at least in this instance, an extremely ironic result. Air Vice-Marshal H. G. Smart (air officer commanding in Iraq in May 1941) to Sir Charles Portal (chief of the air staff), 13 Nov. 1941, AIR 8/549.

Notes for Chapter 9—The Supply of Credit

1. Sir Maurice Peterson (British ambassador in Iraq) to foreign office, 11 Feb. 1939, FO 371/23207, E1216/374/93; memorandum by the export credits guarantee department, 21 Feb. 1939, FO 371/23207, E1368/374/93; Iraqi ministry of foreign affairs to W. E. Houstoun-Boswall (British charge d'affaires in Iraq), 13 April 1939, FO 371/23208, E2821/374/93.

2. Peterson to foreign office, 11 Feb. 1939, FO 371/23207, E1216/374/93; memorandum by the export credits guarantee department, 18 Feb. 1939, FO 371/23207, E1368/374/93; Iraqi ministry of foreign affairs to Houstoun-Boswall, 13 April 1939, FO 371/23208, E2821/374/93.

3. Sir Basil Newton (British ambassador in Iraq) to foreign office, 31 May 1939, FO 371/23215, E4085/1079/93.

4. Peterson to foreign office, 14 Jan. 1939, FO 371/23207, E376/374/93.

5. Memorandum by the export credits guarantee department, 18 Feb. 1939, FO 371/23207, E1368/374/93; Peterson to foreign office, 8 March 1939, FO 371/23207, E1772/374/93; Houstoun Boswall to foreign office, 13 April 1939, FO 371/23208, E2821/374/93.

6. Report by the chiefs of staff, 14 Jan. 1939, CAB 53/43, paper 824; foreign office to export credits guarantee department, 28 Jan. 1939, FO 371/23207, E663/374/93; foreign office to export credits guarantee department, 4 May 1939, FO 371/23208, E2959/374/93.

7. War office to general officer commanding British troops in Egypt, 19 Jan. 1939, CAB 53/45, paper 841; war office to foreign office, 28 April 1939, FO 371/23210, E3200/474/93.

   With the advantage of hindsight we can see that British military leaders overestimated Italy's ability to interfere with the movement of British ships through the Red Sea. Illustrating the ineffectiveness of the Italian naval and air forces in East Africa, between June 1940, when Italy entered the war, and December 1940 fifty-four British convoys sailed through the Red Sea with the loss of only one ship. Major-General I. S. O. Playfair, *History of the Second World War, United Kingdom Military Series: The Mediterranean and Middle East*, Vol. I: *The Early Successes Against Italy* (London, 1954), pp. 248–49.

8. British embassy in Iraq, "Annual Report Economic (A) on Iraq for 1938," 10 May 1939, FO 371/23203, E3556/78/93; minute by J. G. Ward (eastern department of the foreign office), 6 Nov. 1937, FO 371/20800, E6276/65/93.

9. Sir Francis Humphrys (British ambassador in Iraq) to foreign office, 1 Feb. 1934, FO 371/17858, E962/190/93.

10. The text of the railway agreement is in Sir Archibald Clark Kerr (British ambassador in Iraq) to foreign office, 1 April 1936, FO 371/19998, E2117/25/93.

11. Peterson to foreign office, 30 Jan. 1939 and 17 March 1939, FO 371/23207, E793/E2040/374/93; Houstoun-Boswall to foreign office, 13 April 1939, FO 371/23208, E2821/374/93.

12. Export credits guarantee department to treasury, 25 Jan. 1939, FO 371/23207, E663/374/93; foreign office to export credits guarantee department, 28 Jan. 1939, FO 371/23207, E663/374/93; foreign office to export credits guarantee department, 4 May 1939, FO 371/23208, E2959/374/93.

13. Note by the war office, 1 March 1939, FO 371/23190, E1966/88/65; war office to foreign office, 15 March 1939, FO 371/23190, E1966/88/65.

14. Foreign office to air ministry, 28 March 1939, FO 371/23190, E2028/88/65; foreign office to war office, 7 June 1939, FO 371/23190, E3648/88/65.

15. Minute by H. L. Baggalay (eastern department of the foreign office), 25 April 1939, FO 371/23208, E2821/374/93; foreign office to export credits guarantee department, 4 May 1939, FO 371/23208, E2959/374/93.

16. Export credits guarantee department to treasury, 8 May 1939, FO 371/23208, E3440/E3441/374/93.

17. Treasury to foreign office, 18 May 1939, FO 371/23208, E3728/374/93.

18. Foreign office to treasury, 6 June 1939, FO 371/23208, E3728/374/93; ex-

port credits guarantee department to treasury, 25 May 1939, FO 371/23208, E3993/374/93; treasury to foreign office, 16 June 1939, FO 371/23208, E4534/374/93.

19. Newton to foreign office, 25 May 1939 and 6 June 1939, FO 371/23208, E3871/E4122/374/93; Iraqi ministry of foreign affairs to British embassy in Baghdad, 13 June 1939, FO 371/23208, E4472/374/93.

20. Newton to foreign office, 6 June 1939 and 21 June 1939, FO 371/23208, E4122/E4450/374/93.

21. Export credits guarantee department to foreign office, 15 June 1939, FO 371/23208, E4344/374/93; treasury to foreign office, 19 June 1939, FO 371/23208, E4344/374/93; treasury to export credits guarantee department, 10 July 1939, FO 371/23209, E4953/374/93; export credits guarantee department to foreign office, 11 July 1939, FO 371/23209, E4959/374/93.

22. Export credits guarantee department to foreign office, 15 June 1939, FO 371/23208, E4344/374/93; treasury to foreign office, 19 June 1939, FO 371/23208, E4344/374/93; memorandum by the foreign office, 30 June 1939, FO 371/23208, E4707/374/93.

23. Newton to foreign office, 1 July 1939, FO 371/23208, E4753/374/93.

24. Foreign office to export credits guarantee department, 6 July 1939, FO 371/23208, E4707/374/93; treasury to export credits guarantee department, 10 July 1939, FO 371/23209, E4953/374/93; export credits guarantee department to foreign office, 11 July 1939, FO 371/23209, E4959/374/93.

25. Newton to foreign office, 16 Aug. 1939, FO 371/23209, E5860/374/93.
   Because the Iraqi government had recently been able to pay a portion of its outstanding bill with British manufacturers for railway material, Britain now offered only £460,000 in commercial credits rather than £650,000 which was the amount stipulated in the original British offer in May 1939. Export credits guarantee department to treasury, 31 Oct. 1939, FO 371/23209, E7294/374/93.

26. Foreign office to export credits guarantee department, 4 Oct. 1939, FO 371/23209, E6773/374/93; foreign office to treasury, 25 Oct. 1939, FO 371/23209, E7115/374/93.

27. Export credits guarantee department to treasury, 11 Oct. 1939, FO 371/23209, E6881/374/93; treasury to export credits guarantee department, 25 Oct. 1939, FO 371/23209, E7183/374/93.

28. Newton to Ali Jaudat (Iraqi foreign minister), 6 Nov. 1939, FO 371/23209, E7809/374/93.

29. Newton to foreign office, 23 Nov. 1939, FO 371/23209, E7392/374/93. The text of the Anglo-Iraqi credit agreement is in FO 371/23209, E7842/374/93.

30. Export credits guarantee department to treasury, 20 Oct. 1939, FO 371/23209, E7115/374/93; treasury to export credits guarantee department, 25 Oct. 1939, FO 371/23209, E7183/374/93; Newton to Ali Jaudat, 6 Nov. 1939, FO 371/23209, E7807/374/93.

31. Major-General G. G. Waterhouse (inspector-general of the Iraqi army and head of the British advisory military mission), "Quarterly Report on the Iraqi Army and Air Force," 29 Feb. 1940, FO 371/24551, E1235/15/93; Newton to foreign office, 10 May 1940, FO 371/24552, E1948/47/93, C. J. Edmonds (adviser to the Iraqi ministry of the interior) to Newton, 4 Feb. 1941, Edmonds' papers, box 2, file 3.

32. Foreign office to war office, 14 Oct. 1939, FO 371/23209, E6859/374/93; foreign office to war office, 10 Nov. 1939, FO 371/23207, E7423/178/93.

33. War office to foreign office, 24 Nov. 1939, FO 371/23207, E7738/178/93; war office to foreign office, 15 Jan. 1940, FO 371/24551, E246/47/93.

Notes for Chapter 10—The Problem of Oil

1. Longrigg, *Oil*, pp. 25–32, 41–47, 66–83; Shwadran, *Oil*, pp. 195–242; Kent, *Oil and Empire*, passim; Mejcher, *Imperial Quest*, passim; Penrose, Edith and E. F. *Iraq: International Relations and National Development* (London, 1978), pp. 56–78, 137–144; Helmut Mejcher, *Die Politik und das Öl im Nahen Osten*, Vol. I: *Der Kampf der Mächte und Konzerne vor dem Zweiten Weltkrieg* (Stuttgart, 1980), passim; Stivers, "International Politics," pp. 517–40; William Stivers, *Supremacy and Oil: Iraq, Turkey, and the Anglo-American World Order, 1918–1930* (Ithaca, 1982), pp. 87–91, 108–37; R. W. Ferrier, *The History of the British Petroleum Company*, Vol. I: *The Developing Years 1901–1932* (Cambridge, 1982), pp. 355–58, 520–22, 580–87.

2. Longrigg, *Oil*, pp. 44, 68–70; Shwadran, *Oil*, pp. 201, 227–28, 238, 249; Penrose, *Iraq*, pp. 56–63, 68.

3. Longrigg, *Oil*, pp. 43, 69; Shwadran, *Oil*, pp. 227–28; Penrose, *Iraq*, pp. 64–65.

4. British embassy in Iraq, "Economic Report (B) on Iraq for 1939," 14 Dec. 1939, FO 371/23204, E8084/78/93; minute by P. M. Crosthwaite (eastern department of the foreign office), 13 June 1940, FO 24547, E2129/213/65; Longrigg, *Oil*, p. 78; Penrose, *Iraq*, pp. 65–66.

5. Longrigg, *Oil*, pp. 69, 73; Shwadran, *Oil*, pp. 227–28, 238; Penrose, *Iraq*, pp. 64, 69–70.

6. Longrigg, *Oil*, pp. 73–75; Shwadran, *Oil*, p. 238; Penrose, *Iraq*, pp. 69–71.

7. Longrigg, *Oil*, pp. 74–75, 80; Shwadran, *Oil*, p. 239, 250; Penrose, *Iraq*, pp. 71, 138.

8. Longrigg, *Oil*, pp. 79–81; Shwadran, *Oil*, p. 250; Penrose, *Iraq*, pp. 138–39.

9. Longrigg, *Oil*, p. 82; Shwadran, *Oil*, pp. 239–40; Penrose, *Iraq*, pp. 139–40.

10. Penrose, *Iraq*, pp. 72–74, 139–44.

11. Longrigg, *Oil*, pp. 76–77; Shwadran, *Oil*, pp. 240–42; Penrose, *Iraq*, p. 139.

12. Longrigg, *Oil*, p. 77; Penrose, *Iraq*, pp. 140, 143–44.

13. Memorandum by Lord Cadman (chairman, I.P.C.), 24 July 1939, FO 371/23215, E5326/1079/93; memorandum by the petroleum department, 8 April 1940, FO 371/24557, E1652/225/93; Longrigg, *Oil*, p. 45; Shwadran, *Oil*, p. 249; Penrose, *Iraq*, p. 143.

14. Memorandum by Cadman, 24 July 1939, FO 371/23215, E5326/1079/93; minute by H. L. Baggallay (eastern department of the foreign office), 8 Aug. 1939, FO 371/23215, E5326/1079/93; memorandum by the petroleum department, 8 April 1940, FO 371/24557, E1652/225/93; Penrose, *Iraq*, p. 143.

15. Memorandum by Baggallay, 3 Feb. 1939, FO 371/23215, E1079/1079/93; Longrigg, *Oil*, pp. 75, 81; Penrose, *Iraq*, pp. 139–40.

16. Sir Basil Newton (British ambassador in Iraq) to foreign office, 27 May 1939,

FO 371/23215, E3884/1079/93; Newton to foreign office, 31 May 1939, FO 371/23215, E4085/1079/93; Longrigg, *Oil,* pp. 75, 83; Penrose, *Iraq,* p. 140.

17. Resolution passed at I.P.C. board meeting, 20 July 1939, FO 371/23215, E5326/1079/93; I.P.C. to the permanent Anglo-French executive committee for oil, 22 Feb. 1940, FO 371/24557, E1125/225/93.

18. Minute by Baggallay, 3 Feb. 1939, FO 371/23215, E1079/1079/93.

19. I.P.C. to the permanent Anglo-French executive committee for oil, 22 Feb. 1940, FO 371/24557, E1125/225/93.

20. *Ibid.*

21. Note by the French delegation to the permanent Anglo-French executive committee for oil, 30 Dec. 1939, FO 371/24557, E1125/225/93; foreign office to petroleum department, 16 March 1940, FO 371/24557, E1093/225/93.

22. The British put this figure at only $7,500,000. Memorandum by the British delegation to the permanent Anglo-French executive committee for oil, 1 April 1940, FO 371/24557, E1443/225/93.

23. Note by the French delegation to the permanent Anglo-French executive committee for oil, 30 Dec. 1939, FO 371/24557, E1125/225/93.

24. Interdepartmental conference, 20 March 1940, FO 371/24557, E1435/225/93; memorandum by the petroleum department, March 1940, FO 371/24557, E1259/225/93; memorandum by the petroleum department, 8 April 1940, FO 371/24557, E1652/225/93.

25. Ministry of economic warfare to mines department, 8 April 1940, FO 371/24557, E1652/225/93; Maurice Pearton, *Oil and the Romanian State* (London, 1971), pp. 244–50; Williamson Murray, *The Change in the European Balance of Power 1938–1939: The Path to Ruin* (Princeton, N.J., 1984), pp. 327–28.

26. Interdepartmental conference, 20 March 1940, FO 371/24557, E1435/225/93; memorandum by the petroleum department, March 1940, FO 371/24557, E1259/225/93; memorandum by the petroleum department, 8 April 1940, FO 371/24557, E1652/225/93.

27. Petroleum department to foreign office, 16 March 1940, FO 371/24557, E1218/225/93; minute by Baggallay, 20 March 1940, FO 371/24557, E1218/225/93; memorandum by the petroleum department, 8 April 1940, FO 371/24557, E1652/225/93.

28. Interdepartmental conference, 20 March 1940, FO 371/24557, E1435/225/93; memorandum by the petroleum department, March 1940, FO 371/24557, E1259/225/93.

29. Interdepartmental conference, 20 March 1940, FO 371/24557, E1435/225/93; memorandum by the petroleum department, March 1940, FO 371/24557, E1259/225/93; memorandum by the British delegation to the permanent Anglo-French executive committee for oil, 1 April 1940, FO 371/24557, E1443/225/93.

30. Memorandum by the petroleum department, 8 April 1940, FO 371/24557, E1652/225/93.

31. Interdepartmental conference, 11 June 1940, FO 371/24547, E2129/213/65; petroleum department to I.P.C., 11 June 1940, FO 371/24547, E2129/213/65; I.P.C. to petroleum department, 12 June 1940, FO 371/24547, E2129/213/65.

32. Foreign office to treasury, 18 July 1940, FO 371/24556, E2198/203/93; foreign office to I.P.C., 3 Aug. 1940, FO 371/24556, E2198/203/93; Longrigg, *Oil,* pp. 78–79; Penrose, *Iraq,* p. 145.

33. Longrigg, *Oil,* p. 117.
34. Basra Petroleum Company to petroleum department, 25 July 1940, FO 371/24557, E2749/225/93.
35. Petroleum department to foreign office, 5 Oct. 1940, FO 371/24557, E2749/225/93; foreign office to Newton, 29 Oct. 1940, FO 371/24557, E2860/225/93.
36. Penrose, *Iraq,* p. 144.

Notes for Chapter 11—The Deterioration of Anglo-Iraqi Relations:
Phrase One—September 1939–October 1940

1. Sir Basil Newton (British ambassador in Iraq) to foreign office, 29 Aug. 1939, FO 371/23211, E6145/474/93; foreign office to Newton, 9 Sept. 1939, FO 371/23211, E6353/474/93.
2. Foreign office to Newton, 11 Sept. 1939, FO 371/23211, E6320/474/93.
3. Admiralty to foreign office, 13 April 1940, FO 371/24548, E1661/1661/65.
4. War office to foreign office, 24 Nov. 1939, FO 371/23207, E7738/178/93; war office to foreign office, 15 Jan. 1940, FO 371/24551, E246/47/93.
5. Newton to foreign office, 25 Aug. 1939, 29 Aug. 1939, and 7 Sept. 1939, FO 371/23211, E5995/E6145/E6352/474/93; Khadduri, *Independent Iraq,* pp. 144–45, 152; Hirszowicz, *The Third Reich and the Arab East,* p. 68.
6. Newton to foreign office, 7 Sept. 1939, FO 371/23211, E6352/474/93.
7. Newton to foreign office, 13 Sept. 1939, FO 371/23211, E6490/474/93; Newton to foreign office, 18 Jan. 1940, FO 371/24559, E495/495/93.
8. Newton to foreign office, 9 Sept. 1939, FO 371/23218, E6406/6263/93; foreign office to war office, 16 Dec. 1939, FO 371/23212, E7532/474/93; Newton to foreign office, 18 Jan. 1940, FO 371/24559, E495/495/93; Khadduri, *Independent Iraq,* p. 146.
9. Khadduri, *Independent Iraq,* pp. 144–45, 152.
10. Ali Jaudat (Iraqi foreign minister) to Newton, 6 Sept. 1939, FO 371/23212, E6557/474/93.
11. Foreign office to Newton, 9 Sept. 1939 and 16 Sept. 1939, FO 371/23211, E6353/E6490/474/93; Newton to Ali Jaudat, 25 Sept. 1939, FO 371/23212, E6805/474/93; foreign office to F. H. W. Stonehewer-Bird (British minister in Saudi Arabia), 10 May 1940, FO 371/24548, E1759/953/65.
12. Khadduri, *Independent Iraq,* pp. 162–65.
13. Newton to foreign office, 8 Dec. 1939, FO 371/23202, E8010/72/93; Newton to foreign office, 3 April 1940, FO 371/24558, E1725/448/93; Khadduri, *Independent Iraq,* pp. 148, 153, 157.
14. Khadduri, *Independent Iraq,* pp. 37, 145, 153, 161–62, 175.
15. Newton to foreign office, 20 May 1940, FO 371/24558, E1732/448/93; Khadduri, *Independent Iraq,* p. 175; Longrigg, *Iraq,* p. 284; Hirszowicz, *The Third Reich and the Arab East,* p. 106; Tarbush, *The Role of the Military in Politics,* p. 170.
16. Foreign office to Newton, 30 May 1940, FO 371/24560, E2024/1123/93; foreign office to Newton, 16 June 1940, FO 371/24561, E2128/2022/93; foreign office to Newton, 23 June 1940, FO 371/24558, E2105/448/93.
17. Newton to foreign office, 18 June 1940, FO 371/24561, E2128/2022/93; Newton to foreign office, 25 June 1940, FO 371/24558, E2105/448/93; Khadduri, *Independent Iraq,* pp. 176, 193.

18. Foreign office to Newton, 16 June 1940, FO 371/24561, E2128/2022/93; foreign office to Newton, 28 March 1941, FO 371/27062, E1154/1/93.
19. Khadduri, *Independent Iraq*, p. 176; Longrigg, *Iraq*, p. 284.
20. Khadduri, *Independent Iraq*, pp. 164–65, 178–79; Hirszowicz, *The Third Reich and the Arab East*, pp. 78–84, 94, 108–09.
21. Khadduri, *Independent Iraq*, pp. 186–91; Hirszowicz, *The Third Reich and the Arab East*, pp. 40–41, 86–94, 115–27; Weber, *The Evasive Neutral*, pp. 57–58, 70.
22. Foreign office to Newton, 14 Nov. 1940 and 21 Nov. 1940, FO 371/24558, E2905/448/93.
23. Newton to foreign office, 7 July 1940, FO 371/24561, E2190/2022/93; Newton to foreign office, 28 Sept. 1940, FO 371/24559, E2790/495/93; Newton to foreign office, 9 Oct. 1940, FO 371/24561, E2997/2022/93; Khadduri, *Independent Iraq*, pp. 176–77; Longrigg, *Iraq*, p. 284.
24. C. J. Edmonds (adviser to the Iraqi ministry of the interior) to Newton, 12 May 1940, FO 371/24561, E2022/2022/93; Newton to foreign office, 27 May 1940, FO 371/24561, E2095/2022/93; memorandum by Edmonds, 31 July 1940, FO 371/24549, E2283/2029/65; Khadduri, *Independent Iraq*, p. 171.
25. Foreign office to Newton, 20 Aug. 1940, FO 371/24549, E2283/2029/65; Newton to foreign office, 31 Aug. 1940, FO 371/24548, E2572/953/65.
26. Foreign office to war office, 1 Aug. 1940, FO 371/24558, E2315/448/93.
27. Conclusions of the war cabinet, 1 July 1940, FO 371/24558, E2228/448/93.
28. Foreign office to war office, 20 June 1940, FO 371/24558, E2105/448/93; foreign office to Newton, 5 July 1940, FO 371/24558, E2228/448/93.
29. Foreign office to war office, 20 June 1940, FO 371/24558, E2105/448/93.
30. Memorandum by the chiefs of staff, 29 June 1940, CAB 80/13, paper 497.
31. Minutes of the chiefs of staff committee, 27 June 1940, CAB 79/5.
32. Newton to foreign office, 18 June 1940 and 3 July 1940, FO 371/24558, E2105/E2228/448/93; minute by A. V. Coverley-Price (eastern department of the foreign office), 20 June 1940, FO 371/24558, E2105/448/93.
33. Memorandum by the chiefs of staff, 29 June 1940, CAB 80/13, paper 497.
34. Minutes of the chiefs of staff committee, 27 June 1940, CAB 79/5; minutes by P. M. Crosthwaite (eastern department of the foreign office), 12 July 1940, and J. W. R. MacLean (eastern department of the foreign office), 24 July 1940, FO 371/24558, E2228/448/93.
35. C.-in C. India to war office, 6 July 1940, FO 371/24558, E2228/448/93; C.-in-C. Middle East to war office, 9 July 1940, FO 371/24558, E2228/448/93; viceroy to secretary of state for India, 9 July 1940 and 11 July 1940, FO 371/24558, E2228/448/93.
36. Minutes of the ministerial committee on military policy in the Middle East, 23 July 1940, CAB 95/2; foreign office to war office, 1 Aug. 1940, FO 371/24558, E2315/448/93.

Notes for Chapter 12—The Deterioration of Anglo-Iraqi Relations:
Phase Two—November 1940–May 1941

1. Foreign office to Sir Basil Newton (British ambassador in Iraq), 14 Nov. 1940 and 21 Nov. 1940, FO 371/24558, E2905/448/93.
2. Newton to foreign office, 27 Nov. 1940 and 30 Nov. 1940, FO 371/24559,

E3010/448/93; Newton to foreign office, 4 Dec. 1940, FO 371/24559, E3020/448/93.

3. Minute by P. M. Crosthwaite (eastern department of the foreign office), 7 Feb. 1940, FO 371/24559, E448/448/93.

4. Foreign office to Newton, 14 Nov. 1940, FO 371/24558, E2905/448/93; chiefs of staff committee to foreign office, 6 Jan. 1941, FO 371/27061, E58/1/93.

5. Petroleum department to I.P.C., 11 June 1940, FO 371/24547, E2129/213/65; I.P.C. to petroleum department, 12 June 1940, FO 371/24547, E2129/213/65; Playfair, *The Mediterranean and Middle East*, I, p. 79; D. J. Payton-Smith, *History of the Second World War, United Kingdom Civil Series: Oil, A Study of War-Time Policy and Administration* (London, 1971), p. 230.

6. Foreign office to treasury, 18 July 1940, FO 371/24556, E2198/203/93; foreign office to I.P.C., 3 Aug. 1940, FO 371/24556, E2198/203/93; Longrigg, *Oil*, pp. 78–79; Penrose, *Iraq*, p. 145.

7. Minute by P. Dean (eastern department of the foreign office), 26 Feb. 1941, FO 371/27061, E647/1/93; foreign office to Newton, 6 March 1941, FO 371/27062, E773/1/93; report by the joint planning staff, 'Oil Demolition', 2 May 1941, CAB 79/11; minutes of the defense committee (operations) of the war cabinet, 5 June 1941, CAB 69/2.

8. W. E. Houstoun-Boswall (British charge d'affaires in Iraq) to foreign office, 13 April 1939, FO 371/23215, E2822/1322/93; minutes by M. J. R. Talbot (eastern department of the foreign office), 23 July 1940, and H. L. Baggalay (eastern department of the foreign office), 25 July 1940, FO 371/24559, E2280/495/93; ministry of food to foreign office, 26 Oct. 1940, FO 371/24561, E2331/2102/93; admiralty, *Iraq and the Persian Gulf*, pp. 457–58, 490.

9. Minutes of a meeting at the ministry of economic warfare, 28 Oct. 1940, FO 371/24556, E2915/203/93; Newton to foreign office, 14 Dec. 1940, FO 371/24559, E3092/448/93; minute by Talbot, 18 March 1941, FO 371/27062, E874/1/93.

10. Newton to foreign office, 14 Nov. 1940, FO 371/24556, E2915/203/93; India office to foreign office, 9 Dec. 1940, FO 371/24556, E3075/203/93.

11. Foreign office to Newton, 21 Dec. 1940, FO 371/24559, E3092/448/93.

12. C. J. Edmonds (advisor to the Iraqi ministery of the interior) to Newton, 3 Jan. 1941, Edmonds' papers, box 2, file 3; Newton to foreign office, 7 Jan. 1941, FO 371/27061, E137/1/93; Paul Knabenshue (United States minister in Iraq) to state department, 8 Jan. 1941, 890G.248/47; Al-Hashimi, *Mudhakkirat*, pp. 365–66, 369, 410–11.

13. Khadduri, *Independent Iraq*, pp. 201, 288; Longrigg, *Iraq*, p. 285.

14. Minute by Crosthwaite, 12 Nov. 1940, FO 371/24558, E2905/448/93; foreign office to Newton, 24 Nov. 1940, FO 371/24558, E2905/448/93.

15. Newton to foreign office, 5 Dec. 1940 and 18 Dec. 1940, FO 371/24559, E3020/E3092/448/93; Khadduri, *Independent Iraq*, p. 202.

16. Foreign office to Newton, 21 Dec. 1940, FO 371/24559, E3092/448/93; Khadduri, *Independent Iraq*, pp. 28–29, 288.

17. Newton to foreign office, 30 Jan. 1941, FO 371/27061, E320/1/93; Edmonds to Newton, 15 Feb. 1941, FO 371/27063, E1317/1/93; Khadduri, *Independent Iraq*, pp. 202–04; Longrigg, *Iraq*, pp. 224, 277, 286.

18. Khadduri, *Independent Iraq*, pp. 197–98, 202–03.

19. Edmonds to Newton, 15 Feb. 1941, FO 371/27063, E1317/1/93; Edmonds to Newton, 1 April 1941, FO 371/27067, E1806/1/93; Khadduri, *Independent Iraq*, pp. 205, 207.

20. Newton to foreign office, 3 Feb. 1941 and 4 Feb. 1941, FO 371/27061, E353/1/93; Khadduri, *Independent Iraq*, pp. 205–06.

21. Newton to foreign office, 1 March 1941, FO 371/27063, E1311/1/93; Edmonds to Newton, 1 April 1941, FO 371/27067, E1806/1/93; Khadduri, *Independent Iraq*, pp. 163–64, 308–09.

22. Newton to foreign office, 2 Jan. 1941, FO 371/27061, E58/1/93; foreign office to Newton, 10 Jan. 1941 and 2 Feb. 1941, FO 371/27061, E58/E333/1/93.

23. Newton to foreign office, 19 Feb. 1941, FO 371/27061, E608/1/93; Newton to foreign office, 1 March 1941, FO 371/27063, E1311/1/93; foreign office to Newton, 28 March 1941, FO 371/27062, E1154/1/93.

24. Foreign office to Newton, 13 Feb. 1941, FO 371/27061, E405/1/93; minute by Talbot, 18 March 1941, FO 371/27062, E874/1/93.

25. Newton to foreign office, 5 Feb. 1941 and 8 Feb. 1941, FO 371/27061, E385/E405/1/93.

26. Foreign office to Newton, 13 Feb. 1941, FO 371/27061, E405/1/93; Newton to foreign office, 4 March 1941, FO 371/27062, E856/1/93; conversation between Anthony Eden (British foreign secretary) and Tawfiq al-Suwaydi, 7 March 1941, FO 371/27092, E1477/146/93.

27. Edmonds to Newton, 1 April 1941, FO 371/27067, E1806/1/93; Cornwallis to foreign office, 28 April 1941, FO 371/27076, E3286/1/93; Khadduri, *Independent Iraq*, pp. 207–08.

28. Memorandum by Knabenshue, 12 Feb. 1941, FO 371/27098, E780/514/93; Al-Hashimi, *Mudhakkirat*, pp. 403–04.

29. Playfair, *The Mediterranean and Middle East*, I, pp. 257–369.

30. *Ibid.*, pp. 391–450.

31. Newton to foreign office, 26 March 1941, FO 371/27067, E1717/1/93; Cornwallis to foreign office, 28 April 1941, FO 371/27076, E3286/1/93; Khadduri, *Independent Iraq*, p. 208; Hirszowicz, *The Third Reich and the Arab East*, pp. 138–39; Tarbush, *The Role of the Military in Politics*, pp. 160, 170.

32. Edmonds to Newton, 1 April 1941, FO 371/27067, E1806/1/93; Cornwallis to foreign office, 28 April 1941, FO 371/27076, E3286/1/93; Khadduri, *Independent Iraq*, pp. 208–09.

33. Khadduri, *Independent Iraq*, pp. 210–12.

34. Foreign office to British embassy in Washington, 4 April 1941, FO 371/27062, E1254/1/93; Cornwallis to foreign office, 7 April 1941, FO 371/27063, E1343/1/93; foreign office to Cornwallis, 10 April 1941, FO 371/27063, E1343/1/93.

35. Foreign office to Cornwallis, 3 April 1941, FO 371/27062, E154/1/93.

36. Foreign office to Cornwallis, 5 April 1941, FO 371/27062, E1276/1/93.

37. Khadduri, *Independent Iraq*, p. 211.

38. Cornwallis to foreign office, 4 April 1941, FO 371/27062, E1276/1/93.

39. Cornwallis to foreign office, 4 April 1941 and 5 April 1941, FO 371/27062, E1277/E1291/1/93.

40. Cornwallis to foreign office, 7 April 1941, FO 371/27063, E1337/1/93.

41. Cornwallis to foreign office, 7 April 1941, FO 371/27063, E1337/1/93.

42. Cornwallis to foreign office, 4 April 1941, FO 371/27062, E1276/1/93.

43. Cornwallis to foreign office, 9 April 1941, FO 371/27063, E1386/1/93; Cornwallis to foreign office, 28 April 1941, FO 371/27076, E3286/1/93; Khadduri, *Independent Iraq*, pp. 212, 214; Batatu, *The Old Social Classes*, pp. 453, 461; Hirszowicz, *The Third Reich and the Arab East*, p. 139.

44. Cornwallis to foreign office, 7 April 1941, FO 371/27063, E1343/1/93.

45. Foreign office to Cornwallis, 10 April 1941, FO 371/27063, E1343/1/93; foreign office to British embassy in Ankara, 11 April 1941, FO 371/27063, E1363/1/93.

46. Khadduri, *Independent Iraq*, pp. 215–16.

47. Foreign office to British embassy in Cairo, 7 April 1941, FO 371/27062, E1292/1/93; foreign office to Cornwallis, 8 April 1941, FO 371/27063, E1359/1/93.

48. Wavell to war office, 7 April 1941 and 10 April 1941, FO 371/27063, E1359/E1385/1/93.

49. Viceroy to secretary of state for India, 9 April 1941, FO 371/27064, E1436/1/93; memorandum by Wavell, "Operations in Iraq, Syria and Persia May 1941–January 1942," 18 Oct. 1942, FO 371/52341, E2219/2219/65.

50. Minutes by Winston S. Churchill (prime minister), 20 April 1941, and C. W. Baxter (head of the eastern department of the foreign office), 21 April 1941, FO 371/27066, E1623/1/93; minutes of the chiefs of staff committee, 21 April 1941, CAB 79/11.

51. Minutes of the defense committee (operations) of the war cabinet, 9 April 1941, CAB 69/2; report on Basra by L. S. Amery (secretary of state for India), 14 April 1941, CAB 80/27, paper 253; minute by Churchill, 20 April 1941, FO 371/27066, E1623/1/93.

52. Viceroy to secretary of state for India, 13 April 1941, FO 371/27064, E1456/1/93; government of India to India office, 21 April 1941, FO 371/27066, E1609/1/93; minutes of the chiefs of staff committee, 3 May 1941, CAB 79/11.

53. Report on Basra by Amery, 14 April 1941, CAB 80/27, paper 253; Dharm Pal, *Official History of the Indian Armed Forces in the Second World War 1939–1945: Campaign in Western Asia* (Calcutta, 1957), pp. 15–18.

54. Conclusions of the war cabinet, 14 April 1941, CAB 65/18.

55. Foreign office to British embassy in Baghdad, 15 April 1941, FO 371/27064, E1450/1/93.

56. Cornwallis to foreign office, 15 April 1941 and 19 April 1941, FO 371/27065, E1508/E1584/1/93.

57. Cornwallis to foreign office, 16 April 1941, FO 371/27065, E1524/1/93; Cornwallis to foreign office, 30 April 1941, FO 371/27067, E1850/1/93.

58. Cornwallis to foreign office, 16 April 1941, FO 371/27065, E1524/1/93.

59. R.A.F. headquarters in Iraq to R.A.F. headquarters in Egypt, 18 April 1941, FO 371/27065, E1586/1/93.

60. Cornwallis to foreign office, 18 April 1941, FO 371/27065, E1565/1/93; Cornwallis to foreign office, 21 April 1941, FO 371/27066, E1616/1/93; Khadduri, *Independent Iraq*, p. 219.

61. Cornwallis to foreign office, 28 April 1941, FO 371/27067, E1790/1/93; Iraqi legation in London to British foreign office, 29 April 1941, FO 371/27067, E1837/1/93.

62. Cornwallis to foreign office, 25 April 1941, FO 371/27067, E1723/1/93;

minute by Sir H. W. Malkin (legal expert at the foreign office), 6 May 1941, FO 371/27092, E2095/146/93; note by the foreign office, 6 May 1941, FO 371/27068, E2034/1/93.

63. Minutes of the chiefs of staff committee, 11 April 1941, CAB 79/10; minutes of the defence committee (operations) of the war cabinet, 14 April 1941, CAB 69/2; minute by Churchill, 20 April 1941, FO 371/27066, E1623/1/93; minute by Baxter, 5 May 1941, FO 371/27092, E2095/146/93.

64. Al-Qazzaz, "The Iraqi-British War of 1941," p. 595.

65. Cornwallis to foreign office, 23 April 1941, FO 371/27066, E1686/1/93; R.A.F. headquarters in Iraq to R.A.F. headquarters in Egypt, 24 April 1941, FO 371/27065, E1592/1/93; general officer commanding Basra to C.-in-C. India, 29 April 1941, FO 371/27067, E1905/1/93.

66. Cornwallis to foreign office, 30 April 1941, FO 371/27068, E1921/1/93.

67. Cornwallis to foreign office, 28 April 1941, FO 371/27067, E1782/E1790/1/93.

68. Cornwallis to foreign office, 6 June 1941, FO 371/27077, E3426/1/93.

69. General officer commanding Basra to C.-in-C. India; 29 April 1941, FO 371/27067, E1905/1/93.

70. On 1 May Rashid Ali expressed this apprehension to the Turkish minister in Baghdad. Sir H. Knatchbull-Hugessen (British ambassador in Turkey) to foreign office, 3 May 1941, FO 371/27067, E1912/1/93. See also Knabenshue to state department, 29 April 1941, 890G.00/590; and George Kirk, *Survey of International Affairs 1939–1946: The Middle East in the War* (London, 1952), p. 69.

71. Denis Richards, *Royal Air Force 1939–1945*, Vol. I: *The Fight at Odds* (London, 1953), p. 314.

72. Memorandum by the war office, "The Iraq Campaign September 1939–May 1941," not dated but probably summer 1941, WO 201/1255; Winston S. Churchill, *The Second World War*, Vol. III: *The Grand Alliance* (Boston, 1950), pp. 256, 259; Kirk, *The Middle East in the War*, p. 70.

73. R.A.F. headquarters in Iraq to British ambassador in Baghdad, 30 April 1941, FO 371/27067, E1802/1/93.

74. Longrigg, *Iraq*, p. 297; Batatu, *The Old Social Classes*, pp. 205, 456–57.

75. By 13 April 1941 axis forces had reached the western border of Egypt, thereby reconquering all the territory in Libya (except for Tobruk) that Britain had seized the previous winter. Confronted with the prospect of overwhelming defeat, between 24 April and 1 May British commanders were compelled to evacuate all of their troops from the mainland of Greece. Playfair, *The Mediterranean and Middle East*, II, pp. 19–41, 83–105.

76. Khadduri, *Independent Iraq*, p. 223; Hirszowicz, *The Third Reich and the Arab East*, pp. 129, 154–55; Warner, *Iraq and Syria 1941*, pp. 85, 94.

77. Air Vice-Marshal J. H. D'Albiac (air officer commanding in Iraq) to air officer commanding-in-chief in Egypt, 28 July 1941, FO 371/52470, E8720/8720/93; Air Commodore F. W. Walker (air headquarters in Iraq) to Sir Charles Portal (chief of the air staff), 11 Nov. 1941, AIR 8/549; Air Vice-Marshal H. G. Smart (air officer commanding in Iraq in May 1941) to Portal, 13 Nov. 1941, AIR 8/549.

78. Edmonds to F. Ashton-Gwatkin (Chatham House), 7 Sept. 1948, Edmonds' papers, box 13, file 1.

79. Khadduri, *Independent Iraq*, p. 228.

80. R.A.F. headquarters in Iraq to R.A.F. headquarters in Egypt, 30 April 1941,

FO 371/27067, E1802/1/93; Cornwallis to foreign office, 30 April 1941, FO 371/27067, E1815/1/93.

81. Cornwallis to foreign office, 30 April 1941, FO 371/27067, E1818/1/93.

82. R.A.F. headquarters in Iraq to R.A.F. headquarters in Egypt, 30 April 1941, FO 371/27067, E1802/E1817/1/93; Cornwallis to foreign office, 30 April 1941, FO 371/27067, E1815/1/93; minutes of the defence committee (operations) of the war cabinet, 30 April 1941, CAB 69/2.

83. Cornwallis to foreign office, 30 April 1941, FO 371/27067, E1815/1/93; foreign office to Cornwallis, 30 April 1941, FO 371/27067, E1815/1/93.

84. Playfair, *The Mediterranean and Middle East,* II, p. 183.

Notes for Chapter 13—The Hostilities of May 1941

1. Brigadier-General John B. Glubb, *The Story of the Arab Legion* (London, 1948), pp. 251–303; Mackenzie, *Eastern Epic,* I, pp. 82–106; Richards, *Royal Air Force,* pp. 310–24; Christopher Buckley, *Five Ventures: Iraq-Syria-Persia-Madagascar-Dodecanese* (London, 1954), pp. 3–38; Playfair, *The Mediterranean and Middle East,* II, pp. 177–97; Pal, *Campaign in Western Asia,* pp. 77–112; Lieutenant-General Sir John B. Glubb, *Britain and the Arabs: A Study of Fifty Years 1908 to 1958* (London, 1959), pp. 235–48; Hirszowicz, *The Third Reich and the Arab East,* pp. 134–72; Mahmud al-Durra, *Al-Harb al-Iraqiya al-Britaniya* (The Iraqi-British War of 1941) (Beirut, 1969), pp. 233–391; Bernd Philipp Schroder, *Deutschland und der Mittlere Osten im Zweiten Weltkrieg* (Gottingen, 1975), pp. 63–149. Several of these works also describe the campaigns in Syria and Iran which followed the fighting in Iraq and which are briefly mentioned later in this chapter.

2. Although German paratroopers did not land in Crete until 20 May, they and their transport aircraft, together with the fighter and bomber aircraft needed to support them, had been earmarked for this task for several weeks previous. Playfair, *The Mediterranean and Middle East,* II, pp. 121–48.

3. *Ibid.,* p. 195.

4. *Ibid.,* p. 196.

5. Hirszowicz, *The Third Reich and the Arab East,* pp. 163–64.

6. *Ibid.,* p. 165.

7. *Ibid.,* p. 154.

8. Al-Durra, *Al-Harb,* p. 209.

9. *Ibid.,* p. 209.

10. *Ibid.,* p. 209.

11. *Ibid.,* p. 210.

12. British military mission in Iraq, "Quarterly Report on the Iraqi Air Force," 30 Nov. 1941, FO 371/31366, E1108/101/93.

   The Iraqi air force had such a large proportion of unserviceable aircraft because, like many other air forces then and now, it invested excessively in glamorous and conspicuous items like new planes (for the purchase of which lucrative sales commissions were often available to high ranking officers) and inadequately in more mundane but essential items like spare parts and maintenance personnel. Wing Commander S. D. Culley (inspector of the Iraqi air force), "Quarterly Reports on the Iraqi Air Force," 31 May 1939, FO 371/23204, E4283/79/93; 31 Aug. 1939, FO 371/23205, E6649/79/93;

31 May 1940, FO 371/24561, E1236/1236/93; 31 Aug. 1940, FO 371/24561, E2017/1236/93.

13. The civilian vehicles had been hastily requisitioned in Palestine to carry food, water, and ammunition. However, many of them broke down en route and had to be abandoned because they were in poor condition and generally lacked spare parts and extra tires. Sir Alec Seath Kirkbride, *A Crackle of Thorns: Experiences in the Middle East* (London, 1956), p. 132.

14. The Indian troops included Gurkhas from Nepal and, more important, a sapper unit from Madras which provided invaluable assistance to the British forces in crossing water obstacles on the march to Baghdad. Mackenzie, *Eastern Epic*, I, pp. 102–04; Playfair, *The Mediterranean and Middle East*, II, p. 189.

15. General John B. Glubb, the commander of the Arab Legion, puts the British strength in this operation at 1,450 men. However, the war office maintains that the true number was only 1,200. Field-Marshal Lord Wilson, the British commander in Palestine and Transjordan, gives a figure of 1,200 to 1,400. Glubb, *Britain and the Arabs*, p. 245; memorandum by the war office, "Iraq Campaign September 1939–May 1941," not dated but probably summer 1941, WO 201/1255; Field-Marshal Lord Wilson, *Eight Years Overseas 1939–1947* (London, n.d.), p. 108.

16. Memorandum by the war office, "Iraq Campaign September 1939–May 1941," not dated but probably summer 1941, WO 201/1255; Glubb, *Arab Legion*, pp. 259, 287.

17. Glubb, *Arab Legion*, pp. 280–81, 298.

18. Glubb, *Britain and the Arabs*, pp. 245, 248.

19. Schroder, *Deutschland und der Mittlere Osten*, p. 137.

20. Hirszowicz, *The Third Reich and the Arab East*, pp. 171–72.

21. Robert Lewis Melka, "The Axis and the Arab Middle East: 1930–1945" (Ph.D. dissertation at the University of Minnesota, 1966), p. 269.

22. The Italian planes did not enter combat until 29 May. Playfair, *The Mediterranean and Middle East*, II, p. 188; Richards, *Royal Air Force*, pp. 320, 322.

23. Memorandum by Squadron Leader A. G. Dudgeon, "The Defence of Habbaniya and the Subsequent Air Operations During the Iraqi Rebellion, May 1941," 21 July 1941, AIR 20/6026.

24. Al-Durra, *Al-Harb*, p. 246.

25. German foreign ministry to the German legation in Iran, 22 May 1941, United States, department of state, *Documents on German Foreign Policy 1918– 1945*, Series D (1937–1945), Vol. XII: *The War Years* (Washington, 1962), p. 853; Hirszowicz, *The Third Reich and the Arab East*, p. 169; Schroder, *Deutschland und der Mittlere Osten*, p. 121.

26. Playfair, *The Mediterranean and Middle East*, II, p. 189; Richards, *Royal Air Force*, p. 322.

27. British embassy in Iraq, "Report on the Leading Personalities of Iraq for the Year 1940," 29 June 1940, FO 371/24562, E2329/2329/93; Khadduri, *Independent Iraq*, p. 216.

28. British embassy in Iraq, "Report on the Leading Personalities of Iraq for the Year 1940," 29 June 1940, FO 371/24562, E2329/2329/93; Khadduri, *Independent Iraq*, pp. 117, 216; Batatu, *The Old Social Classes*, pp. 451–52, 458; Husry, "The Political Ideas of Yunis al-Sabawi," pp. 166, 172–75.

29. Khadduri, *Independent Iraq*, pp. 120–230; Beeri, *Army Officers in Arab Politics*, pp. 20–37, 367–72; Batatu, *The Old Social Classes*, pp. 205, 451–52, 456–57.
30. British embassy in Iraq, "Report on the Leading Personalities of Iraq for the Year 1940," 29 June 1940, FO 371/24562, E2329/2329/93; C. J. Edmonds (adviser to the Iraqi ministry of the interior) to Sir Basil Newton (British ambassador in Iraq), 15 Feb. 1941, FO 371/27063, E1317/1/93; Husry, "The Political Ideas of Yunis al-Sabawi," p. 166.
31. Newton to foreign office, 10 Feb. 1941, FO 371/27062, E815/1/93.
32. Kedourie, *The Chatham House Version*, pp. 268–69.
33. Hiroshi Shimizu, "Anglo-Japanese Competition in the Textile Trade in the Inter-War Period: A Case Study of Iraq, 1932–1941," *Middle Eastern Studies*, Vol. 20 (1984), p. 280.
34. Khadduri, *Independent Iraq*, p. 13.
35. Kedourie, *The Chatham House Version*, pp. 268–69.
36. Batatu, *The Old Social Classes*, p. 47.
37. Kedourie, *The Chatham House Version*, p. 253.
38. Phebe Ann Marr, "Yasin al-Hashimi: The Rise and Fall of a Nationalist" (Ph.D. dissertation at Harvard University, 1966), p. 333.
39. See Chapter 8.
40. British embassy in Iraq, "Report on the Leading Personalities of Iraq for the Year 1940," 29 June 1940, FO 371/24562, E2329/2329/93; British air headquarters in Iraq to air ministry, 6 April 1941, FO 371/27064, E1424/1/93; British air headquarters in Iraq to air ministry, 8 April 1941, FO 371/27063, E1368/1/93.
41. British air headquarters in Iraq to air ministry, 27 April 1941, FO 371/27067, E1742/1/93; political resident in the Persian Gulf to government of India, 16 May 1941, FO 371/27071, E2432/1/93; Rajaa Hussain al-Khattab, *Tasis al-Jaysh al-Iraqi wa Tatawwur Daurhi al-Siyasi 1921–1941* (The Establishment of the Iraqi Army and the Development of its Political Role 1921–1941) (Baghdad, 1979), p. 253.
42. W. G. Elphinston, "The Kurdish Question," *International Affairs*, Vol. 22 (1946), p. 99; C. J. Edmonds, "Kurdish Nationalism," *Journal of Contemporary History*, Vol. 6 (1971), pp. 95–96.
43. Sir Kinahan Cornwallis (British ambassador in Iraq) to foreign office, 28 June 1941, FO 371/27077, E3422/1/93.
44. *Ibid.*
45. Cornwallis to foreign office, 11 July 1941, FO 371/27078, E4231/1/93.
46. See Chapter 5.
47. Sylvia G. Haim, "Aspects of Jewish Life in Baghdad under the Monarchy," *Middle Eastern Studies*, Vol. 12 (1976), p. 192; Cohen, "The Anti-Jewish Farhud," p. 9.
48. Memorandum by Colonel H. C. Smith (director-general of the Iraqi State Railways), 19 Aug. 1941, FO 371/27109, E5229/3025/93.
49. Memorandum by the general staff of the war office, "Notes on the Iraqi Army," February 1951, FO 371/91659, EQ 1201/4.
50. Glubb, *Arab Legion*, p. 284.
51. One British participant in the fighting maintains that in certain important respects, such as machine-guns and mortars, the Iraqi army's weapons were

of a more modern type than those of the British forces which were ranged against it. Glubb, *Britain and the Arabs*, p. 246.

52. Minutes of the defence committee (operations) of the war cabinet, 3 May, 6 May, and 8 May 1941, CAB 69/2.

53. During the fighting the Iraqis did halt oil deliveries through the pipeline to Haifa, but the flow was fully restored within four weeks of the armistice. Pal, *Campaign in Western Asia*, pp. 73–74; Payton-Smith, *Oil*, pp. 238, 357–58; Buckley, *Five Ventures*, p. 38.

54. Indicating the British government's determination not to allow itself to be deterred from military action by threats to the safety of its civilians in Iraq, on the eve of the conflict, L. S. Amery, the secretary of state for India, coldly stated that "[we should not] hamper either our diplomacy or our actual operations by any considerations of a purely sentimental character. Our women and children are facing the bombs here every day." Amery to Anthony Eden (foreign secretary), 29 April 1941, L/P&S/12/2863, P.Z. 2203/41.

　　In the event, no harm came to the British civilians in Iraq. Longrigg, *Iraq*, pp. 290, 296.

55. Playfair, *The Mediterranean and Middle East*, II, pp. 191, 193; Glubb, *Arab Legion*, p. 303; Pal, *Campaign in Western Asia*, pp. 84, 102, 104; Buckley, *Five Ventures*, p. 36.

　　It is interesting to observe the number of different racial or ethnic groups who fought, invariably with distinction, under the British flag in this campaign. Where would Britain have been without them?

56. Officially the Iraqi government put its losses at 500 dead and 700 wounded. Buckley, *Five Ventures*, pp. 36–37.

57. In the seven years that followed the fighting in May 1941, over 1,400 officers were expelled from the Iraqi army. Batatu, *The Old Social Classes*, p. 30.

58. Khadduri, *Independent Iraq*, pp. 13, 235–38, 249, 252–87, 299–306, 358–68; Majid Khadduri, *Republican Iraq: A Study in Iraqi Politics since the Revolution of 1958* (London, 1969), pp. 1–61; Batatu, *The Old Social Classes*, pp. 30–32, 345, 478, 764–807; M. A. Saleem Khan, *The Monarchic Iraq: A Political Study* (Aligarh, India, 1977), p. 95.

Notes for Chapter 14—Conclusion

1. Khadduri, *Independent Iraq*, pp. 163–64, 308–09.

2. Jamil al-Midfai and Ali Jawdat, for example. Ireland, *Iraq*, pp. 256, 258, 326; Maurice Peterson, *Both Sides of the Curtin: An Autobiography* (London, 1950), p. 138.

Bibliography

UNPUBLISHED SOURCES
Public Record Office

Air Ministry
AIR 5 Papers of the air historical branch.
AIR 8 Papers of the chief of the air staff.
AIR 9 Papers of the directorate of plans.
AIR 20 Unregistered papers of the air ministry.
AIR 23 Papers of overseas commands.
AIR 40 Papers of the directorate of intelligence.

Cabinet Office
CAB 2 Minutes of the committee of imperial defence.
CAB 4 Memoranda of the committee of imperial defence.
CAB 16 Subcommittees of the committee of imperial defence.
CAB 23 Conclusions of the cabinet.
CAB 24 Memoranda of the cabinet.
CAB 27 Committees of the cabinet.
CAB 51 Middle East committees of the committee of imperial defence.
CAB 53 Chiefs of staff committee of the committee of imperial defence.
CAB 65 Conclusions of the war cabinet.
CAB 66 Memoranda of the war cabinet.
CAB 69 Defence committee (operations) of the war cabinet.
CAB 79 Minutes of the chiefs of staff committee of the war cabinet.
CAB 80 Memoranda of the chiefs of staff committee of the war cabinet.
CAB 92 Committees of the war cabinet.
CAB 95 Middle East committees of the war cabinet.

Colonial Office
CO 730 Colonial office papers on Iraq.
CO 935 Colonial office confidential print.

Foreign Office
FO 371   General correspondence of the foreign office.
FO 406   Foreign office confidential print.
FO 624   British embassy in Baghdad.

War Office
WO 201   Middle East forces.

India Office Library and Records

L/P&S/12   Correspondence of the India office's political and secret depart-
            ment.
L/P&S/18   Memoranda of the India office's political and secret department.
R/15/1   Bushire political residency.
R/15/5   Kuwait political agency.

Middle East Centre, St. Anthony's College, Oxford

C. J. Edmonds' papers.

National Archives, Washington

Decimal   Records relating to the internal affairs of Iraq.
File 890G

PUBLISHED SOURCES
Documents

Great Britain, colonial office. *Special Report by His Majesty's Government in the United
    Kingdom of Great Britain and Northern Ireland to the Council of the League of
    Nations on the Progress of Iraq during the period 1920–1931.* London, 1931.
Great Britain, colonial office. *Report by His Majesty's Government in the United
    Kingdom of Great Britain and Northern Ireland to the Council of the League of
    Nations on the Administration of Iraq for the period January to October, 1932.*
    London, 1933.
Hurewitz, J. C. (ed.). *The Middle East and North Africa in World Politics: A Docu-
    mentary Record,* Vol. II: *British–French Supremacy 1914–1945.* New Haven,
    Conn., 1979.
United States, department of state. *Documents on German Foreign Policy 1918–
    1945,* Series D (1937–1945), Vols. X–XIII: *The War Years.* Washington,
    1957–64.
United States, department of state. *Foreign Relations of the United States: Diplo-
    matic Papers 1940,* Vol. III and *Diplomatic Papers 1941,* Vol. III. Washing-
    ton, 1958–59.

Books

Amery, L. S. *My Political Life,* Vol. II: *War and Peace 1914–1929.* London, 1953.
Antonius, George. *The Arab Awakening: The Story of the Arab Nationalist Move-
    ment.* London, 1938.

Arfa, Hassan. *The Kurds: An Historical and Political Study.* London, 1966.

Ashworth, William. *An Economic History of England 1870–1939.* London, 1960.

Atiyyah, Ghassan R. *Iraq: 1908–1921, A Socio-Political Study.* Beirut, 1973.

Barker, A. J. *The Neglected War: Mesopotamia 1914–1918.* London, 1967.

Barnett, Correlli. *The Collapse of British Power.* London, 1972.

Batatu, Hanna. *The Old Social Classes and the Revolutionary Movements of Iraq: A Study of Iraq's Old Landed and Commercial Classes and of its Communists, Bathists, and Free Officers.* Princeton, N.J., 1978.

Beeri, Eliezer. *Army Officers in Arab Politics and Society.* New York, 1970.

Beloff, Max. *Imperial Sunset,* Vol. I: *Britain's Liberal Empire 1897–1921.* London, 1969.

Bentwich, Norman. *The Mandates System.* London, 1930.

Bond, Brian. *British Military Policy between the Two World Wars.* Oxford, 1980.

Bowyer, Chaz. *The Encyclopedia of British Military Aircraft.* London, 1982.

Browne, Brigadier-General J. Gilbert. *The Iraq Levies 1915–1932.* London, 1932.

Buckley, Christopher. *Five Ventures: Iraq-Syria-Persia-Madagascar-Dodescanese.* London, 1954.

Busch, Briton C. *Britain, India, and the Arabs, 1914–1921.* Berkeley, Calif., 1971.

Churchill, Winston S. *The Second World War,* Vol. III: *The Grand Alliance.* Boston, 1950.

Cohen, Michael J. *Palestine: Retreat from the Mandate, The Making of British Policy, 1936–45.* New York, 1978.

Collier, Basil. *History of the Second World War, United Kingdom Military Series: The Defence of the United Kingdom.* London, 1957.

Connell, John. *Auchinleck: A Biography of Field-Marshal Sir Claude Auchinleck.* London, 1959.

Connell, John. *Wavell: Scholar and Soldier, To June 1941.* London, 1964.

Darwin, John. *Britain, Egypt and the Middle East: Imperial Policy in the Aftermath of War 1918–1922.* London, 1981.

Dodwell, H. H. (ed.). *The Cambridge History of India,* Vol. VI: *The Indian Empire 1858–1969.* Delhi, n.d.

Al-Durra, Mahmud. *Al-Harb al-Iraqiya al-Britaniya* (The Iraqi-British War of 1941). Beirut, 1969.

Ferrier, R. W. *The History of the British Petroleum Company,* Vol. I: *The Developing Years 1901–1932.* Cambridge, 1982.

Foster, Henry A. *The Making of Modern Iraq: A Product of World Forces.* Norman, Oklahoma, 1935.

Fraser, David. *And We Shall Shock Them: The British Army in the Second World War.* London, 1983.

Gallagher, John. *The Decline, Revival and Fall of the British Empire: The Ford Lectures and other Essays.* Cambridge, 1982.

Glubb, Brigadier-General John B. *The Story of the Arab Legion.* London, 1948.

Glubb, Lieutenant-General Sir John B. *Britain and the Arabs: A Study of Fifty Years 1908 to 1958.* London, 1959.

Great Britain, admiralty, naval intelligence division. *Iraq and the Persian Gulf.* London, 1944.

Haldane, Lieutenant-General Sir Aylmer L. *The Insurrection in Mesopotamia, 1920.* Edinburgh, 1922.

Al-Hashimi, Taha. *Mudhakkirat Taha al-Hashimi* (Memoirs of Taha al-Hashimi), Vol. 1: *1919–1943.* Beirut, 1967.

Higham, Robin. *Britain's Imperial Air Routes 1918 to 1939: The Story of Britain's Overseas Airlines*. London, 1960.

Higham, Robin. *Armed Forces in Peacetime: Britain 1918–1940, A Case Study*. London, 1962.

Hirszowicz, Lukasz. *The Third Reich and the Arab East*. London, 1966.

Horne, Alistair. *A Savage War of Peace: Algeria 1954–1962*. London, 1977.

Hyde, H. Montgomery. *British Air Policy Between the Wars 1918–1939*. London, 1976.

Ireland, Philip W. *Iraq: A Study in Political Development*. London, 1937.

Ismael, Tareq Y. *Iraq and Iran: Roots of Conflict*. Syracuse, N.Y., 1982.

Joseph, John. *The Nestorians and their Muslim Neighbors: A Study of Western Influence on their Relations*. Princeton, N.J., 1961.

Kedourie, Elie. *England and the Middle East: The Destruction of the Ottoman Empire 1914–1921*. London, 1956.

Kedourie, Elie. *The Chatham House Version and Other Middle-Eastern Studies*. New York, 1970.

Kedourie, Elie. *In the Anglo-Arab Labyrinth: The McMahon-Husayn Correspondence and its Interpretations 1914–1939*. Cambridge, 1976.

Kedourie, Elie. *Islam in the Modern World and Other Studies*. London, 1980.

Kennedy, Paul. *The Rise and Fall of British Naval Mastery*. London, 1976.

Kennedy, Paul. *The Realities Behind Diplomacy: Background Influences on British External Policy, 1865–1980*. London, 1981.

Kent, Marian. *Oil and Empire: British Policy and Mesopotaminan Oil 1900–1920*. London, 1976.

Khadduri, Majid. *Independent Iraq 1932–1958: A Study in Iraqi Politics*. 2nd ed. London, 1960.

Khadduri, Majid. *Republican Iraq: A Study in Iraqi Politics since the Revolution of 1958*. London, 1969.

Al-Khattab, Rajaa Hussain. *Tasis al-Jaysh al-Iraqi wa Tatawwur Daurhi al-Siyasi 1921–1941* (The Establishment of the Iraqi Army and the Development of its Political Role 1921–1941). Baghdad, 1979.

Kirk, George. *Survey of International Affairs 1939–1946: The Middle East in the War*. London, 1952.

Kirkbride, Sir Alec Seath. *A Crackle of Thorns: Experiences in the Middle East*. London, 1956.

Klieman, Aaron S. *Foundations of British Policy in the Arab World: The Cairo Conference of 1921*. Baltimore, 1970.

Laqueur, Walter. *A History of Zionism*. New York, 1972.

Longrigg, Stephen H. *Iraq 1900 to 1950: A Political, Social, and Economic History*. London, 1953.

Longrigg, Stephen H. *Syria and Lebanon under French Mandate*. London, 1958.

Longrigg, Stephen H. *Oil in the Middle East: Its Discovery and Development*. 3rd ed. London, 1968.

Lorimer, J. G. *Gazetteer of the Persian Gulf, Oman, and Central Arabia*, Vol. II. Calcutta, 1908.

Mackenzie, Compton. *Eastern Epic*, Vol. I: *September 1939–March 1943 Defence*. London, 1951.

Main, Ernest. *Iraq: From Mandate to Independence*. London, 1935.

Margalith, Aaron M. *The International Mandates*. Baltimore, 1930.

Marlowe, John. *Late Victorian: The Life of Sir Arnold Talbot Wilson*. London, 1967.

Marr, Phebe. *The Modern History of Iraq.* Boulder, Colorado, 1985.

Mehrotra, S. R. *India and the Commonwealth 1885–1929.* London, 1965.

Mejcher, Helmut. *Imperial Quest for Oil: Iraq 1910–1928.* London, 1976.

Mejcher, Helmut. *Die Politik und das Öl im Nahen Osten,* Vol. I: *Der Kampf der Mächte und Konzerne vor dem Zweiten Weltkrieg.* Stuttgart, 1980.

Milward, Alan S. *The Economic Effects of the Two World Wars on Britain.* London, 1970.

Moberly, Brigadier-General F. J. *History of the Great War Based on Official Documents: The Campaign in Mesopotamia 1914–1918,* 4 vols. London, 1923–27.

Murray, Williamson. *The Change in the European Balance of Power 1938–1939: The Path to Ruin.* Princeton, N.J., 1984.

Pal, Dharm. *Official History of the Indian Armed Forces in the Second World War 1939–1945: Campaign in Western Asia.* Calcutta, 1957.

Payton-Smith, D. J. *History of the Second World War, United Kingdom Civil Series: Oil, A Study of War-time Policy and Administration.* London, 1971.

Pearton, Maurice. *Oil and the Romanian State.* London, 1971.

Penrose, Edith and E. F. *Iraq: International Relations and National Development.* London, 1978.

Peterson, Maurice. *Both Sides of the Curtin: An Autobiography.* London, 1950.

Playfair, Major-General I. S. O. *History of the Second World War, United Kingdom Military Series: The Mediterranean and Middle East,* Vol. I: *The Early Successes against Italy (to May 1941).* London, 1954.

Playfair, Major-General I. S. O. *History of the Second World War, United Kingdom Military Series: The Mediterranean and Middle East,* Vol. II: *The Germans Come to the Help of their Ally (1941).* London, 1956.

Pollard, Sidney. *The Development of the British Economy 1914–1967.* 2nd ed. London, 1969.

Porath, Y. *The Palestinian Arab National Movement: From Riots to Rebellion,* Vol. II: *1929–1939.* London, 1977.

Postan, M. M. et al. *History of the Second World War, United Kingdom Civil Series: Design and Development of Weapons: Studies in Government and Industrial Organisation.* London, 1964.

Prasad, Sri Nandan. *Official History of the Indian Armed Forces in the Second World War 1939–1945: Expansion of the Armed Forces and Defence Organization 1939–1945.* Calcutta, 1956.

Richards, Denis. *Royal Air Force 1939–1945,* Vol. I: *The Fight at Odds.* London, 1953.

Rubin, Barry. *The Arab States and the Palestine Conflict.* Syracuse, N.Y., 1981.

Saleem Khan, M. A. *The Monarchic Iraq: A Political Study.* Aligarh, India, 1977.

Schroder, Bernd Philipp. *Deutschland und der Mittlere Osten im Zweiten Weltkrieg.* Gottingen, 1975.

Shwadran, Benjamin. *The Middle East, Oil and the Great Powers.* 3rd ed. New York, 1973.

Sluglett, Peter. *Britain in Iraq 1914–1932.* London, 1976.

Stafford, Lieutenant-Colonel R. S. *The Tragedy of the Assyrians.* London, 1935.

Stivers, William. *Supremacy and Oil: Iraq, Turkey, and the Anglo-American World Order, 1918–1930.* Ithaca, N.Y., 1982.

Tarbush, Mohammad A. *The Role of the Military in Politics: A Case Study of Iraq to 1941.* London, 1982.

Taylor, A. J. P. *English History 1914–1945.* London, 1965.

Thornton, A. P. *The Imperial Idea and its Enemies: A Study in British Power.* London, 1959.

Toynbee, Arnold J. *Survey of International Affairs 1925,* Vol. I: *The Islamic World since the Peace Settlement.* London, 1927.

Toynbee, Arnold J. *Survey of International Affairs 1928.* London, 1929.

Toynbee, Arnold J. *Survey of International Affairs 1930.* London, 1931.

Toynbee, Arnold J. *Survey of International Affairs 1934.* London, 1935.

Toynbee, Arnold J. *Survey of International Affairs 1936.* London, 1937.

Warner, Geoffrey. *Iraq and Syria 1941.* London, 1974.

Weber, Frank G. *The Evasive Neutral: Germany, Britain and the Quest for a Turkish Alliance in the Second World War.* Columbia, Missouri, 1979.

Wigram, Reverend W. A. *Our Smallest Ally: A Brief Account of the Assyrian Nation in the Great War.* London, 1920.

Wilson, Field-Marshal Lord. *Eight Years Overseas 1939–1947.* London, n.d.

Woodward, Sir Llewellyn. *British Foreign Policy in the Second World War,* Vol. I. London, 1970.

Wright, Quincy. *Mandates Under the League of Nations.* Chicago, 1930.

Articles

Cohen, Hayyim J. "The Anti-Jewish *Farhud* in Baghdad, 1941." *Middle Eastern Studies,* Vol. 3 (1966).

Cohen, Michael J. "A Note on the Mansion House Speech, May 1941." *Asian and African Studies,* Vol. 11 (1977).

Cox, Jafna L. "A Splendid Training Ground: The Importance to the Royal Air Force of its Role in Iraq, 1919–32." *The Journal of Imperial and Commonwealth History,* Vol. 13 (1985).

Darwin, John. "Imperialism in Decline? Tendencies in British Imperial Policy Between the Wars." *The Historical Journal,* Vol. 23 (1980).

Edmonds, C. J. "Kurdish Nationalism." *Journal of Contemporary History,* Vol. 6 (1971).

Elphinston, W. G. "The Kurdish Question." *International Affairs,* Vol. 22 (1946).

Haim, Sylvia G. "Aspects of Jewish Life in Baghdad under the Monarchy." *Middle Eastern Studies,* Vol. 12 (1976).

Hemphill, Paul P. J. "The Formation of the Iraqi Army, 1921–33." In Kelidar, Abbas (ed.). *The Integration of Modern Iraq.* London, 1979.

Hursy, Khaldun S. "The Assyrian Affair of 1933." *International Journal of Middle Eastern Studies,* Vol. 5 (1974).

Husry, Khaldun S. "King Faysal I and Arab Unity, 1930–33." *Journal of Contemporary History,* Vol. 10 (1975).

Husry, Khaldun S. "The Political Ideas of Yunis al-Sabawi." In Buheiry, Marwan R. (ed.). *Intellectual Life in the Arab East, 1890–1939.* Beirut, 1981.

Khadduri, Majid. "General Nuri's Flirtations with the Axis Powers." *Middle East Journal,* Vol. 16 (1962).

Orr, Colonel G. M. "The Military Forces in India." *Army Quarterly,* Vol. 18 (1929).

Porath, Y. "Britain and Arab Unity." *Jerusalem Quarterly,* Vol. 15 (1980).

Porath, Y. "Nuri al-Said's Arab Unity Programme." *Middle Eastern Studies,* Vol. 20 (1984).

Porath, Y. "Abdallah's Greater Syria Programme." *Middle Eastern Studies,* Vol. 20 (1984).

Al-Qazzaz, Ayad. Review of *Memoirs of Taha al Hashimi*, by Taha al-Hashimi. *Middle East Forum*, Vol. 45 (1969).

Al-Qazzaz, Ayad. "The Iraqi-British War of 1941: A Review Article." *International Journal of Middle Eastern Studies*, Vol. 7 (1976).

Sheffer, Gabriel. "The Involvement of Arab States in the Palestine Conflict and British-Arab Relationship before World War II." *Asian and African Studies*, Vol. 10 (1974).

Shimizu, Hiroshi. "Anglo-Japanese Competition in the Textile Trade in the Inter-War Period: A Case Study of Iraq, 1932–1941." *Middle Eastern Studies*, Vol. 20 (1984).

Silverfarb, Daniel. "The British Government and the Question of Umm Qasr 1938–1945." *Asian and African Studies*, Vol. 16 (1982).

Stivers, William. "International Politics and Iraqi Oil, 1918–1928: A Study in Anglo-American Diplomacy." *Business History Review*, Vol. 55 (1981).

Taggar, Y. "The Iraqi Reaction to the Partition Plan for Palestine, 1937." In Ben-Dor, Gabriel (ed.). *The Palestinians and the Middle East Conflict*. Ramat Gan, Israel, 1978.

Tomlinson, B. R. "India and the British Empire, 1880–1935." *The Indian Economic and Social History Review*, Vol. 12 (1975).

DOCTORAL DISSERTATIONS

Amin, Mudhaffar Abdullah. "Jamaat al-Ahali: Its Origin, Ideology, and Role in Iraqi Politics 1932–1946." University of Durham, 1980.

Marr, Phebe Ann. "Yasin al-Hashimi: The Rise and Fall of a Nationalist." Harvard University, 1966.

Melka, Robert Lewis. "The Axis and the Arab Middle East: 1930–1945." University of Minnesota, 1966.

Niama, Khadim Hashim. "Anglo-Iraqi Relations During the Mandate." University College of Wales Aberystwyth, 1974.

Sassoon, Yosef. "Economic Policy in Iraq 1932–1950." Oxford University, 1980.

Simon, Reeva Spector. "Iraq Between the Wars: The Creation and Implementation of a Nationalist Ideology." Columbia University, 1982.

Index

Abadan, 3, 66, 115, 133, 142
Abd al-Ilah, Prince, *see* Regent
Abu Dhabi, 25, 57
Aden, 3, 23
Ahmad, Shaykh of Kuwait, 66, 68, 69, 143
Air ministry (Britain), 23, 26–27, 31, 54, 55
Air route, Egypt-Australia, 3, 23, 87
Airbases, British, in Iraq, 3, 12, 22, 23–32. 44, 51–52, 80–87 *passim*, 115, 142, 144, 145. *See also* Basra; Habbaniya; Hinaidi; Mosul; Shaiba
Aircraft: 23, 47, 83, 84, 85, 116, 168 (n. 62); German, committed to Iraq, 131, 133
Airfields: Iranian, 116; Iraqi, as refueling stops for British, 24, 26
Airlift, German, Rhodes to Iraq, 134
Aleppo, 57
Alexandretta, 57, 74
Amadia, revolt by Kurds in, 36
Amman, motor route from, to Kuwait, 67
Ammunition, 79
Ammunition factories, Iraqi, 84
Ancillary services to Royal Air Force, 53, 54
Andrew Weir, 119
Anglo-French declaration (Nov. 1918), 6
Anglo-Iranian Oil Company, 67–68, 94–98 *passim*, 142
Anglo-Iraqi railway agreement (March 1936), 89
Anglo-Iraqi treaty of 1930, 21–22, 30–31, 36–37, 60, 82, 106, 107, 115, 124; annexure article 4, 48–49; article 5 *vs.* article 4, 127–28; and employment of British "foreign experts" in Iraq, 88; military equipment acquisitions clause, 22, 77

Anglo-Italian agreement of 1938, 59, 60
Anglo-Ottoman convention of 1913, 67
Anti-aircraft guns, 78, 79, 84, 116
Anti-tank guns, 79, 84
Arab nationalism, 52, 56–64 *passim*, 140, 145
Arab tribesmen massacre Assyrians (1933), 42
Arab unity, 56–64 *passim*, 66
Arabs, 47; British concessions to during World War I, 5–6, 114; and Jerusalem riots (1929), 21; Palestinian, 115; Sunni, *see* Sunni Arabs; Shiite, *see* Shiites
Armed forces, Iraq, 87, 132, 139. *See also* Iraqi army; Iraqi air force
Armenians, 33, 34
Armored car companies, British 48
Arms smuggling, Kuwait to Iraq, 66
Arms supplies, Iraqi, 74–86, 92–93, 97, 143, 144; diversification of sources, 83–84, 85; German offers of, 89; non-British, and bribery, 168 (n. 63)
Army cooperation aircraft, 23, 83, 168 (n. 62)
Arnhem (Holland), battle of, 55
Artillery, horse-drawn, 78
Artillery ammunition, 79, 84
al-Askari, Jafar, 25, 143
Assets, British, seized by World War I foes, 16
Assyrians, 16, 33–46, 75, 130, 132, 142; ex-levies, armed, and the 1932 revolt, 48; massacre of, 42, 138, 143; recruited as levies, 47 (*see also* Levies); revolt against Ottoman empire, 33–34, 33
Atrocities committed by Iraqi armed forces (1935–37), 81
Australia, 3
Autonomy, Assyrian, 33, 38
Aviation fuel, 101